THE ROAD FROM WIGAN PIER

A Biography of Les Cannon

by

OLGA CANNON
& J. R. L. ANDERSON

LONDON
VICTOR GOLLANCZ LTD
1973

To Those who Care

Printed in Great Britain by
The Camelot Press Ltd, London and Southampton

CONTENTS

ACKNOWLEDGEMENTS

THE AUTHORS WISH to thank the many people who have helped them in the preparation of this book. They include members of the Cannon family, friends and associates of Les Cannon in his career, and in particular Mr Woodrow Wyatt and the many others who have given permission to quote both from published work and from correspondence, and who have provided information and guidance. The authors are also grateful to the Executive Council of the ETU for permission to quote from Minutes.

The short passages quoted on pp. 88, 89 and 91 are from *The Nuremberg Trials* by R. W. Cooper, Penguin Books, 1947; the extract from a BBC broadcast that appears on pp. 166–7 cannot be acknowledged because those who took part were anonymous.

Wherever possible the sources of photographs have been acknowledged; but the authors are grateful to the many photographers whom it has been impossible to trace.

LIST OF ILLUSTRATIONS

THE ROAD FROM WIGAN PIER

WIGAN

WIGAN, 1920. BRIEFLY, it seemed not a bad world to be born into. The ghastly years of war were over: the ghastliness of what turned out to be only a counterfeit peace was yet to come. The Wigan of Orwell's *The Road to Wigan Pier* was half a generation in the future.

Europe seemed freed from the hateful militarism of Prussia. In spite of clamour that he should be hanged, the Kaiser (Wilhelm II of Germany) had been allowed to go quietly to exile in Holland. There was no longer an Emperor of Austria, no longer an empire to be ruled from Vienna. The nationalities that had groaned under the Hapsburg yoke were emerging on their own; Czechoslovakia, under the great Thomas Masaryk (president 1918–35), one of the bright hopes for a modern democratic State.

The British Empire was at its height, victorious in the greatest war in history, apparently invincible. King George V, celebrating the tenth anniversary of his succession, was setting a new and rather comforting pattern for the British monarchy. For nearly half his reign Britain had been at war, and he had stood out as a brave and dignified symbol of his embattled nation. Now he and Queen Mary were settling to a middle age of family life, kindlier than that of his awesome grandmother, Queen Victoria, much more respectable than the life of his father, King Edward VII. King George and Queen Mary were immensely popular.

In class-consciousness the England of 1920 was still nearer to the nineteenth century than to the twentieth century, but there was a new dignity in being working-class. Most manual workers were materially better off than they had ever been; wartime wage rates had not yet been slashed, and in that brief period of post-war boom there was plenty of work. The Labour

Party was a new force in politics. In the first post-war election
it had broken with the Liberals to stand on its own and won
59 seats. The Liberals themselves were in hopeless disarray,
split between those supporting Mr Lloyd George's Coalition
and those demanding independence. In the election of 1918
the independent Liberals were all-but wiped out of Parliament,
winning only 26 seats against Labour's 59. Labour could feel
sanguine about the future. Britain seemed moving towards a
much more genuine democracy. Even women (true, not all
women—they had to be over thirty) had the vote.

Outside Parliament, too, organised Labour was flexing its
muscles, and enjoying the feeling. The miners, the railwaymen
and the transport workers revived their "Triple Alliance"—on
paper, at least, the most formidable of all trade union groups
established before the war. It seemed capable of calling on its
own a strike that would be not much less crippling than a
general strike: it might have called such a strike in 1914 had
not war intervened. It nearly came into action in the autumn
of 1919, but the railwaymen, under J. H. Thomas, got what they
wanted from the Government after a short strike of their own,
without needing to call on their allies. The dockers were able
to improve their lot with a commission of inquiry which brought
Ernest Bevin into national prominence. The miners got the
Sankey Commission, whose chairman actually recommended
nationalisation, although since the Commission as a whole was
unable to produce an agreed report it accomplished nothing.
For the moment, however, the miners did not do badly.
They kept their wartime wages, and they got a seven hour
working day by act of Parliament.

In May 1920, Ernest Bevin's dockers in London refused to
load a ship called the *Jolly George* with munitions to support
British intervention against the Bolsheviks in Russia. The whole
Labour movement supported them, threatening a general strike
if British intervention persisted. The Government, which was
sick of such a futile war, was only too glad to give way, and
intervention ceased. It seemed a splendid victory. In July of
that same year a group of radical British socialists and shop
stewards met to form the Communist Party of Great Britain.
It was clearly opposed to most of the things the Labour Party
stood for, though it did not seem so at the time. Lenin, however,

took the point in his famous letter, saying, "We will support Henderson [Arthur Henderson, leader of the Labour Party] as a rope supports a man who is hanged."

Wigan, then (as now), could scarcely be called an attractive town. It is about sixteen miles north-west of Manchester, and for most of its history it was an inconspicuous settlement in the valley of the River Douglas, which takes water from the high moors inland to the Ribble estuary. The Romans apparently knew it, for a Roman altar found nearby is built into the tower of All Saints Church. The first (and in some ways the worst) phase of Britain's industrial revolution changed the whole of the South Lancashire countryside, and Wigan with it. The coal that was vital to the Lancashire cotton industry lies underground here, and as more cotton mills were built, more coal was wanted. So the mills came to the coalfield, and the coalfield served the mills. Coalowners and millowners grew rich, and built street after street of little mean houses for the human labour they needed to get the coal and work their mills. There was no planning; anyone with a bit of waste land could build what he wanted on it. Wigan and its neighbouring villages became absorbed in the huge industrial complex of South Lancashire. Pittances as nineteenth-century industrial wages usually were, they were still better than what could be earned on the land, and vastly better than a farm labourer's wage in Ireland. So men flocked to the new industrial towns, and they attracted a constant stream of immigrants from Ireland. One must be careful about applying twentieth-century standards of housing and hygiene to the conditions of the nineteenth century. Horrible as the older rows of working-class dwellings in Lancashire seem now, when they were built they gave most of their inhabitants more than they had ever been accustomed to. A standpipe in a yard was a considerable advance on fetching water from a well. And hard as life was in mine and mill, it brought a warmth of human companionship to the men and women who toiled there.

The miners were, as they are still, always a little apart from other manual workers. Their job is like no other, they face greater dangers than any other group of workers (except deep-sea fishermen), their very lives are dependent on one another.

The intense group-loyalty of the coalfields grows out of the very nature of the miner's life—he could not exist without confidence in his mates. This sense of community extends from pit to home; it colours every aspect of a mining family's being. With it goes a deep pride, part personal, part communal, in *being* a miner. In colliery districts the miner is the aristocrat of manual workers. His pride matches the aristocrat's—and sometimes, in resistance to change or clinging to old habits of thought, it can be as narrow and as obstinate as the aristocrat's pride of lineage.

Wigan, 1920. A town, almost a way of life, stranded by history, rather as a whale may be stranded after a storm-tide. The whale is left to die, his great strength useless in a strange environment. The old Wigan is about to die, but its people do not know it. They are conscious of their corporate strength; their industries, coal and cotton, still seem the pillars of the British economy. The coalowners and the millowners have done well out of the war; momentarily, they are doing even better in the post-war boom. Some of this prosperity spills over to the workers. Few people bother much about the future—everybody is thankful that the war is over, life is getting back to normal, and "normality" looks like being a good deal better than it was in 1914. The desperate need of reorganisation in the coal industry, to meet what in reality is a contracting market, is ignored. The most profitable coal-seams have been worked to destruction during the war; the profits have been spent, and little capital put back in equipment to develop new workings. Capital has poured into the cotton industry—short-sightedness as calamitous as the lack of capital for the mines, for in a few years the Lancashire cotton industry will be grossly over-capitalised on an obsolete pattern, quite incapable of meeting competition from newly-developed textile industries in India and Japan. In 1920 these problems went unrecognised. They were soon to affect the whole nation; with their accompanying imbalance of distorted economics, the whole world.

National history is the sum of the stories of the lives of individuals. Every child born in that year of 1920 was to have his life shaped—often grievously mis-shaped—by the events that followed that brief post-war boom, a boom that was itself but a symptom of the world sickness that had broken out in the war of 1914–18. Most of that "Class of 1920", as of the children born in any year, merged into the great anonymous multitude who have no memorial, save perhaps their own children, but whose lives collectively form the history of their time. This book tells the story of one who did not merge, of a boy born in Cudworth Street, Wigan, on February 21, 1920, whose reaction to the experiences of his childhood was a fierce determination to change society. Les Cannon did not accomplish more than a tithe of what he tried to do: he did not live long enough to make sure even of that tithe. But the world is a better and a cleaner place because Les Cannon lived. He was the most creative force in British trade unionism over two decades of this century. He was one of the most remarkable men of his generation. Even if some of the trade union reforms that he worked and fought to achieve seem to have come to an end with his death, even if the great trade union movement itself seems, as he put it when he lay dying, "to have lost its way", his life was much more than one man's passing triumph. The things he stood for are not dead. He may be temporarily forgotten as his ideals go temporarily out of fashion, but the historians of the next century will recognise him as the truly formative influence he was.

Les was the fourth of seven children born to Jim Cannon, a Wigan miner, and his wife Nellie (née Turner). The Cannons were Irish immigrants from Sligo. Jim Cannon's father came to England around the middle of the last century. Like many of his fellow-emigrants from Ireland he went first to London, where there was sometimes labouring work to be had in the docks and markets. The work was there all right, but usually there were far too many men competing for it, and it was as easy to starve in mid-Victorian London as in Ireland. So the immigrant Cannon drifted North, and finally got work in the Lancashire coalfield. He married a Lancashire woman, who was one of the few working girls of her generation who could read and write. This gave her some standing in the community, for the neighbours came to her when they wanted letters written, or when they had some document that they could not themselves read. Literacy, however, brought few material benefits to a working-class mother in nineteenth-century Wigan. Seventeen pregnancies, and coping somehow with her enormous brood, left Jim's mother exhausted and prematurely aged. Life was simply too much for her, and the home in which Jim Cannon grew up was dirty and neglected. Nevertheless, his mother's literacy must have played some part in his early years. Although he was young enough to benefit from the 1870 Education Act, that first generation of literate children often lost interest in reading if their parents were illiterate. Somehow that exhausted, worn-out woman must have found the spirit to encourage young Jim's reading. Perhaps she herself was—or had been—able sometimes to escape from her surroundings with a book. The ability to immerse himself in reading so that he was oblivious of all material things became a marked characteristic of Jim Cannon. He left school at twelve to follow his father down the pit, but, solely by his own reading, educated himself to an astonishingly high standard. He began reading political philosophy in his teens, spending every spare penny on books. He read all the works of Marx and other socialist writers that he could lay hands on, became a convinced Socialist, and joined the British Communist Party soon after it was formed in 1920.

Had Jim Cannon been born a little later he would almost certainly have found his way to a polytechnic, perhaps to a university, where his intellectual ability would have been recognised. He was a natural scholar, and all his interests were intellectual. As it was, the society into which he was born offered nothing to a boy-labourer whose schooling stopped at twelve. His response was to develop an extraordinary detachment from life, in which he turned to books almost as to a drug. This was to cause his own family much heartache later.

Although he was always a scholar rather than a man of action Jim Cannon had to work in the pits. His learning marked him off from his fellows, who looked to him for leadership, which he gave as far as he could. As a young man he was in the thick of industrial politics and a regular speaker at meetings in support of trade union candidates who, with Liberal help, were beginning to get into Parliament. It was at a by-election meeting that he met his wife. She was a Tory supporter, and she came to the meeting to heckle the Labour speakers. Jim Cannon rather liked hecklers; he had a quick mind, capable of sharp sarcasm, and dealing with hecklers added spice to the proceedings. On this occasion, however, the girl annoyed him—she seemed to be saying the same thing over and over again. Finally he said to her, "If you are really interested, wait after the meeting, and I'll answer all your questions for you." The girl did wait, they had a long discussion, and arranged to meet again. The girl's name was Nellie Turner.

After a year's courtship they were married on August 4, 1914—the day on which England declared war on Germany. That grim event was barely understood at the time, and it did nothing to damp the spirits of the young couple or their guests. Their wedding was a gay affair, with bridesmaids in pink and blue, and a coach and pair to take the bride and bridegroom to the reception. After a honeymoon in London, Jim Cannon and his bride came back to a house in Cudworth Street, Wigan, furnished for them by Nellie's father.

The Turners were not all that pleased about their daughter's marriage, for they considered that she was marrying beneath her. The Turners themselves were highly respectable, regular churchgoers, and staunch Tory voters. Nellie's father had a barge on the Liverpool–Manchester canal, and their house, on the banks of that canal, was a large terraced house, with a bakehouse and big rooms. In their eyes Jim Cannon was an "Irish-socialist coalminer, poor as a church mouse, hopeless about the house, given to reading books by the dozen and to endless talk about politics". Nevertheless, he was Nellie's "chosen", and a working-class family does not abandon its children for making unsuitable marriages, whatever families in higher social strata may sometimes do. The Turners gave their daughter a "posh" wedding, and provided bedroom and dining-room furniture for her new home. There were carpets on the floor and curtains for the windows. The Cannons returned from their honeymoon to find a full set of crockery—complete with sugar bowl and cream jug—displayed on the dining-room sideboard, and a row of new pots and pans on the kitchen shelf, together with a box of cutlery for six. Their new neighbours called to admire all this finery.

Their first son, Terry, was born in 1915, followed by a second son, Jimmie, eighteen months later. A year after Jimmie's birth, Terry, at the age of three, contracted polio. The war years pressed hard on miners' families, for food prices were high, and rationing—unlike the scheme introduced in the Second World War—did not become really effective until nearly the end of the war. Nellie Cannon was determined to get the best help she could for her crippled child. The specialist at Wigan Infirmary recommended daily hospital treatment, and every day for the next two years Nellie Cannon took the little boy to the infirmary, carrying him two miles each way to save the tram fare. Terry partially recovered the use of his limbs and repaid his mother with a lifetime of devotion.

A third son (Frank) was born in 1918 and a fourth (Les) in 1920. Each birth was a difficult one, and at each a doctor was present, and instruments had to be used. The doctor who assisted at Les's birth arrived considerably the worse for drink, with his instruments rusty and neglected. Nellie Cannon's sister, Martha, seething with anger, screamed at him, "If there are complications I shall haul you before the Courts myself." There were no complications, but the doctor never sent a bill.

Leslie, the name chosen for the baby, was held to be a very "pretty" name. Nellie Cannon thought it "posh". She always called him "Leslie", and disliked the abbreviated "Les", which Les himself, and his friends, always used.

Two more children arrived within the customary eighteen-months' pattern, both girls—Ann in 1921 and Joan in 1923. A seventh child, and fifth son, Brian, followed a decade later, in 1933.

When Les was born, in February 1920, the Cannon family were already feeling the cost of Terry's illness. As more children arrived their home began to lose its shine. The embroidered mats and covers were put away, the sideboard lost its polish. Most of the pretty cups were broken. Nellie's family, the Turners, helped where they could, but such help as they could give did not go far in a family with six children, one a semi-invalid. Jim Cannon earned around £3 a week, usually a bit less than £3. Such earnings seem almost unbelievable today, but in 1920 anything over £2 15s (£2.75) a week was considered a reasonable wage. Many an unskilled labourer brought up a family on 30s (£1.50) a week, and many a country parson or non-conformist minister had an income of no more than £100 a year. When his fourth son was born Jim Cannon could look forward to a life of hard work in return for just about enough to live on. Politically, he could look forward to a better future as the socialism in which he believed made greater and greater headway in changing national life.

But Les Cannon's arrival in the world marked the peak of his father's material success. Before Les was one year old the post-war boom had broken, and the coal industry entered a period of acute distress. Many things contributed to this. Basically, the mines in all the older coalfields, Lancashire among them, were obsolete. The newer (and geologically more favoured) coalfields in Nottinghamshire and the East Midlands were (as they are still) highly profitable, but the older pits were already uneconomic. Their economic sickness had been masked by the war, when every ton of coal, produced at almost any cost, was needed; and their sickness remained hidden during the short post-war boom. As the boom came to an end, however, the organic sickness of the coal industry began to be felt. And all over the world the boom was coming to an end. Commodity prices were falling, and the primary-producing countries, which had provided a brisk market for British textiles and other manufactured goods, could no longer afford to buy them. British ships, no longer able to find cargoes, were being laid up. As ships were laid up, orders in the shipyards fell off. Manufacturing industry, which had seemed to have an insatiable appetite for coal, reduced consumption as production was cut back.

During the war the Government had taken control of the coal industry, and in 1920 the industry was still controlled. The price of control was massive subsidies to maintain uneconomic pits. In October, when Les was seven months old, the miners struck for higher wages, and it seemed possible that the Triple Alliance —the railwaymen and transport workers—would support the strike. Mr Lloyd George gave way, the miners got more or less what they wanted and the Triple Alliance was not called upon to act. It was a hollow victory. The Government was retrenching everywhere and decided to hand back the mines to private control on March 31, 1921. The mines in fact had never ceased to be in private ownership—controls and subsidies had left ownership unaffected. The abandonment of Government control, however, was of critical importance to the miners.

Wartime (and briefly post-war) controls had given the miners *national* minimum rates of pay, as distinct from their old *district* agreements. Under the old system men in the profitable coalfields earned more, while those in the older, uneconomic pits had to be content with less: the alternative was the threat of closure and unemployment. The whole industry required fundamental reorganisation, which was not to come until after the Second World War. Even then, and with nationalisation, the re-structuring of the coal industry required over a quarter of a century—and it is still not complete.

In 1921 there was no nationalisation. The coalowners, told to go it alone, were quite incapable of long-term economic strategy. As they saw it, the only way of keeping the older collieries in business was to return to district wage agreements, so that uneconomic production could be subsidised by lower wages. The miners refused to accept district agreements, and the day after the coal industry returned to private control—on April 1, 1921—the miners were locked out.

Now the miners were in desperate need of help from the Triple Alliance. They expected their allies, the railwaymen and the transport workers, to support them, and a strike was duly announced for a fortnight later—to begin on Friday, April 15, 1921. But the situation had changed. With the mines under Government control a strike involved the Government in direct negotiation with the strikers. How could railwaymen and transport workers negotiate with coalowners? The Government could no longer make terms; the most it could do was to mediate. By its nature, mediation involved compromise, and compromise meant that no one could get everything he wanted.

The miners refused to compromise. With the Government's mediation they were offered a temporary settlement providing that all existing wage-rates should remain unchanged pending negotiations for the establishment of a "national pool" (by a levy on coal prices and perhaps a continuing subsidy) to equalise wage-rates between more and less profitable coalfields. J. H. Thomas, the railwaymen's leader, and Ernest Bevin, the leader of the transport workers, thought that the terms offered a reasonable basis for negotiation, and that the miners ought to accept them. Frank Hodges, then secretary of the Mineworkers Federation (the National Union of Mineworkers did not come until after the Second World War), was in favour of acceptance, but Herbert Smith, the mineworkers' president, wanted to fight. By a majority of one vote the Federation's executive supported Smith.

So the lock-out continued. But the allies were no longer ready to fight. Holding that they had done all they could in getting at least a basis for settlement offered to the miners, Bevin and Thomas called off the strike fixed for Friday, April 15. This is still known as "Black Friday" in militant Labour memories. The miners regarded it as betrayal. They fought on alone and stayed out until the end of June, when they were forced back to work by sheer need—there were no social welfare payments to strikers' families then.

Was "Black Friday" a betrayal? The historian A. J. P. Taylor regards it rather as a conflict of attitudes:

> "Black Friday" (he writes in *English History 1914–45*) marked a clash between two conceptions of union policy— the old outlook of class war, to be fought with the bull-headed obstinacy of the trenches, and a new unionism, aiming at compromise, or even partnership. Herbert Smith spoke for the past. Thomas and Bevin for the future.

That seems a fair historical judgement. The clash of attitudes is still unresolved. That first trade union crisis of Les Cannon's infant life was in essence the same as the conflict between old conceptions of class war and new forms of creative trade unionism which was to dominate his later life.

The miners came out of that particular crisis badly. They held out for three months and then had to go back on the coal-owners' terms, which meant substantial wage-cuts in many districts. They would have done far better to negotiate on the provisional settlement offered them in April, but the majority of their leaders did not look at things like that. They had lost one battle of the class war, but they had fought, and they would fight again. The solidarity with which miners and their families had endured the strike was a noble thing—the one fine quality in an unhappy, muddled dispute. To endure a strike (or lock-out) in those days meant real suffering. There was no alternative work, no income tax to be recovered, only a mockery of "welfare"—destitution meant starvation, or the miseries of the still largely Victorian Poor Law and the workhouse. Other unions held collections for the miners, or made donations from their own funds, but such help could not go far. Things were not quite so bad as they became later; there had been the brief strike in October 1920, but there had been no prolonged stoppage since before the war. There were small personal savings to be drawn upon, homes still held a few bits and pieces that could be pawned, or sold. The Co-op and the little shops in the streets where miners lived gave a certain amount of credit— that helped, but it was a point of honour that credit given during a strike should be paid back as soon as there were wages to be earned again, and most miners' wives hated the idea of getting into debt. The habit of buying on hire-purchase was not so ingrained then as it is now. Clothing clubs were a form of hire-purchase that was traditionally respectable, but in a family with several young children the benefit from a clothing club was soon exhausted. The Cannon family, with their neighbours, tightened their belts and hung on.

1921 was a grim year. Wages were cut in industry after industry, but in spite of wage-cutting there was heavy unemployment. In June 1921 the unemployment figures rose to two millions. In the Lancashire cotton industry—the main domestic market for Lancashire coal—unemployment was particularly heavy.

In 1922 things improved a bit, but not in the Lancashire coalfield. There was work, but at pitifully low wages, and the Cannons were hard pressed to make ends meet. The coming of a Labour Government in 1924—the minority Government led by Mr Ramsay MacDonald—seemed briefly to offer new hope, and in the summer of 1924 the miners secured a new wage-agreement which gave them rather better conditions. But although it looked as if this was Labour coming into its own, in reality the miners got their wage-agreement because coal was enjoying a short artificial boom. The French, intent on punishing Germany for the war, did not want a revival of the coal industry in the Ruhr. For a time the circumstances of French occupation of the Ruhr effectively crippled the West German coal industry, and British collieries reaped the benefit. But the Ruhr coal industry was too important to the rest of

Europe to remain crippled. It revived, and with its revival the European market for British coal fell off again. By the middle of 1925 all the coal industry's endemic troubles were again apparent. The owners gave notice to rescind the 1924 wage-agreement, and offered a new agreement with reductions in wage-rates. The miners refused, and were again threatened with a lock-out. This time the General Council of the TUC took a hand and threatened to "black" all transport of coal. The Government, by now a Conservative Government under Mr Baldwin, was ready enough to mediate, but it could no more coerce the coalowners than the TUC could shift the mine-workers' leaders from their adamant refusal to compromise. Trouble was bought off temporarily by the Government's offer of a subsidy to maintain existing wages and colliery profits for nine months, during which a Royal Commission would inves-tigate conditions in the coal industry. The Commission, under Sir Herbert Samuel, made a number of reasonable proposals for reform, including the nationalisation of mining royalties, the grouping of collieries into large units, and the provision of amenities such as pithead baths. In the existing economic plight of the industry, however, it also found it necessary to recommend a reduction in wages. The Commission achieved nothing. The coalowners would have nothing to do with reforms and the miners were not prepared to consider any reduction in wages.

The subsidy ran out at the end of April 1926. The owners at once insisted that wage-rates must be reduced. The miners again refused to accept any reduction. On May 1 the coal industry was again brought to a standstill by a lock-out. On May 3 the whole trade union movement rallied to the support of the miners with a General Strike. After a nine days' wonder that generated a vast deal of excitement and precious little else the General Strike was called off. The miners proceeded to go it alone. They endured their lock-out doggedly for another six months and were then forced back to the pits on worse terms than ever.

This is not the place to attempt an analysis of the General Strike. Apart from producing a magnificent demonstration of trade union solidarity, it was a total failure. It did nothing whatever for the miners, and weakened the unions—and the whole Labour movement—for a generation. Fundamentally, its failure was the outcome of the same clash of attitudes that broke the Triple Alliance in 1921—the conflict between the advocates of old-fashioned class war and the "new" trade unionists who preferred the conference table to the battlefield. Bevin, Thomas and their fellows represented the ablest working-class brains of their generation, which is to say that they were among the ablest men of their time drawn from any social class. They lacked formal education, but they were brilliant, self-trained advocates, inspired organisers and formidable business men. They were often far abler than the industrialists with whom they had to negotiate, and could make rings round them in argument. The miners had had one such leader in Frank Hodges, but he was over-ruled in 1921 and by 1926 he had been succeeded by A. J. Cook, an Old Testament prophet among class warriors, spell-binding as a speaker, politically almost an anarchist. His response to appeals for compromise was adamantine rejection, with the battle-cry "Not a penny off the pay, not a minute on the day".

The General Council of the TUC, although widely accused in the coalfields of betrayal, had not simply abandoned the miners. There were complex meetings with go-betweens and emissaries from the Government, the chief of whom was Sir Herbert Samuel, late of the Samuel Commission. He suggested the setting up of a board to work out wage reductions, which were not, however, to be imposed until the coalowners had accepted the reforms proposed by his Commission. The TUC regarded this as a basis for negotiation. The miners did not. So the General Strike was called off and the lock-out went on.

Had the miners possessed a Bevin as their leader it is probable that they could have won important concessions, and secured at least the beginnings of that reorganisation for which the coal industry had to wait another twenty-one years—until nationalisation in 1947. But these are the "ifs" of history—fascinating to contemplate, and equally, futile to consider. The reality was pure tragedy for the miners. The General Council of the TUC considered them obstinate. They regarded themselves as betrayed and withdrew into a private world of misery. Suffering during the six months for which they continued to hold out was acute. When, finally, they were driven back to the pits, there was no work for many of them. Unemployment in the

coalfields was, and remained, heavy. Jim Cannon was a lodge
official of his union, and had taken a prominent part locally
and nationally in the dispute. He had spoken at rallies, and he
had gone to London with a miners' deputation. Naturally he
was a marked man. Mine managers could pick and choose
whom they wanted to employ—and they did not want men
they regarded as agitators. Jim Cannon never worked in the
coalfields again.

UNEMPLOYMENT

THERE REALLY *WAS* a Wigan Pier. It had gone by the time that George Orwell visited Wigan in the 1930s and he recorded that "even the spot where it used to stand is no longer certain". Orwell was wrong here, for the "pier" was a loading platform on the Leeds and Liverpool canal, near the bottom of Cudworth Street where the Cannon family lived.

Four rows of mean terraced houses, of which the Cannons' home was one, were compressed into a small area of what had been waste land between the River Douglas and the canal. The district was known locally as "the Potteries". Along the bottom of the little streets ran an unfenced single-track railway line, connecting "Owd Nat's" pit with the coal-loading wharf at Wigan Pier. The top of the street was enclosed by a high wall surrounding the weaving sheds of Eckersley's cotton mill. Across a small paved backyard behind the Cannons' home was the lavatory, flushed by waste water from the kitchen tap. Sewage went straight into the River Douglas, a shallow and evil-smelling stream which bordered the yard, protected by a low stone wall and iron railing.

Beyond the railway was an open space adjoining Wigan Corporation's Transport Depot. Somewhat idealistically, this was called Swan Meadow. It may have been a meadow once, but in Les Cannon's childhood it provided only a hard clinker football pitch, surrounded by a mixture of coarse grass, nettles and rubbish. In the middle of Les's childhood the family moved a little way away, but the surroundings were equally depressing.

Many years later—in 1954—Les wrote a description of the view from their back window; the scene had not changed very much. "Looking out of the window of the back room," he wrote, "is really terribly depressing. First you see the old shed which was built in the early 1930s—we used to make ice-cream in it. Now the protective tar-felting is hanging off it in shreds. Over that, you see the slate roof of the lavatory. Filling the third quarter of the window is the railway embankment, with a few dirty green sods sprouting here and there. Thus three-quarters of the window-space is filled. Above, one can see the sky, until a train passes; then the sky is obliterated except for the part you can see under the carriages, and the room becomes noticeably darker."

The Cannons were fortunate in one respect—their house had three small bedrooms instead of the more usual two. It was about all they were fortunate in, for their street had suffered from subsidence and the whole house was twisted out of shape. No door fitted its frame properly, and doors could be kept shut only by wedges. The three small upstairs rooms were built with the utmost economy of space. The three doors opened on to a minute landing, just big enough to hold a galvanised iron bucket, which served as the only lavatory indoors.

Downstairs were the kitchen-living-room and a tiny front room, or "parlour". The wedding present carpets of 1914 had long gone and by the time the children were growing up the front-room floor was covered by cheap linoleum, the living-room had bare flagstones, scrubbed every day and whitened by Nellie Cannon, using the "rubbing stone" provided by the rag and bone man in return for whatever rags he could collect. This was the home in which seven children were brought up, with a father out of work for ten years.

There is shameful housing in Britain still, but in the 1920s the Cannon family lived in conditions that were considered normal for working-class areas in the industrial North. And with their three rooms upstairs they were better off than many; and at least they had a house, instead of one room in a tene-ment. All the same, it is right to look back in anger at the conditions that a rich society—and Britain then was relatively much richer than Britain now—expected its poorer members to tolerate. In a sense it was no one's fault—the fault was a collec-tive national sin among the well-to-do in preferring not to notice how the other half of the community lived. People are as guilty of deliberate blindness and sectional selfishness now as ever they were, but in not quite the same way. Housing reform is lamentably slow, but no one nowadays would *defend* the conditions in which Les Cannon and his brothers and sisters were brought up. Really disgraceful housing in Britain now is exceptional rather than normal for the working-class, and however slowly reforms come, the need for reform is admitted. For most of Les Cannon's childhood reformers were regarded as impractical visionaries, and the bulk of reformist political effort went into trying to protect the unemployed and the low-paid wage earners from *cuts* in their appalling living standards rather than in trying to rebuild Britain. Orwell, whose books did so much to open middle-class eyes to the bitterness of the human poverty around them, has written of the "utter hopelessness" he saw in the face of a working-class wife in Wigan. But Orwell's books belong to the thirties. When the Cannon family tightened their belts to face long-term unemployment, Orwell's books, the Left Book Club, and other manifestations of political determination to shake complacency were still half a generation away.

It is impossible to approach Les Cannon's life without trying to understand the anger that his childhood left in him. All men, of course, are conditioned by their childhood. With Les it was more than that: he dragged himself up in a world that seemed fashioned of harshness and injustice. The good things in life, even the very minor good things that nowadays are taken for granted, the nice things advertised in newspapers or seen in shop windows, were not for the Cannons. He saw his father, the best-read man in the whole neighbourhood, obviously capable of doing almost anything, cast aside and unwanted. He saw his mother, denied every sort of comfort or convenience, over-tired always, ground down by pinching, scraping and slaving to keep their home together. The savage injustices of unemployment, the assaults on human dignity, the ugliness of Wigan's back streets were in the air he breathed. Life was like that, but as he became old enough to think he did not believe that life had to stay like that. Anger at the hardships and indignities that society apparently expected his family to put up with became part of his being.

Unemployment is hard enough to endure today, but it needs a hard effort of imagination to try to *feel* what it was like half a century ago. First, it was something new. There had been slumps before, of course, and much suffering when men were out of work, but an endemic disease of unemployment, with apparently no hope at all for men cast out by industry, was not experienced until the 1920s. The idea that to be out of a job was somehow a man's own fault died hard. That had never been wholly true, but for most of British history the permanently unemployed were mostly the unemployable—the drunkards, the psychiatric cases, the few who would not rather than could not work. We recognise now that large-scale unemployment is no more the fault of the individuals who suffer from it than cholera is the fault of those who contract it during an epidemic; that such unemployment is an economic sickness that the individual is powerless to avert. This was not widely recognised then, and outside the actual areas of heavy unemployment there was a comfortable feeling that the unemployed were largely work-shy. This might affect a man's own feelings about himself —he might *know* that he was a good workman, that he had done nothing to merit being thrown out of a job, but as year succeeded year of unemployment he might begin to feel that he was somehow a personal failure. Under the stress of despair his relations, or his wife's relations, might sometimes tell him so. This added a new dimension of unhappiness to the bitterness of being out of work.

Since 1911 there had been unemployment benefit of a kind. The first Unemployment Insurance Act applied only to workers in the building trades and some other industries which were regarded as particularly subject to ebbs and flows of work. The scheme was not intended to do more than to alleviate short periods of unemployment; if a man was out of work for more than six months his insurance benefit came to an end and he and his family were left to the miseries of the old Poor Law. Inadequate as it was, the 1911 scheme was vastly better than nothing. It was extended to some other groups of workers during the 1914–18 war, and on demobilisation after the war it was extended (temporarily) to ex-Service men who might have difficulty in finding civilian employment. In 1920, again primarily to assist ex-Service men, unemployment insurance was made all-but universal (there were still a few exceptions) for wage-earners earning less than £5 a week.

The insurance scheme, however, still did not envisage long-term mass unemployment. When this came the scheme was quite unable to deal with it. By 1926 the insurance scheme had been patched up in various ways to provide so-called "uncovenanted benefit" after the period of insurance benefit had run out. Later legislation established the hated Means Test and set up the Unemployment Assistance Board to provide relief to men whose theoretical "insurance benefit" had long been exhausted. At best these schemes, known collectively as "the dole", provided only pittances; at worst they offended every instinct of human decency and dignity. Historians have argued since that the introduction of the dole prevented revolution. If so, the price was savage—and it is being paid still.[1]

There was no National Health Service. An unemployed man might succeed in remaining on a doctor's "panel", but there was not even this vestigial form of access to medical treatment for wives and children. They had to depend on the out-patients' departments of hospitals, or on charity. There were no free medicines—a child's bottle of cough mixture could mean a financial crisis in the family budget. If you had toothache, you endured it, or paid sixpence ($2\frac{1}{2}$p) to have the aching tooth pulled out by a neighbour who practised tooth-pulling. To save sixpence there were methods of self-help— strong thread put round a tooth and tied to a door, which you then slammed, was a recognised do-it-yourself way of pulling out a tooth. If eyesight began to fail, you gave up reading, or tried a junk-shop for a second- or third-hand pair of spectacles which might bring some benefit. Or you could buy new spectacles at Woolworths. There was a card on the counter for do-it-yourself eye-testing, and you tried on pair after pair of spectacles in the hope of coming across one which helped you to see better. Again the cost, although it might be only one shilling (sixpence for each lens—$2\frac{1}{2}$p) could be crippling. Crude as this sounds, Woolworths and other cheap shops which sold ready-made

[1] Cf. A. J. P. Taylor, *English History 1914-45.* "Unemployment insurance . . . took the edge off discontent. Even when the unemployed rioted, this was to get higher rates of benefit, not to bring down a system which had made them unemployed . . . Thanks to Lloyd George, barricades were not set up in English streets."

spectacles, provided a service of real value. If you had any incipient eye-disease, self-help of this nature might assist you to go blind. But if your sight was failing simply through age, a pair of ready-made or second-hand spectacles might be of enormous benefit. Society in the 1920s did not much care, either way.

Jim Cannon became unemployed after six months on strike. During the strike he had such minute help as the union could give, but no other benefit of any kind, for himself or his family. By the time he was classed as "unemployed" instead of being on strike the family was more or less destitute. When Jim got his unemployment relief it came to just over £2 a week *for the whole family*. The rates varied a bit from time to time, but averaged about 24s (£1.20) a week for himself and his wife, with 3s (15p) a week for each child—£2 2s (£2.10) a week all told. The family might just survive, but could not live on this. Nellie Cannon and the children came to the rescue.

The eldest son, Terry, was eleven in 1926, Jim Junior was ten, Frank eight, Les six, Ann five and Joan three. Terry, who had contracted polio as a baby and who owed his recovery to his mother's devotion, was still often in poor health. Ann had been gravely ill with double pneumonia as a baby. Les suffered from an ear-discharge, and was also often ill. In spite of these physical setbacks they were a tough family and this toughness, allied to Nellie Cannon's moral courage, made them undefeatable—by illness, unemployment or anything else. Nellie Cannon's first step towards economic self-help was to organise a paper round. She collected evening papers in bulk from a wholesaler, and the boys went round selling them as soon as they came home from school. This was hard work, and in winter cold work, but it brought in a pound or so a week, and for years was the mainstay of the family. Paper-selling took three forms. The first (and easiest) was delivery to regular customers in their own homes. But there were not enough regular customers. So the boys would take papers to their "pitches" at street corners, and sell to passers-by. Then, on Saturday evening, there was the round of clubs and pubs. For both "pitches" and club-selling there was stiff competition, but the Cannon boys were alert, ingenious and quick off the mark—they always managed to hold their own, and usually got in first. Selling newspapers was a serious business, and full of intricacies. This was in the days before radio, and newspapers, particularly local evening papers, with racing results, news of football and other sports, were more nearly a necessity of life than they are now. Saturday was the busiest day of the week, with four editions of the evening papers in the afternoon, and then—about 8 p.m.—the first editions of the Sunday papers. The boys would start by selling programmes outside the football ground. Then the evening papers would come out with half-time scores, and at three-quarter time in the local match they would be allowed into the ground. Everybody was interested in football, and business was brisk. Nellie Cannon would come round with banana sandwiches for the boys, but sometimes there was no time to eat them.

Paper-selling was essentially a family business. With all the boys able to take part, if one brother was ill, the others saw to it that the rounds were kept going.

The Cannons developed other small enterprises. When the evening paper rounds were finished, the boys would go to Wigan open-air market to pick up whatever orange boxes or broken crates they could persuade the stallholders to let them have. The boxes were taken home for Jim Cannon Senior to chop them into firewood. This was tied up in bundles, which the boys sold in the streets from a home-made wooden barrow at a penny or a halfpenny a bundle.

Then there was coal-picking. There is always some usable coal mixed with the slag from collieries, and hunting the slag heaps for burnable bits of coal is an age-old custom of the poor in colliery districts. Nominally, the coal still belongs to the colliery, and coal-picking is technically stealing, but the custom in those days was so widespread that it was commonly winked at. Very occasionally there might be a prosecution to establish the colliery company's rights in the coal, but nobody regarded such a prosecution as bringing any disgrace, and if a fine were imposed it would be met by a whip-round among the neigh-bours. Coal-picking, however, was subject to keen competition, particularly from women, known locally as "the pit-brow lasses", who made it almost a regular job. The Cannon boys would glean whatever bits of coal were missed by the women,

and take it home for their mother to use. If they were lucky
enough to have any surplus they kept it to make up into hundredweight bags which they sold for a shilling (5p), undercutting
the local coal-merchants' price of 1s 6d ($7\frac{1}{2}$p) a hundredweight.

Almost as important as the dole in preventing unemployed
miners and their families from seething into riot was this
access to coal. In other parts of England the miseries of unemployment were made worse by the fact that an unemployed
man's home was almost always cold—indeed, the homes of
the poor in winter were almost expected to be cold. In coalmining areas even the unemployed could usually keep a fire of
some sort going. There was coal to be picked, or a neighbour in
work might let an unemployed family have some of the con-
cessionary coal that was a traditional fringe-benefit for miners.
Poor as they were, the Cannons had their kitchen fire. Nellie
Cannon never relaxed her standards of cleanliness and good
housekeeping, and even when she was reduced to having only
one pair of sheets for each bed, her sheets were always washed
every week.

The boys had yet other ways of earning odd coppers. No
self-respecting housewife in Wigan—in the North of England
generally—would fail to keep her kitchen floor and front door-
step rubbed and whitened. If a tired woman had a few coppers
to spare she would gladly pay a boy to do her floor for her. The
young Cannons earned a name for good work with the rubbing-
stone, and this, too, added pennies—ocasionally a whole sixpence—to the family income.

For a short time the indefatigable Nellie Cannon tried to run
a small shop in her front room. She sold cigarettes and sweets,
but the profits were so minute that it is doubtful if the shop
ever really covered expenses. Another attempt at family business was an ice-cream round. Nellie Cannon made the ice-
cream, and a younger brother of Jim Cannon Senior, working
with another man, tried to sell it in the streets during the day.
In the evenings, when the boys had finished their newspaper
rounds, they would take out the push-cart. This business did
not prosper. There was heavy competition from established
ice-cream merchants, who had brightly painted horse-drawn
vans opposed to the Cannons' home-made push-cart. Another
cause of failure was the Cannons' reluctance to throw away

B

good food. If the boys came back in the evening with unsold ice-cream, the neighbours were invited to have it free. The prospect of free ice-cream in the evening naturally discouraged earlier sales. Burning wheat to keep up the price, or destroying today's good ice-cream in the interests of tomorrow's sales, were not practices that came naturally to the Cannons.

Apart from the pittance of Jim Cannon Senior's dole, the family was supported by Nellie Cannon and her boys. Why did Jim Cannon, outstandingly able and intelligent, apparently abdicate his family responsibilities?

Jim Cannon was always something of an enigma. His childhood as one of seventeen children brought up on a miner's wages was deprived in every material sense. He must have got some encouragement in his own reading from his literate mother, but she, exhausted by incessant pregnancies and the burden of her huge family, cannot have given him much. At the age of twelve he followed his father into the pit—apart from being helped to a job in coalmining, what other encouragement he got from his father one does not know. One suspects that it cannot have been much. Yet somewhere in his origins was a gene of towering intellectual ability, which not only enabled him to educate himself but gave him a profound understanding of politics. And he was not just self-educated; he was a man of wide culture, with a deep love of music. Again self-taught, he was a talented player of the mandolin.

When still in his teens, in the early 1900s, he began lecturing for the Workers' Educational Association and the National Council of Labour Colleges, and he was in demand as a lecturer throughout his life. He could lecture—and talk well—on almost anything, from the Labour Theory of Value to everyday problems of current wages. Whatever he undertook to speak about was studiously prepared, and he approached a lecture with real mastery of his facts, and prepared to deal with any supplementary question that might come up. He had a remarkable debating technique, keeping quiet and good-tempered while his opponent made the running, then suddenly coming in with a devastating reply.

Yet with all this, there was something lacking. He had tireless intellectual energy, but no practical drive. He was a scholar, not a man of action. His political reading, and his first-hand experience of injustice to working men and women, made him a convinced socialist, but he neither attempted to stand for Parliament (where he would certainly have made his mark) nor to achieve more than local trade union office. He had plenty of courage, and unshakeable loyalty. In the bitter strike of 1926 he took part in every miners' march and demonstration, even when such demonstrations came in for rough handling by the police—half a century ago the authorities, and often the public, were less sympathetic to trade union demonstrations than is customary today. He was sufficiently active in militant opposition to the coalowners to be black-listed after the strike and debarred from working as a miner. But from then on he did not fight, or rather, he was prepared to fight only intellectually. His neighbours called him "The Professor", and there was indeed something of the absent-minded professor about him. On one occasion two of the boys quarrelled while he was reading a book. Tempers flared as the quarrel turned into a fight— he simply went on reading. Finally, a relative was called to separate the boys. Jim Cannon took no notice and remained deeply immersed in his book.

He was ready enough to put his abilities at the disposal of other people—as long as (it seemed) he did not benefit himself. In those harsh days a miner made chronically sick by pneumoconiosis (a lung disease brought on by the inhalation of dust) or nystagmus (an eye disease caused by working in the pits) had often to fight to secure the meagre compensation that the law then provided for the victims of industrial disease. Although it might be self-evident that pneumoconiosis or nystagmus was due to working in the pits, a man still had to prove that his disability was caused by his work, and the medical representatives of insurance companies or the coalowners could deploy a host of cynically clever arguments to fog the issue. Jim Cannon had the intellectual skill to meet such arguments, and he used often to represent injured mineworkers at compensation tribunals. He was at his best on such occasions—cool, clearheaded, and of devastating forensic ability. This work was, of course, unpaid.

Although it was abundantly clear that Jim Cannon would never work again in the Wigan coalfield, he seems never to have contemplated going elsewhere in search of work; indeed, he seems to have made no great effort to look for work outside coalmining. He was once offered a job by the Co-operative movement which would have taken him to London. He declined it, on the ground that if he accepted it would mean doing some unemployed Londoner out of a job.

He was content—or seemed content—to leave the burden of supporting his family to his wife and young sons. Naturally, this exposed him to criticism—Les Cannon, in particular, as he grew up, felt bitterly about his father. Nellie Cannon, and the rest of the family, were all for self-help. Jim Cannon Junior, Les Cannon's elder brother, in some notes contributed to this biography, writes of the paper-selling, the coal-picking and the rest, and adds: "The picture I am trying to paint is that we would all, either individually or collectively, try anything to improve our standard of living."

But not the father of the family. The picture does not make sense. Jim Cannon Senior was a gentle, compassionate man. He was not an overbearing husband, a beer-swiller, determined to get what he could out of life for himself, at whatever cost to his family. Jim Cannon hardly touched beer—it was a rare occasion for him to enter a pub. Orwell, and other middle-class observers of unemployment between the wars, were struck by the fact that an out-of-work man would hardly ever lift a finger to help his wife with the housework—and that working-class wives did not expect, would even resent, such help. A man long unemployed has little left of human dignity; it is as if the last shreds of private dignity require that a man must not demean himself by doing "women's work", and as if his wife does not want her husband so "demeaned". However illogical, cruel, too, this attitude may seem, it was certainly real then, and perhaps still is in some industrial communities. Tradition, or herd instinct—for a man, however intelligent, can seldom wholly contract out of his herd—may explain Jim Cannon's detachment from housework. It cannot explain his detachment from the business of breadwinning, for that same tradition which requires a man to leave housework to women requires *him* to be the breadwinner. There was some much deeper psychological cause for Jim Cannon's unrealistic attitude to life.

It was unrealistic, not contemptible. His family might criticise

Jim Cannon for his detachment from breadwinning, but he kept their respect, and affection. They could not understand him, they could be very much irritated by him, but they remained exceedingly proud of him. And they learned much from him; his wide reading and philosophical approach to life fertilised all their minds.

Jim Cannon Senior was important to Leslie's development not least because he gave Les an angry determination not to contract out of life as his father apparently had done. Yet this is an over-simplification of two highly complex personalities. Jim Cannon did not contract out of life in the sense that a hippie does: he remained alert and keenly interested in politics, he was deeply concerned for the welfare of the working-class as mankind, if less immediately concerned for the income of his family. He is perhaps most nearly understood in early medieval terms, as a sort of anchorite whose vision is so fixed on the life to come that he has no eyes for his own surroundings. Jim Cannon was no religious visionary—he shared the Communist condemnation of religion as the opium of the people. He was a visonary nonetheless, his promised land the Socialist common-wealth where no man exploited another, and all could lead full lives without injustice.

Fifty years on, we have lived through another world war and long periods of Cold War, and we have seen the cynical imperialism with which Communist Russia treats her smaller neighbours. In the 1920s the Russian Revolution was still new, it still seemed to offer mankind a new vision and a new hope. It is necessary to try to think oneself back to fifty years ago. The clearest analogy is with the early Christian church, which looked to the Day of Judgment and the Second Coming as imminent events, likely to occur in a man's own lifetime. Many people in the 1920s expected world revolution and universal Communism to come in their own lifetime. In the coalfields, particularly, it seemed that social revolution *must* come in Britain; the miners, isolated by the conditions of their work, were so convinced of the justice of their case for an end to capitalist exploitation that it seemed inconceivable that things could long continue as they were. The prolonged strike of 1926 is understandable only in terms of the miners' belief that if they hung on long enough, events would somehow come to their rescue. Had not the Russian miners contributed a million roubles to their strike fund? Surely it was but a question of time before the whole working-class in Britain joined with the mineworkers to compel a new social system?

It did not turn out like that. Bevin, Thomas and the other dominant members of the TUC were not revolutionaries, nor were MacDonald, Snowden and the main political leaders of the Labour movement. Nor, indeed, were the workers in the newer and more prosperous British industries, most of whom wanted motor bicycles far more than revolution. The Labour Party made no effort to organise the unemployed; whatever it might preach in the way of socialism, its practical concern was for better doles. The miners *were* isolated, in their thinking as well as by the geography that (in the days before the motor car) kept the coalfields as places rather apart from the rest of Britain.

Jim Cannon's self-education was profoundly influenced by his experiences as a mineworker. His passionate loyalty was to his fellow-miners. His own black-listing, a savage sentence to a kind of economic death, was a form of martyrdom, to be endured patiently in the interests of his fellows. To leave the coalfields to look for work elsewhere would have seemed to him a sort of betrayal. That keeping faith with himself meant hardship for his wife and family was something that he could not help. His own vision sustained him.

That vision, however, was not a simple faith in Communism. Jim Cannon was a highly intelligent man, and one decade was enough to convince him that Communism allied to Russian power-politics was not the road to socialism for Britain. Although he had been a founder-member of the Wigan branch of the Communist Party in 1920, he broke with the Communists in 1929. The breach came—significantly—over a clash of loyalties, to the Communist Party on the one hand, to the mineworkers on the other. The miners' national leader, A. J. Cook, was not a Communist. His ideals were Communist almost in the sense of the Sermon on the Mount, he was a passionate preacher and widely regarded as a revolutionary. But he was never prepared to toe the Communist Party line, and if he disapproved of Communist political policy, he said so. At one election meeting he spoke against the Communists'

Harry Pollitt. This was too much for the Communists in the Mineworkers' Federation, who decided to conduct a campaign against Cook. Cannon supported Cook. Finally, he was told that he must either endorse the campaign against Cook, or leave the Communist Party. He left.

The elder Cannon's break with the Communist Party foreshadowed in a curious way the much more resounding break with the Communists later made by his son. When Les Cannon in his teens began to take an active part in politics, Jim Cannon Senior advised him not to join the Communist Party. It was typical of the father's intellectual honesty that when, in 1939, his son ignored his advice and did join the Party, the older man made no recrimination. What Leslie did was Leslie's business. Jim Cannon Senior would advise, but he would not nag.

The great slump that began with the American stock market crash in 1929 could not make things much worse for the Cannons, because by then Jim Cannon had already been out of work for four years. The real blow came in 1931 with the introduction of the Means Test. This was a brutal attack on such human dignity as an unemployed family might have left. In theory, the Means Test was supposed to prevent the abuse of unemployment relief by withholding benefit from those who did not really need it. In practice, since virtually every unemployed family needed every penny of the ungenerous dole, it brought intolerable unhappiness. The regulations required that the income—if any—of every member of a family living in the same home, from grandparents down to grandchildren, must be taken into account in reckoning an unemployed man's entitlement to relief. This had savage effects on family life, for many a teenage child who had just started in a job would leave home rather than let his earnings count against his father's dole. The administration of the test demanded endless snooping of the most unpleasant sort. Week by week the Means Test man would come round to discover if there had been any change in a family's circumstances. He would inspect the house for any sign that something new had been bought; if he noticed a new frying pan he wanted to know where the money to buy it had come from. Of course such snooping invited subterfuge: if a family had been given some new stick of furniture, it would

be taken to a neighbour's house until the Means Test man had
come and gone. Children who had any sort of job might go—
or at least go nominally—to live with relatives who were in
work, and therefore not subject to the Means Test. The Cannons were marginally better off than many because the boys
were not paid wages for their newspaper-selling, and earnings
fluctuated so greatly that it was hard for bureaucracy to assess
them. Even so, Jim Cannon's dole was cut as often as it could
be. It was a grim time.

In 1931 Jim Cannon had what seemed a chance of escaping
from the miseries of the Means Test, and a last chance of
returning to the coal industry. Being black-listed as an "agitator"
he could not hope for work as a miner, but there was one job
he could get, that of checkweighman. The checkweighman at a
colliery is a recognised mineworker, but he is not employed by
the management. His job is to check the weight of coal on
which pieceworkers are paid, and he is employed by the miners
themselves, through their union. Historically, a job as checkweighman has several times come to the rescue of individuals
in the coal industry persecuted for their views. Arthur Horner,
later to become General Secretary of the National Union of
Mineworkers, was black-listed in South Wales just as Jim
Cannon was in Lancashire. Horner returned to the coal industry as checkweighman of Mardy and he made that particular
checkweighman's job famous throughout Britain.

Checkweighmen are elected by their fellow-members of the
union, and when a vacancy occurred at Jim Cannon's old
colliery he stood as a candidate for the job. When the votes
were counted, the result was a tie. The issue was settled by the
toss of a coin. Jim Cannon lost.

That, however, was not the end of the matter. It turned out
that the successful candidate suffered from deafness, and he
was unable to do the job properly because he could not
always hear the weights called out for him to check. So he
resigned, and there was another election. Votes were cast by
the miners as they came off shift, and the sealed ballot-box
had to be kept somewhere overnight. With touching faith in
other people's integrity, Jim Cannon agreed that the box
should spend the night unguarded.

The curious result was that Jim Cannon had fewer votes than

he had polled before, an outcome, given his popularity for his work at compensation tribunals and the miners' traditional loyalty, that was very strange indeed. The family was heartbroken. Here, at last, was a real chance of getting back to regular wages, a chance that everything in Jim Cannon's record certainly merited. And it had gone against him, by reason of his own unrealism in trusting the ballot-box to remain unsupervised. Or so it seemed. Nothing could be proved: these things happen; but the happening was hard to bear. Nellie Cannon took it badly, threatening wildly—for the only time in her gallant life—to kill herself. Jim Cannon took the blow philosophically. Remarking, "I have been very careless", he returned to his books.

Jim's detachment often made him seem immune to his surroundings. His sister-in-law recalls seeing him walking in a Wigan street one day, pursued by a woman who did not share his political views, and who was screaming at him, "Bolshie, Bolshie, you bloody Bolshie". He didn't turn a hair, but continued his walk, immersed in whatever he was thinking about.

On another occasion he got into trouble with his mother-in-law for frying a piece of bacon in a pan that had been used for frying fish. How could anyone possibly put bacon in a fish pan? To Nellie Cannon's mother, and, no doubt, to Nellie, this seemed almost the last word in reprehensible absent-mindedness. Jim Cannon could not understand what the fuss was about.

His detachment, however, was from practical life, not from what he regarded as the realities of discussion, philosophical argument, and music. If his unrealism made him a bad father in some ways, his readiness to discuss things which his children, or anyone else who cared to come along, made him an intellectually exciting man to live with. In spite of his own atheism, a regular visitor to the home was a local clergyman who had long discussions with him about the Bible. The clergyman did not shake Jim Cannon's atheism; what effect he had on the clergyman's faith is unknown. The two men had apparently little in common, but they obviously enjoyed talking to each other, for they met regularly for some years. Jim might consider that an opponent in debate was wrong, but he respected sincerely-held convictions even when he did not agree with them. This readiness to listen to another man's arguments was one of the things that made him so formidable in debate.

He would spend hours with his mandolin, delighting particularly in airs from the Gilbert and Sullivan operas, large chunks of which he knew by heart. There was no television then, and families, especially poor families, had to make their own entertainment. Singing with Dad to the mandolin gave the Cannon family some of their happiest times together. Both Jim Cannon Junior and Leslie tried to learn to play the mandolin. Both became fair performers, but neither could match their father.

In 1936, after ten years on the dole, Jim Cannon at last got a job—as a lavatory attendant at the bus station in Wigan's Market Square. It was not much of a job, but the regular wages brought a little relief to Nellie Cannon. Jim was, as always, philosophical about it, observing that at any rate he was once more working in a basic industry. One of his jobs was to hand out clean towels to those who came for a wash and brush up. Among his clients one day was a Labour MP, for whom in the past he had often written speeches. The MP left him tuppence as a tip. It needed all Jim Cannon's philosophy to stomach that.

III

TOWARDS POLITICS

FROM THE AGE of five to the age of fifteen, throughout his most formative years, the dominant theme of Les Cannon's life was unemployment. He and his brothers and sisters lived with insecurity. When other children are just starting to go to school, Les was earning vitally important pennies to help to feed the family. Paper-selling, coal-picking, scrubbing a neighbour's floor, were not for fun or pocket-money—they were jobs that earned food. He had to go to school too, of course, so that his share of the work had to be done after school hours.

He did not enjoy good health. The ear-discharge from which he had suffered from infancy often caused sores on his neck and face, and he had a pronounced stutter. He learned to live with these disabilities, his lively outdoor activities unimpaired.

The stable factor in his world was his mother. However tired she was—and she must often have been desperately tired—she kept her sense of humour throughout her life. The one luxury she allowed herself in those days was an occasional visit to a cinema, where she promptly fell asleep. She kept their home spotless, saw to it that clothes were clean and mended, and produced the best meals she could. Nellie Cannon always provided cooked meals of some sort for her family—the children were not sent off for a penn'orth of chips from the fried-fish shop. Sometimes there was no more than bread and margarine when the children came home from school, but the bread was always freshly baked at home. The crusts were a reward for the first child home, a bonus keenly sought. She could buy only the cheapest meat, scrag end, bacon ends and the like, but she planned carefully and cooked well.

Les was deeply attached to his mother. To see her always working, always tired, made him angry, and added to his sense of resentment about his father. In his child's eyes, his father should have done more to help, and he determined that if he himself grew up to have a family he would find ways of keeping them all properly. Les never understood his father's detachment—how could a child understand it? Later in life he realised that it was not indolence, but some much more complex psychological state, but he was never able to understand it—his father's detachment was utterly alien to his own passionate sense of responsibility for others. These feelings towards his father certainly helped to mould his own attitude to life.

His father's unemployment dominated Les's childhood, but, of course, his father was but one of a multitude of unemployed in Wigan. Half of Les's generation grew up in the same world of insecurity; unemployment, Means Testings, the indignities that the poor were expected to accept, were in the air he breathed. Les did not accept them. Even as a child he did not blame his father for unemployment; he did blame him for not putting his abilities to work in other ways, but he understood well enough that unemployment in the coal industry was a national sickness, and nothing to do with individual miners. Reading his father's books, talking to his father, gave him a political education with his primary schooling. Of course he did not formulate things clearly as a schoolboy: he did feel instinctively that to leave a man like his father unemployed was a crime by somebody, and that he himself was going to do whatever he could to change the system. Dreams of youth . . . but Les's dreams were built on the harsh facts of unemployment in the 1920s and early thirties.

It was a hard childhood, but not a bleak one. There are checks and balances in life, and the ugliness of unemployment in Wigan's mean streets was redeemed by a close-knit sense of community. Nellie Cannon saw to it that the family was always a warm, compact group, and the community of Wigan's "Potteries" was in many ways an enlargement of the family. Everybody knew everyone else. The clinker of Swan Meadow was a universal playground, and the grey streets of little terraced houses were instinct with human companionship of all ages. The Cannons were not pub-goers—there was no money— but the neighbourhood's one pub, also called Swan Meadow, was a focus of interest in their lives. The children would gather

outside the door at closing time on Friday evenings, to wait for
a kindly old miner known as Old Sheppy. He would emerge a
trifle mellow and roll pennies in the road for the youngsters
to chase after. There were strict rules to this game. The children
had to line up along a wall, and the old man would roll a
penny down the line. As soon as the penny passed the end of
the line the kids were free to chase it, and whoever got the
penny kept it. The chase was enlivened, and given a spice of
danger, by the occasional passing of cart-horses—there was
hardly any motor traffic then. Sometimes a child would have
to dive under the belly of a horse to get at the elusive penny.
Les, always alert and agile, was particularly good at this.

He had his share of childhood adventures. Once he managed
to get his head stuck in the iron railings that walled off the
River Douglas from the backyards of Cudworth Street. All his
mother's efforts with margarine as a lubricant failed to release
him, and the Fire Brigade had to be called to cut him free.
There was a great occasion when workmen came to knock a
hole in the Corporation Transport Depot at Swan Meadow.
The hole was to make a new entrance for buses, but while it
remained just a hole it was a wonderful cave for games. The
boys called it "Red Gulch", a romantic-sounding name from
one of Tom Mix's cowboy films.

At five, Les went to the local Church of England school,
a gaunt Victorian building, with high Gothic windows. He
joined the Sunday School and enjoyed the annual Sunday
School treats, usually an outing to Blackpool. It was on one of
these outings that he first came across a fruit machine. It took
pennies, with the promise of rich rewards. Les had two pennies,
which he entrusted to the machine. It kept the pennies, but
returned nothing. So his spending-money was gone. He was
bitterly disappointed, and there and then made a resolution
to have nothing more to do with gambling machines—a
resolution which he kept throughout his life.

The school had little to offer but the rudiments of reading
and arithmetic, which Les acquired quickly because he was
naturally bright. He hated the rigid authority of the school,
however, and was often in trouble.

Just after his twelfth birthday he won a scholarship to the
Junior Technical School of Wigan and District Mining and

Technical College. This was a real achievement, for competition for such scholarships was keen. Only sixty-four awards,
some from Wigan Borough, some from Lancashire County
Council, were given each year, and to qualify for an award a
boy had to show outstanding ability. Les was helped by his
remarkable command of English, brought about by the wide
reading encouraged by his father. The immediate effect of his
scholarship, however, was an acute financial problem for his
mother.

Boys at the Junior Technical College wore suits which
were regarded as their school uniform. It was unthinkable that
Les should be dressed differently. But the school uniform cost
£2, and Nellie Cannon did not have £2—£2 was large sum
then, and Florrie's readiness to lend it was an act that neither
Nellie Cannon nor her son ever forgot.

The school-leaving age was then fourteen. Unless a parent
could afford school-fees there were few opportunities for secon-
dary education. There were some free places at grammar
schools, but not many, and even if a boy were able enough to
win a free place his parents might be unable to keep him while
he stayed at school. Les's scholarship gave him three years of
general education, with a good grounding in technical skills
such as woodwork and metalwork. One of his teachers, Mr H. C.
Lillicrap, remembered him well nearly forty years later, and
wrote of him in 1971: "He was consistently good in physics,
woodwork and English. At the age of fourteen he wrote con-
fidently and fluently; his essays were well-ordered, thoughtful,
and, like his handwriting, exceptionally mature."

When he was fourteen Les joined a Church Guild and attended classes in religious instruction that were held on Monday
evenings. He showed such aptitude that the Church offered to
provide for his further education so that he could be trained for
the priesthood. This alarmed his atheist father, who promptly
set Les reading and discussing political philosophy. After a few
months no more was heard of the priesthood.

At fifteen and a half Les left school for a job as a van-boy
at an oil depot hard by the old Wigan Pier. His teachers and
his mother were disappointed; they wanted him to stay on at
school, and by that time he had shown such obvious ability
that he could almost certainly have got a grant. Les enjoyed

learning, but at that time—1935—the prospects even for well educated boys were dim; many of his older schoolmates, even those with really good qualifications, were on the dole. Moreover, Les had always before him the example of his own father —a highly educated man who had been on the dole for years. In Wigan in the mid-1930s there did not seem much purpose in acquiring education. And above all else, Les wanted to try to help his mother. So when the chance of a job at the oil depot came along, he took it.

It was not much of a job. He worked with the driver of a van delivering paraffin. The van carried paraffin in bulk, from which deliveries were made in two-gallon cans. It was the van-boy's job to measure paraffin into the cans, to carry the cans from van to customer, and to bring back empty cans. In the depot he was responsible for cleaning and polishing the van. He also had an unofficial job, which was more important (at least to the driver) than all his other duties. The van-boy sat beside the driver in the cab of the van, and it was his job to note the mileage whenever the driver was able to cruise with the engine shut off. The van was supposed to run so many miles to a gallon of petrol, and when it had run a sufficient number of "free" miles the driver would syphon the equivalent quantity of petrol from the tank into two-gallon cans. This petrol would then be sold to certain garages at a cut price. (Petrol, then, was still frequently sold to motorists in cans, so there was a ready market.) A skilful driver could add quite a bit to his wages in this fashion, and the money was important to him, for a driver's wages in Wigan in those days averaged not much more than £2 a week.

Most of the drivers working for the depot were cheerful souls, and they normally gave a proportion of this unofficial mileage-bonus to their boys. Les's driver was a surly individual, who gave him nothing. He was not a pleasant man to work for.

Experience in the depot was not much happier. At the end of his first week, at noon on Saturday, Les was polishing the mudguard of his van before it went into the garage for the weekend. He was feeling rather proud of the gloss he was putting on the mudguard when the depot superintendent came up and asked him how he liked the work. Les, whose surly driver had not quenched his enthusiasm for earning a living, replied that he liked it very much.

"Take your cap off and call me Sir when you speak to me," said the superintendent.

Les did not stay in that job long. About three weeks later one of the more friendly drivers warned him that he was about to get the sack. This had nothing to do with Les's work, but was the outcome of a deal made by one of the salesmen with the owner of a hardware store. The salesman had succeeded in getting a fairly large order for paraffin previously supplied by a rival oil company, but one of the terms of the deal was that a job should be found at the depot for the shopkeeper's nephew. The commission on that particular deal was paid out of Les's livelihood.

Les was now on the dole himself. For a brief moment there seemed something almost manly in telling his mates, "I'm going to sign on tomorrow," but the bitterness of being out of work soon made itself felt. There just *were* no jobs. Les undertook a planned campaign to look for work. He divided the whole Wigan industrial area into sectors, and every morning he would set off on his bicycle to call at every cotton mill and engineering works in a particular sector to ask for work. One major field of possible work was barred to him because of his name—the coal industry. As Jim Cannon's son, the son of a black-listed agitator, there would be no work for him in the Lancashire coalfield, so it was no use trying there. He went far outside Wigan to all the neighbouring cotton towns. But it was no good. At one mill he did get a temporary job sweeping out a weaving shed. He went to his sweeping-up job in his old Wigan Technical College cap. The foreman recognised the cap, told Les that it was a shame that a lad with his education should be able to find nothing better than a sweeper's job, and encouraged him to keep on trying for something else. The foreman's kindliness could not provide a job, but it shone out in Les's memories of a miserable period.

He still helped with the family's paper rounds. The night of October 3, 1935, brought wonderful business, though for a sad reason. The papers that night carried the headline, "Italy Invades Abyssinia". With the fear of war in everybody's mind people rushed out to buy papers, and Les sold bundle after bundle. He did not get home until 1 a.m.—his pockets weighed down with pennies—to find his mother still waiting for him. It was a Wednesday, the evening when the family supper was sausage and tomato—one of Les's favourite meals. Late as it was, his mother had his supper ready for him.

In terms of the calendar Les's unemployment lasted only for about two months, though it seemed an eternity at the time. Shortly before his sixteenth birthday his fine school record came to the rescue, and he was taken on as an apprentice electrician by Wigan Corporation, which maintained its own Electricity Department.

Les was lucky to get an apprenticeship with a local authority employer. There was no national agreement then governing apprentice-wages, and the tradition that an apprenticeship to a skilled trade was to be paid for by a parent rather than an employer was still strong. Many a local contractor charged a premium for taking an apprentice. Sometimes the premium would be paid back in wages—in very small sums, like half a crown (12½p) a week—over the period of the apprenticeship. Sometimes a boy would be paid nothing at all, being amply recompensed (it was argued) by being permitted to learn a trade. This was the old principle of apprenticeship, when a journeyman's skills were guarded by the medieval Trade Guilds, and entry to professions such as medicine and the law as well as crafts like printing and woodworking was alike achieved by apprenticeship. And this, indeed, is still the basis for the sharp distinction in status between the skilled tradesman and the labourer. The system, however, was always open to abuse by encouraging the employment of apprentices as cheap labour, and in the heavy unemployment of the early 1930s many apprentices were deliberately so used, and sacked as soon as they became entitled to a journeyman's rates of pay. A local authority, particularly one in an industrial area, could not behave like this, and Wigan Corporation was reckoned a good employer. No premium was asked for Les's apprentice-ship, and he was paid 14s (70p) a week, rising by stages to 25s (£1·25) a week. He was also encouraged to go back to school, and in 1937 he returned to Wigan Technical College to begin the three-year course of part-time day study required for the Ordinary National Certificate in Electrical Engineering. He did extremely well. At the end of his first year he was awarded the First Senior Course Prize, and a year later he won the Electrical Engineering Course Prize. His early schooling had been notable for his ability in English. He began now to show outstanding ability in maths, getting 96 per cent in an examination on the calculus. Mathematics appealed to something deep in his nature—its orderliness, perhaps, the precision with which effect can be calculated from cause, gave him intense intellectual satisfaction. In other circumstances he might well have become a mathematical philosopher; he was sensitive not alone to the usefulness but to the sheer beauty of mathematical conceptions. But the physical setting of his life at seventeen did not go with academic philosophy. He was interested in too many other things. Moreover, in 1938 the future of everybody and everything seemed dominated by the rising power of the dictators, Hitler and Mussolini. If there was to be a future for any sort of human decency, that power had to be challenged. As he grew into his later teens, Les threw himself more and more passionately into politics. Although he easily qualified for his Ordinary National Certificate in Electrical Engineering, he never sat for the Higher Certificate.

Les Cannon's political apprenticeship, which culminated in his decision to join the Communist Party in 1939, will be discussed in the next chapter. Here we are concerned with other influences of his teenage years which helped to form the personality that later threw itself into politics. Those influences were diverse. Poverty was endemic, its influence all-embracing, but by no means wholly destructive. Les knew, for instance, that his mother had had to borrow the money for his first suit of school clothes; he hated the indignity she had suffered for his sake, but, in a way, the knowledge that he could not afford school clothes added to his sense of achievement in winning the scholarship that took him to the Technical College. His family might be poor, but in his school work he could match boys from far richer homes. School gave him confidence, and the nervous stutter which had affected him earlier gradually diminished. Poverty also heightened all enjoyment: little

things, taken for granted in today's relatively affluent society—
the buying of a paperback book (Penguins then cost 6d—2½p)
or a visit to the cinema—were acts of positive pleasure. Poverty
of the sort that the Cannon family endured is not ennobling.
It is an affront to the human spirit, and, in so far as British
society is rid of it, people are well rid of it. But where such
poverty did not destroy, it undoubtedly stiffened character.
Les Cannon's determination to fight against poverty, his
courage and his endurance, derived in part from poverty itself.

Keen as he was on books and political discussion, Les was
no withdrawn intellectual. He was a lively teenager and enjoyed swimming, rugby and soccer. Girls found him very
attractive, and though he was shy he had a number of girl
friends. He was particularly keen on dancing and enrolled in
the classes of a well-known dancing school in Wigan. He
became an excellent dancer and a member of a (competition)
formation-dancing team. It was typical of him that he took
everything to do with dancing very seriously. When he went to
a dance he dressed for it with elaborate care, with the assistance
of his sister and aunt. There was no bathroom at home—a bath
was still a tub in front of the kitchen fire—and Les was scrupulous about personal cleanliness. He used to go regularly to
the house of his aunt, who had a bathroom, to have baths.

On May Day, 1936, two months after his sixteenth birthday,
Les joined the Electrical Trades Union as an apprentice-
member and he became a regular attender at the weekly
meetings of the Wigan branch of the ETU. In common with a
number of trade union branches then, meetings were held in
public houses, and drinking was permitted at branch meetings.
Les's first job in the Union was as a "waiter" in the Wigan
branch: he carried trays loaded with pints of beer to the
branch meeting-room, first in the Crofter's Arms, later in the
Fleece Hotel.

He enjoyed those meetings, held every Friday evening. There
was little general political discussion, but much detailed argument about working conditions. In the mid-1930s, the cost of
living was falling slightly and wage-levels were more or less
static. Nowadays one of the main bases for trade union discussion is the effect of the annual Budget. It was not of much
concern to trade unionists then. There was no PAYE, and few

wage-earners earned enough to pay much income tax. Cigarettes were ten for 6d (2½p), the smaller brands such as Players *Weights* and Wills's *Wild Woodbine* ten for 4d—such prices seemed part of the natural order of things and remained unchanged throughout the thirties (until the first Budget of the war). Trade unionists in the 1930s were chiefly concerned with staying in work, and one of the main topics of discussion at ETU branch meetings was the application of an embargo limiting the amount of work it was permissible for a contracting electrician to perform during a working day. If any member was accused of violating the embargo he was brought before the branch and charged with the offence. If found guilty he was fined, sometimes quite heavily—there were cases in which fines of £20 were imposed, a huge sum in those days.

Few things cause such anti-trade union feelings as restrictions on the amount of work a man is permitted to do. Employers naturally resent such restrictions, the public feels that it suffers from them, they raise leader-writers' hackles. Deliberately to tell a man to work at a slower pace than he is capable of working, slower, perhaps, even than he himself wants to work, seems an offence against all nature. Yet at times of heavy unemployment, or even when there is fear of unemployment, restrictions on output are still the most effective weapon that trade unions can employ in defence of jobs. Of course they harm national production, tend to make industries uncompetitive, and all the rest of it. But what matters to a man in Wigan is that *he* should have a job next month: it is no use telling him that in the long run the national economy will be better off if he abandons restrictive practices, if, in the short run, the price *to him* is to work himself out of a job. Human life is lived in the short run, from day to day, from week to week. That there should *be* a wage packet next week matters far more to a wage-earner and his family than the most impressive economic forecasts on what may happen next year. In the 1970s, with trade unions infinitely stronger than they were forty years ago, insecurity is still the basic fear in people's lives, and the unions are still reluctant to abandon defences that have proved effective in protecting *their own members*, whatever untoward side-effects they may have on the nation's livelihood. Political and industrial statesmanship have failed to create any real confidence that for an individual to act in the "national interest" instead of his own brings anything but personal disaster. This is a national tragedy which Les's later work on education and productivity sought to mitigate. But that is looking ahead.

In the 1930s every man in a job, however poor the job might be, knew that there was at least one other man who wanted it—in the older industrial areas, like Wigan, where unemployment was particularly severe, there might be two, three or four other men after every job there was. Among men who are desperate for work there will always be some who are ready to take a job for less than the going rate of wages—in the 1930s, when welfare benefits were minimal, the poorest paid work was better than being on the dole. There were good and bad employers then as there always have been, but there were enough employers ready to take advantage of cheap labour if it offered itself to threaten the security of every man in work. Trade unions cannot be blamed for clinging to their defences. Unhappily, there was a need for defences within each working group, as well as against the outside world. The existence of more men than jobs did not always bring out the finer traits of character among trade unionists. Men who were younger than their mates, or who enjoyed better health or physique, might always be tempted to show that they could work harder than the rest, in the hope that when slack times came they would be the last to be laid off. The union's counter to this very human frailty was to try to insist that no man should work harder than another, to present each man's performance as exactly the same. This led then, as similar practices do still, to endless petty jealousies and frictions. No wonder there was plenty to talk about at meetings of the Wigan branch of the ETU without going deeply into national politics.

The apprentices were more directly concerned with trade union practices then than most youngsters seem to be now. Many of them feared that as soon as they qualified for a journeyman's wage they would be sacked; thus they felt it very much in their own interests that work should be spun out. Moreover, as apprentices, they were covered by no agreement, and they looked hopefully to the union to try to get them one. Apprentices were among the most regular attenders at branch meetings of the Wigan ETU in those days. There would be from five to twenty boys at every meeting—a wonderful turn-out by today's standards.

In 1938 the apprentices' grievances came to a head. Many of them were still working for nothing at all, and nothing ever seemed to be done for them. They decided to raise their problems at a branch meeting, and appointed Les as their spokesman. It was not an easy task. By no means all the men were sympathetic to the boys, and some members challenged the right of boys to put a motion to a branch meeting. Les, however, won the argument here, and it was agreed that local employers should be asked to increase apprentice wages.

This got no one much forrader. The branch duly submitted the boys' request, to receive a formal answer that there was no national agreement about apprentice wages, but that if and when there was one the Wigan employers would certainly abide by it. This do-nothing formula angered the boys. Les and his mates forced another branch decision to go back to the employers to say, "If there is no national agreement, then there is nothing to stop the Wigan employers from making a local agreement about apprentices."

This was a minor victory, but it was no use; the branch officers felt that they had no power to help the boys. The boys, however, were now out to help themselves. They insisted that the branch should request another meeting with the employers, and (perhaps wisely) they also asked that an apprentice-representative should accompany the branch delegation. Les got the job, and at eighteen set out on his first trade union negotiation with employers.

Here is his own recollection of the occasion:

The meeting took place in the upstairs room of an old pub. As I waited there with the chairman and secretary of our branch, I kept nipping out to the "gents" as anticipation of the ordeal got to work on my nervous system. I had written down all that I wanted to say, and I had come armed with the levels of wages of all the various apprentices employed by the gentlemen I was about to meet.

We were called upstairs. The branch chairman and secretary, for some reason I have never understood, sat on some leather wall-seats some yards away from the conference table, where the employers were, leaving me to sit facing them alone.

According to the advice of my father, I did nothing more than state my case. I didn't attempt to explain it, still less to prove it. "See what's in their mind first" was his advice.

But there was nothing new in their mind. The employers' chairman (with whose son I later became very friendly) told me in a tone of rather too-obvious patience what he had already told the branch officials.

"If there is no national agreement," I replied, "and you are not empowered to reach a local agreement, then that means that each of you individually has the power to fix the wages of each of your apprentices." Having got that much agreed, I added, "If that is the case, then each of you can individually raise the wages of your apprentices, and according to the information I've got here," I went on, cheekily brandishing the information about apprentice wages, "they certainly need raising."

This was a good move. The employers were obviously anxious that the wages they paid to their respective apprentices should not be disclosed to one another. I was immediately side-tracked by the astute secretary of the employers' side, who announced that in spite of everything that had been said they had been considering the problem of apprentice wages and were, in fact, proposing to grant an increase to all apprentices in line with the operation of a new wage-award to adults.

So my move succeeded. But I feel now that I ought to have done better. One of the things I learned from ruminating over that experience was never again to allow myself to be robbed of the initiative as I had been by the secretary's smart interruption.

Shortly before his triumph as the apprentices' champion Les was in another fight, which ended less successfully. One of the attractions of the bi-annual Fair held in Wigan's Market Square was a boxing booth run by a man called Bert Hughes. He engaged various professional boxers, some of them quite well known in their day, who were prepared to take on all

comers. There was a prize of ten shillings for anyone who sur-
vived three rounds against Bert Hughes's man. Les wanted
ten shillings. Standing up to punishment in the boxing booth
seemed a hard way of earning it, but Les was game to try and
he agreed to fight a particularly powerful opponent. Mr Ted
Hamill, a contemporary of Les, who was with him at the time,
recalled the scene for this book:

Les at this time was about seventeen, and one brick thick,
as they say. His opponent was superbly muscled and magnificent. I can see poor old Les now, in my mind's eye,
painfully thin, pallid in the extreme, with his pants held up
by his braces tied round his waist as a belt. With his shirt
removed, he stood in stark contrast to his Black Panther
of an opponent.

Les's only assets were his heart and guts. The wide disparity in boxing skills allowed the professional boxer to
ridicule Les's clumsy efforts to put in a blow. He repeatedly
made Les miss him by about a yard, and kept kicking him
in the pants as he blundered by. The crowd was greatly
amused by this exhibition. But at the end of the first round
Les, his temper blazing, whispered to me, "I'll kill him in
the next round."

Round Two, however, was a replica of Round One, and a
caricature of a contest. Suddenly Les's temper snapped, and
I heard him hiss at his opponent words that repudiated the
legitimacy of his birth. As the full significance of Les's insult
sank into the big fighter, he went berserk, and tore into the
helpless boy with frightening ferocity. He crashed his gloved
fist incessantly into Les's face, and the crowd shouted to the
referee to stop the fight.

Thankfully (because the crowd was getting really angry)
Bert Hughes did call a halt to things, and with commendable
alacrity of thought announced that Les's opponent would
be disqualified for the rest of their stay in Wigan. This
mollified the crowd, and averted what had become a po-
tentially dangerous situation. Meanwhile, Les was in a bad
way, floored and outed. His bloody and battered face presented a sorry spectacle as I did my best to help him. Eventually
I dressed him, and got him outside into the cool air, which

revived him considerably. I thought it utterly characteristic of him when he muttered to me through bruised lips, "I'm going into strict training from now on, and when this man comes again I'll murder the guy."

Les did not even get his ten shillings.

IV

THE THIRTIES

WHEN RAMSAY MACDONALD split the Labour Party in 1931 by forming his "National" Government to try to meet the economic crisis that came with the world slump, Les Cannon was eleven. His father had left the Communist Party in 1929, but he remained a Marxist, and his political teaching was on wholly Marxist lines, regarding the performance of MacDonald, Snowden, Thomas and their followers as a betrayal of everything the Labour movement stood for. The cuts in unemployment benefit that the "National" Government imposed were seen as a further betrayal, putting the interests of bankers before those of men and women on the dole. Of course the Cannons were politically to the Left. In their circumstances they couldn't be anything else. Les imbibed Left-wing political thinking with every meal that the capitalist system seemed to grudge the unemployed.

The 1930s were an appalling decade in British political life. No one under fifty now recalls anything about them, and even those of us whose youth was formed (or malformed) by the events of the thirties find it hard to picture now the full political beastliness of that unhappy period. It requires a deliberate effort of will as well as of memory to think back to a time that we should much rather forget. To understand the political development of Les Cannon such effort of both will and memory is imperative. Those under fifty, who *can* remember nothing of the thirties, must try to comprehend emotionally as well as intellectually the history of the time.

The early thirties were barely half a generation away from the slaughter and the suffering of the First World War. The war of 1939–45, though it brought greater suffering to civilians, was not comparable with the war of 1914–18 in its emotional shock. That first war produced the senseless slaughter of the Western Front and destroyed everything that had seemed ordered and stable in the Western world. Political thinking in Britain through most of the thirties was not merely dominated by the fear of war, it was all-but paralysed by it. This led to betrayal after shameful betrayal of every moral standard that was once supposed to govern international relations. The dictators, Hitler and Mussolini in Europe, the Japanese in the Far East, laughed at moral standards, while thinking people in Britain agonised over them. So the dictators won every time —in Manchuria, Abyssinia, Spain, Czechoslovakia and Austria cynical aggression seemed the one policy that worked. The dreadful thing in Britain was that nobody seemed capable of doing anything about it. Every British Government in the thirties—MacDonald's, Baldwin's, Chamberlain's—seemed alike unwilling and unable to take any effective action to check the dictators. And the reports coming out of Germany and Italy and the countries they controlled became more and more horrifying as the decade advanced.

The Labour Party, apart from that discredited section of it which followed MacDonald into the National Government, was in opposition throughout the decade. But what did it oppose? Labour leaders might protest about the sufferings of the unemployed, they might make brave speeches about the need to help democracy in Spain, but they did nothing to rally the nation into any real opposition to the Government. The Liberals, also split between "National" Liberals and the rest, were equally ineffective in giving political opposition any cutting edge.

The leader of the Labour Party after the defection of Ramsay MacDonald and his "National" supporters was George Lansbury, an idealist and a convinced pacifist. He was greatly respected and greatly loved, and even those who did not share his wholly pacifist views felt it unthinkable that Labour should ever support another war. In 1935, when Mussolini invaded Abyssinia, the question had to be faced—would the British people go to war if necessary in support of the League of Nations to resist an aggressor? The answer, as determined by most of the country's political leaders, was that they would not. Even the imposition of economic sanctions against Italy, half-heartedly as they were applied, caused intense heart-searching. Support of the League of Nations was official Labour policy, but the vociferous Left wanted nothing to do with it, holding that the League was a capitalist instrument—it was denounced in a famous phrase by Sir Stafford Cripps, then a leader of the Socialist Left, as no more than "an international burglars' union". The pacifists feared sanctions as a first step towards war. Lansbury argued that the only honourable attitude towards aggression was passive resistance.

Lansbury's extreme pacifism was becoming an embarrassment to the Labour Party and after a savage attack upon him by Ernest Bevin at the Party conference in October 1935, he resigned as leader, to be replaced by Clement Attlee. This did little to clear the murky political air. Labour, under Attlee, Morrison and Dalton on the parliamentary side, and Ernest Bevin, on the trade union side, paid lip-service to the League of Nations and even to sanctions against Italy, but resisted every suggestion for the rearmament that would have put teeth into British international policy.

The Conservatives in the "National" Government were no clearer and (if possible) even more dishonest. The League of Nations was to be supported, of course, but far from pressing sanctions against Italy to the point of war, diplomatic effort was directed towards buying off Mussolini at the expense of Abyssinia. The policy of "appeasement" (though the word was not much in use until the later thirties) was in the air. There is a theory nowadays that Winston Churchill, then in the political wilderness, and his band of patriotic stalwarts were active throughout the 1930s in pressing for rearmament and a determined stand against the dictators. That is largely myth. True, Churchill and his friends warned against Germany, and in their private studies had a political and military realism that the major parties shied away from, but they *did* little or nothing to rally national opinion. They were inhibited always by the fear that real resistance to the Western dictators would end by strengthening Soviet Russia.

There were brave individual voices raised in Britain in those desolate years, but the only coherent party line against aggression was that of the Communists. After Russia joined the League of Nations in 1934 they differed from the Socialist Left in advocating full-blooded support for the League. They were not afraid of war in what they regarded as a good political cause. When the Spanish Civil War thickened the international miasma the Communists sent many of their best young men to fight and die with the International Brigade raised to support the Spanish Government. Their fortitude and courage became legendary—one of the few redeeming features of a dreadful decade.

But the Communist Party of Great Britain had no hope of securing political power. In the General Election of 1935 they managed to get one Member (Willie Gallacher) returned to Parliament, but in the British Parliamentary system that was at best a political idiosyncrasy. What the Communists could do, and tried very hard to bring off, was to promote an alliance of men and women of all shades of opinion who could be persuaded to come together in a Popular Front, animated by a common disgust at the ignominy of national policies against the dictators, and a common readiness to fight.

Given the support of any significant leadership from the main political parties such a Popular Front might have carried the day in Britain; it probably came nearer to expressing the real feelings of the inarticulate mass of the British people than any of the established parties. But no such leadership was forthcoming. Churchill, who always commanded a nucleus of potential support in the country, would have nothing to do with anything that smacked of Communism. The Labour Party was adamant against any alliance that might include Communists. The TUC, having had endless bickering in the 1920s with splinter groups supporting the Red International of Labour Unions formed by the Comintern, was ready to go to any lengths to resist Communist infiltration: Ernest Bevin was said (with the truth often embodied in a popular catch-phrase) to regard the Soviet Union as a breakaway from the Transport and General Workers Union. The idea of a Popular Front attracted a good deal of Liberal support, but that counted for little in real political terms. It achieved one notable victory in 1938, when Vernon Bartlett, essentially a Popular Front candidate, was returned as an Independent MP at a by-election in Bridgwater, Somerset. Historically, the agitation for a Popular Front in the 1930s may be said to have played a large part in bringing about the sweeping Labour victory in 1945, but that is another matter. In the 1930s, the years of young Les Cannon's political apprenticeship, it was at best a safety-valve for political frustration, enabling people to *feel* that they were trying to do something, whether they accomplished anything or not.

That is in practical terms. In another sense, in promoting political thinking among people who might otherwise have given little thought to politics, the 1930s formed a genuinely creative decade. The creative element that sprang from frustration was manifested in an extraordinary fashion in something quite other than any normal form of political expression—the success of an individual publisher's book club. The late (Sir) Victor Gollancz's Left Book Club, founded in March 1936, wound up in November 1948, was an institution unique in British political history. It had some collateral relationship with the eighteenth-century pamphleteers and with Robert Blatchford's later *Clarion* activities, but differed from all predecessors in the field of literary politics in the range and sustained quality of the books it published month by month over more than ten years.

Isolated in Wigan, Les derived political and educational sustenance from the Left Book Club. He never joined the Club in the sense of contracting to buy its "Book of the Month" and going on its mailing list—he had little enough spending money to find even half a crown (12½p) a month. But his cousin Edna was a member, and so were a number of his friends. The books they got from month to month were passed round, and Les read them avidly.

Wigan had a rather special place in the Left Book Club, for it provided the title for George Orwell's *The Road to Wigan Pier*, perhaps the most seminal study of working-class conditions in the 1930s ever published. It was issued as the Left Book Club's "choice" for March 1937, and it is interesting to note that companion volumes issued as supplementary books in that same month included *Freud and Marx* by Reuben Osborn and *Defence of Madrid* by Geoffrey Cox.

The club was not, and never attempted to become, a political party. It was the expression of Popular Front feeling, and its meetings drew speakers from the whole range of political life. They included Wilfred Roberts and Richard Acland, both

Liberal Members of Parliament, Robert (Lord) Boothby, a Conservative with a strongly independent streak, Harry Pollitt and Palme Dutt, both leading Communists, Eleanor Rathbone, who sat in Parliament as Independent Member for the (then) University constituency representing Universities outside Oxford, Cambridge and London, the Dean of Canterbury (The Very Rev. Hewlett Johnson, known for his political views as "The Red Dean"), and (then) Labour rebels or near-rebels including Aneurin Bevan, Russell Strauss, Ellen Wilkinson and Harold Laski. Another moving spirit in the Club was John Strachey, later to become a Minister in Mr Attlee's Government, but then strongly sympathetic to the Communists. Strachey and Harold Laski, with Victor Gollancz, were the selectors of LBC books.

The Left Book Club was the Open University of the 1930s, biased, as its name quite clearly stated, on the side of Left-wing causes, but so it had to be. Here the imperative stressed at the beginning of this chapter must be brought in again—those aged over 50 must deliberately think themselves back into the 1930s, those under 50 must try by an effort of imagination to reconstruct the political frustration of that horrible decade. The cynical description of life as a comedy for those who think, a tragedy for those who feel, will not do. The 1930s were tragic alike for those who thought, or felt. There seemed no hope in the actions of any Western European Government. The performances of governments in Germany, Italy and their satellites were loathsome. The destruction of democracy in Spain, openly fostered by Germany and Italy, connived at by Britain and France with their ignoble policy of non-intervention, was agony to think about. The Spanish Civil War was perhaps the last war in history in which the issues seemed wholly simple and clear-cut—the Fascist forces of evil were marshalled against all the decent forces of good. It was not, of course, in reality so simple, but it seemed so. In the war of 1939–45 one could feel simply enough that Hitler, Mussolini and the Japanese dictatorships must be destroyed, but the betrayal of almost everything for which men thought they died in the First World War was still lively in the minds of those of us who fought in the Second. In Spain, between 1936 and 1939, it seemed that if only Franco could be defeated the whole world would be a cleaner place.

A gallant few went off to fight in the International Brigade. The rest of us subscribed to food-ships for Spain, attended Left Book Club rallies, and felt ashamed—ashamed of earning our livings, saving up for a second-hand Austin Seven, going out with girl friends, while our Government connived at General Franco's victory.

In the United States, Roosevelt's New Deal and such great experiments as the setting up of the Tennessee Valley Authority seemed to offer some hope of a genuine attack on human poverty —the United States, after the Wall Street collapse, was not regarded as the Imperialist Colossus so feared and hated after the Second World War. "Buddy, Can You Spare a Dime?" at least aroused fellow-feelings in Wigan. But in the days before television and transatlantic flights, the United States seemed a long way from Europe. In Europe, the only real hope seemed to be in Soviet Russia.

This was the essence of the political tragedy of the 1930s. The apologists for Russia were either so dazzled by the bright hopes of the Russian Revolution that they could not see the brutalities of Russian Communism, or so horrified by the alternatives of Fascism and National Socialism that they chose not to see them. On the other side of the fence, people were so terrified of the performance of Russian Communism that they chose not to see, or at least not to think about, the ghastly things done in Germany, in Italy, in Spain, in the name of anti-Communism. Forty years on, and looking back, one tends to see this conflict of fear as sharply polarised. It was not so then. Fear had no sharp edges, it was more a general miasma of fear, of Nazism, of Communism, of war, of losing one's job, of being on the dole. Nothing was clear-cut. A simple church-goer might be so sickened by the hypocrisy of non-intervention in Spain that his fear of Communist persecution of religion was overcome by disgust at the behaviour of the anti-Communists. Men otherwise instinctively sympathetic to every cause of human decency might be so terrified of Communism that they almost approved of Hitler, or hoped vaguely that Hitler and Stalin might somehow cancel one another out.

By the middle of the decade political alliances, though still far from clear, were at least a little clearer. The majority of

Les Cannon's mother

An early portrait

Les as a young man

Les with TU colleagues: Harry Nicholas is on his left (*photo Jersey Evening Post*)

the British people, though not formally pacifist, wanted peace at almost any price. This was the strength of the Baldwin and Chamberlain Governments: uninspired and uninspiring, they were unopposed rather than supported by the mass of those who voted for them. The official Labour Opposition was equally uninspiring: it offered a change of faces rather than a change of policies. Official Labour was as hamstrung by fear of Russia as the Government. In 1938 the Labour Party actually sent out an official letter to the secretaries of local Labour parties warning them against the activities of the Left Book Club as "embarrassing to Constituency Labour Parties". It went on to voice the astonishing grievance, "One group has taken the initiative in holding public meetings on Spain, Czechoslovakia, etc. and in directing attention to the problems of the distressed areas. For some years there has been no activity of this kind in the district."[1]

"*For some years there has been no activity of this kind in the district. . . .*" One might think that the Labour Party *disapproved* of meetings about Spain or Czechoslovakia, or calling attention to the problems of the distressed areas in Britain. So, in a way, it did—yet it was not so much disapproval of the *cause* as of its allies in what might be, or become, a Popular Front including Communists. In no circumstances would official Labour countenance an alliance with the Communists—rather let democracy drown than get into a lifeboat with Communists among the crew. Labour's deep suspicion of the Communists was well founded; what was so tragically wrong was that it offered no alternative leadership.

Although called "The Communist Party of Great Britain", the British Communist Party was a tool of Russian foreign policy. The Labour Party's paralysis of will played into Russian hands—Labour's implacable hostility to any broadening of British radicalism rendered impossible the emergence of any genuinely British Marxist Party, or any radical grouping, which could really have commanded mass support. Individual Communists were articulate, aggressive, clever, often politically brilliant, but as a Party the Soviet brand of Communism had

[1] John Lewis, *The Left Book Club, an Historical Record* (Gollancz, 1970).

C

no real roots in the British working-class. The late Morgan Phillips's observation that British Socialism owed more to Methodism than to Marx embodied a good deal of truth. Communism, as presented to the British people in the 1920s and 1930s (and since), was an alien creed, emotionally more attractive to middle-class intellectuals than to the mass of working men and women. It came nearer towards achieving a mass appeal in the late 1930s, before the cynical about-turn of the Molotov–Ribbentrop Pact, than at any time in its history. But it was appeal by default. The hungry sheep looked up and were not fed, except by the Communists, all too eager to cram Soviet propaganda down their throats. The young particularly (but almost anyone brought up in a truly liberal tradition) were at first hurt and disgusted, then despairing and ashamed, about unemployment, Manchuria, Abyssinia, Spain, Austria, Albania, Czechoslovakia—the list of despairs lengthened bitterly with the decade. They looked in vain for political leadership from the established parties in Britain, then either hid their heads, ostrich-like, in the sands of personal life, or turned avidly to the strange consortium brought together by the Left Book Club.

In its early days, the Club seemed to have some hope of winning official Labour support. Mr Attlee was invited to contribute a book, and his *Labour Party in Perspective* appeared as a club "choice" in 1937. But it was a dreary, uninspiring work, with none of the fire of Orwell's *Road to Wigan Pier*, Snow's *Red Star over China*, or any of half a dozen others which appeared in the same year. Soon Labour's tepid support turned to active hostility, and that was the end of any hope of coalescing idealism and radical feeling into a political force with any real prospect of coming to power in Britain.

Against Labour's hostility, Popular Front feeling, of which the LBC was the most significant expression, could not make much headway among the mass of Labour's traditional supporters. Apart from the Communists, and a sprinkling of working-class members of the Labour Party who felt strongly enough to defy official disapproval, the Left Book Club was never really able to become more than a middle-class movement, primarily attracting the more intellectual members of that class—school teachers, university lecturers, scientific workers, journalists and the like. Women, particularly married women, then far less likely to work outside their homes than now, were a strong section of the Club's membership, devoting much time and effort to the organising and running of local groups. In Hackney—then almost wholly a working-class district of east London—a local group of eighteen had only seven manual workers, and this proportion (because of the working-class nature of Hackney) was high.

The effect of LBC books, Popular Front rallies and other such activities on Les Cannon was considerable. He had always enjoyed intellectual discussion with his father; now he could read books on current affairs by some of the keenest and most acute political writers of his time. Given his background, and his father's political teaching, he could have no patience with the theoretical reasoning of middle-class intellectuals. It was natural that he should want to join personally in the political struggle, and equally natural that he should become a Communist. Even so, he did not rush to become a Party member; he did not formally join the Party until he was nineteen, in 1939.

His father, himself an ex-Communist, disapproved. But where else—in 1939—did there seem the slightest hope of genuine progress towards socialism in Britain? Jim Cannon Senior was not a Social Democrat; he was—and in spite of his break with the Communist Party, he remained—a convinced Marxist. Bitter experience of industrial politics in the Mineworkers Federation had persuaded him that the official Labour Party's brand of socialism was not what he understood by socialism. Bitter experience of what he regarded as Communist dishonesty in the affairs of the miners had equally persuaded him that Communism, as practised by the Communist Party of Great Britain, was not for him. At his age, and with his temperament, theoretical Marxism could satisfy him intellectually. It could not satisfy his ardent, fighting son. Towards the end of his life, Jim Cannon Senior came to the conclusion that for all its timidities and faults, the Labour Party, as the traditional embodiment of the political hopes of the British working-class, offered the best road forward for the working-class in Britain. That was a conclusion reached after a lifetime's understanding of the necessity of political compromise, of the value of winning a furlong if you have no real hope of gaining a mile. Les Cannon at nineteen could not think like that; to him, then, Communism seemed the obvious political path to progress.

V

THE ETU

On August 21, 1939, Ribbentrop, once German ambassador in England, then Foreign Minister in Hitler's Government, was formally invited to Moscow. Two days later (August 23, 1939) he and Molotov, the Soviet Foreign Minister, signed the Molotov–Ribbentrop Pact, by which Russia undertook to stay neutral if Germany went to war. In return for this there were clauses (unpublished at the time) by which Germany undertook not to tread too heavily on Russian toes in Poland—that is, after Germany had "liberated" the "oppressed" Germans in Danzig and recovered such alleged ancestral German territory as the Hitler-myth insisted on, Russia would be given a free hand to take what she wanted from the rest of Poland. The Pact was one of the most cynical and sudden reversals of policy in history.

Hitler and Stalin calculated that an apparently supine Britain would be blackmailed by this Nazi–Soviet agreement into running away from military obligations to support Poland against a German invasion. They calculated wrongly. Appalling as the record of successive British Governments in standing up to the dictators had been throughout the 1930s, the Molotov–Ribbentrop Pact suddenly stiffened that mysterious quality in the British people which has shown itself on various occasions in history—call it national pride, patriotism, bloody-mindedness, or what you will. Reluctant as Mr Chamberlain was to declare war on Germany, national feeling was too much for him. Pacifist as so much of the official Labour Opposition had been—and by tradition still was—the idea of knuckling under to Hitler and Stalin was too much for Labour. There was an extraordinary scene in the House of Commons on September 2, when Arthur Greenwood, acting leader of the Opposition in the absence through illness of Mr Attlee, rose to reply to a waffling and evasive speech by Mr Chamberlain. Leopold

Amery, Right-wing Conservative, called across to Greenwood, ex-pacifist, Left-wing Labour, "Come on, Arthur! Speak for England!" And Arthur Greenwood did. On September 3, 1939, Britain sent an ultimatum to Germany and at 11.00 that morning, the ultimatum having been ignored, war was declared.

The Communist Party of Great Britain, which an idealistic young Les Cannon had just joined, now threw away its last chance of establishing itself as a genuinely national party. At first—instructions, presumably, not having arrived from Moscow—it supported the war as a crusade against the vile dictatorship of Hitler. Harry Pollitt, widely popular as a working-class leader, for all his political commitment to Soviet Communism, was notably outspoken in urging support for the British war effort. Pollitt was then official leader of the Communist Party of Great Britain. He was one of the ablest men of his generation, and in many ways one of the nicest, bluff, good-humoured, and with an instinctive understanding of the emotional roots of British working-class feeling. It is a tragedy of political history that Pollitt was so disgusted by the feebleness of the official Labour Party that he turned down the blind alley of Communism and so was lost to the wider Labour movement. In supporting the war he interpreted rightly the mood of working men and women in Britain. For Pollitt to be right, however, counted for nothing with the bureaucrats of the Comintern. The war, with Russia neutral, automatically became an imperialist war, which no good Communist could support. Overnight, the British Communist Party changed its line. In one of those nauseating "confessions" which the Party contrives to extract from those whose deviation from the Party line is important enough to matter, Pollitt admitted that he had erred in regarding a war against the tyranny of Hitler as a war that the British people ought to fight in good heart. A. J. P. Taylor sums up this episode:

> Pollitt, the party leader, was degraded, and compelled to confess his error. This only served to discredit the party. Its membership fell by a third (from 17,000 to under 12,000) and its Left wing associates, such as Gollancz, swung violently away. The Communist Party had an unrivalled consistency

before the war in opposition to Hitler. Now it forfeited, and never regained, this prestige.[1]

In January 1941 the Communist *Daily Worker* (now the *Morning Star*) was banned, with scarcely a protest from anyone. Taylor observes that this banning of the *Daily Worker* "proved an undesigned blessing for the British Communist Party. Unlike the American Party it escaped the embarrassment of actually opposing the war right up to the day on which Hitler attacked Russia."[2]

As Les was debarred from military service by his ear affliction, he was directed to essential war-work at shipyards on the Tyne in his trade as an electrician.

He helped to repair Lord Mountbatten's famous ship *Kelly* when she was brought into the Tyne for repairs.

He drifted out of the Communist Party but he continued to be an active member of the ETU. In June 1941 he returned to Wigan and for a while worked at the Royal Ordnance Factory. After the outbreak of war with Russia, he started work at Leyland, Preston, and he threw himself feverishly into Communist Party activities. He read avidly the despatches from the Russian front, as reported in the *News Chronicle* and his imagination was fired by the heroism of the Red Army and the defenders of Leningrad and Moscow. During the "Aid to Russia" campaign, he spoke at meetings inside and outside the factory and at the Wigan market square. At this time, he was both a Shop Steward at Leyland as well as part-time District Secretary of the ETU. In 1942 he joined the Wigan Trades Council as a delegate from the ETU and soon became a spokesman of the Left.

While attending a conference in London, as an ETU delegate, he met a girl called Barbara, they fell in love and Les proposed marriage. . . .

". . . Les seemed totally involved in his political career, and he tried very hard to convert us to his way of thinking. When he proposed to me, my mother wouldn't give her

[1] A. J. P. Taylor, *English History 1914–45*, p. 559.   [2] *Op. cit.*, p. 612n.

consent, saying that she did not wish me to live in Russia in the people's commune and have her grandchildren brought up in a State creche. But she continued to like him a great deal and to her he was always 'her Leslie'."

Everyone seems to remember him from this period as a courteous young man with a most wonderful sense of humour, fervent in his ideological beliefs.

He kept no diaries, and his political feelings during the war he kept to himself. He did not understand the Party's sudden about-turn from support to opposition of the war against Germany. The original Pollitt surely spoke for Les and his generation of youth in Britain. All who thought politically at all had grown up in the shadow of Hitler, and every decent instinct was to fight him. Les, with his own wide reading and his father's Marxist upbringing, was politically too sophisticated to think in terms of "patriotism"—an emotion his rational mind would have rejected with contempt—but Les was also deeply rooted in the working-class body of English life and the atavistic feelings that have animated the common people of England from Agincourt (or, indeed, from the revolt of Queen Boudicca) onwards were deep within him. Two of his brothers were in the Army. But for his ear affliction, he would have been with them.[1]

This instinctive feeling that the war against Germany had to be fought is well illustrated by the actions of Les Cannon's own union, the ETU. It was not then, as it became later, under Communist control, but it was always well to the Left of the Labour movement, and even in the 1930s Communist influence in the Union was far from negligible. In spite of all this, in May 1940 the Executive Council of the Union decided to make an *interest free* loan of £50,000 to the Government "to assist in carrying on the war against Nazism", and to equip a mobile

---

[1] I am reminded of an occasion many years ago on which Arthur Horner, then general secretary of the National Union of Mineworkers, and (like Pollitt) an essentially *British* Communist, and I were travelling back by train together from a trade union conference in Margate. For some reason we were momentarily alone together in our compartment. It was late evening and the gentle Kentish countryside had a quality almost of fairyland as the train ran through it. Arthur and I sat looking out of the train windows. Suddenly he said, "You know, John, I'd never lift a finger actually to *hurt* this bloody country."—J.R.L.A.

canteen, known as "The Electrical Trades Union Unit" to serve the Forces. At a Union conference in July that year the delegates united Left-wing politics with wholehearted support of the war in a fashion typical of the national state of mind. Having approved the interest-free loan of £50,000 to the Government, the delegates went on to pass a unanimous resolution castigating that same Government for its inclusion of Ministers "who were responsible for the Munich surrender". The resolution concluded:

> We declare our uncompromising hostility to Nazism in any form and in order to ensure the utmost assistance towards this end we call for the conscription of wealth in addition to Labour.[1]

Hitler's invasion of Russia in June 1941 cleared the political air. The war which had changed overnight for the Communists in 1939 from a crusade against tyranny to an exercise in imperialist aggression changed back to a noble war to be fought and won at all costs. The Communists as a party in Britain were so discredited that there was little anti-Communist feeling and the Russians were popular allies. Churchill's famous broadcast on June 22, 1941, declaring: "The cause of any Russian fighting for his hearth and home is the cause of free men and free people in every quarter of the globe," expressed the national mood—and Britain then had so few allies (this was before the United States came into the war) that to feel that at least one other great nation was having to fight Hitler brought a sense of immense relief. The national courage of the Russians was heartening, and the defence of Stalingrad was followed in Britain with a reverent and hushed excitement. Something like the loose "Popular Front" grouping of 1936–39 reappeared to campaign for intensifying the war effort, particularly by hastening the opening of a Second Front in Europe to take some of the German pressure off Russia. Les Cannon was not the sort to go round chalking on walls "*Second Front Now*", but the renewed unity of the Left was a relief to his deeply troubled spirit; he could do whatever war-work he was on without any schizophrenic feelings.

[1] *The Story of the ETU* (published by the Electrical Trades Union), p. 167.

In 1943 he was able to use his local influence in the Electrical Trades Union to make a major contribution to the effectiveness of Britain's war at sea. The Russians might be holding the Germans on land, but at sea almost the whole weight of German naval power was thrown against Britain. Shipping losses mounted appallingly—in the single month of March 1943 nearly half a million tons of shipping were lost. Britain desperately needed replacements for her merchant ships and, even more, additions to the Royal Navy's escort vessels and anti-submarine fleet. To get the most out of round-the-clock working in the shipyards required drastic changes in trade union working practices. Ernest Bevin, then Minister of Labour, asked the ETU to accept a system of group payment by results for electricians which ran counter to all the union's old craft instincts. A special delegate conference was called to consider the request and, in spite of old prejudices, it was agreed to by the substantial majority of 110 votes to 47. In the discussion leading up to this Les was in his element. Later that year Bevin paid a special tribute to the ETU in an address to the Trades Union Congress. He said,

I suddenly had to find 4,000 electricians . . . the ETU, and I pay them this public compliment, agreed with me to take on that pernicious thing (as they always thought it) payment by results. . . . The change they made at their delegate conference was worth about 3,000 to 4,000 men to us, and enabled us to put on the campaign against U-boats at the precise date the Cabinet decided it should operate.

In the whole of the last quarter of 1943 only 146,000 tons of shipping were lost, compared with close on half a million tons in the single month of March. Of course, not all this great gain towards victory in the war at sea was brought about by the ETU's acceptance of a change in working practices. Many other things contributed and all would have been useless without the heroism of seamen. But the ETU's collective readiness to help out was not the least of the factors that combined to make possible the massive improvement in the fortunes of war for the Allies.

By the end of 1943 Les enrolled once more at his old school,

Wigan Technical College, this time for classes in Russian. He abandoned these after one session (1943–4), for he was now becoming prominent as a local trade unionist, serving on Wigan Trades Council, the Ministry of Labour's joint Industrial Committee, and a number of other bodies. He had simply too much to do to continue studying the Russian language, which was a pity, for the more purely intellectual side of him—always prominent in his make-up, but seldom given a fair chance—would dearly have liked to master Russian, to be able to read Tolstoy, Dostoevski and other great Russian writers in the language in which they wrote.

With the end of the war the pace of his trade union and political activities quickened. In 1945 he was elected to the National Executive of the ETU for the Lancashire district of the Union. He was then just twenty-five—the youngest member of the National Executive ever to be elected.

The ETU has always had strong links with Lancashire. From 1907 to 1931, when it moved to London, its head office was in Manchester, and when, in 1940, it was bombed out of its London headquarters it moved back near its old home to temporary offices at Ollerenshaw Hall, Whaley Bridge. Les Cannon's return to Lancashire in 1943 thus brought him near the war-time headquarters of ETU power, and this fortuitous proximity undoubtedly helped his rapid rise to national office in the union. He would have risen in any case, for he was a brilliant negotiator and had an extraordinary understanding of the real, if often inarticulate, feelings of those he represented. And (as we shall see) his simultaneous rise to influence in the Young Communist League, and so in the Communist Party, would have helped him to power in the ETU. But the accident of his own deep roots in Lancashire, and the chance that transferred him from the shipyards of the Tyne to the engineering works at Leyland in 1943, were certainly factors in his swift achievement of a place on the national executive of the ETU.

At this same time, when Les was on top of the world with his success as a young trade union leader, the possibility of an alternative career was opened to him. He attended the wedding of one of his cousins in Wigan, and in proposing a toast to the bride and bridegroom at the reception afterwards in the Cooperative Café in Standishgate, he made a speech which was markedly different from the usual run of such affairs at wedding receptions. For one thing, it went on for half an hour; for another, nobody noticed how long it was until they looked at their watches afterwards.

Les's wedding speech was both personal and social, light and serious, touching on hopes for the future of the post-war world as well as wishing happiness to the newly married couple. People listened to him with a kind of enthralled attention.

Among the guests at that reception were one or two prominent members of the constituency Labour Party. They had heard of Les as a rising young trade unionist, but had not before met him. The upshot of it all was that Les was invited to consider standing as Labour candidate in the 1945 election.

He did not pursue the invitation. He was not then greatly interested in Parliament, and he had all his father's contempt for the performance of the official Labour Party. He was, of course, a Communist, which would have debarred him from being a Labour candidate in any case, though that was a barrier that could have been got over easily enough had he wanted to get over it. Many members of the Labour Party have Communist, or what it became fashionable to call "fellow-travelling", pasts, and they are not the worse Labour men for that. But Les did not want then to identify himself with the Labour Party. He was far more interested in the trade union side of the Labour movement, where he felt that real power lay, and he was beginning to understand the force of Lenin's maxim that Communists should penetrate the unions and remain in them, "carrying on Communist activities inside them at all costs". So nothing came of that invitation to stand for Parliament. It is interesting to speculate on what might have happened had Les chosen to follow that alternative road. He would certainly have been elected, and almost as certainly he would soon have been given office in Mr Attlee's Government. Labour's landslide victory in 1945 brought to the House of Commons many bright young men who had turned to socialism as the result of Service experience, but the Labour benches were short of young trade unionists. That was at least one of the reasons for Mr George Brown's rapid rise to office.

In the bitter Bevanite in-fighting that distracted the Parliamentary Labour Party in the 1950s, Les Cannon's sympathies would have been with the Left, but he was far too able a man to have indentified himself with the sillier aspects of what came (with considerable unfairness to Aneurin Bevan) to be called "Bevanism", and which brought such discredit on the Labour Party in the country. Moreover, Les was a trade unionist who had first-hand knowledge and understanding of that strange complex of courage and obstinacy, prejudice, suspicion and shining human decency which is summed up in the words "trade union loyalty". He would have brought weight to the Left wing of the Parliamentary party, solid trade unionism allied to a quick mind, great political ability, and much personal charm. In the election for the leadership that followed Hugh Gaitskell's death it seems at least possible that Les Cannon would have succeeded him. In which case Les would have become a Labour Prime Minister. . . . But these are the might-have-beens of history, fascinating to speculate upon, fruitless to pursue. Things did not happen in that way.

In considering the way in which things *did* happen in Les Cannon's life, it may be convenient here to give a brief account of the trade union which has figured so prominently in his career.

The Electrical Trades Union is almost as old as the electrical industry in Britain, although in its early days it represented only a handful of the linesmen and mechanics engaged in the new-fangled trades the industry created. The electric telegraph and then the telephone were the first electrical industries— electric lighting, apart from private installations on a very small scale, did not begin seriously to challenge gas until the turn of the last century. In the 1880s small groups of telegraph and telephone linesmen in the industrial districts of Lancashire and Yorkshire, and in London, began to come together in rudimentary unions or "trade societies". Among the earliest of these was a London organisation known as "The Union of Electrical Operatives", but it had no members outside London. In 1889, a Manchester group, uniting a number of small trade associations in Lancashire and Yorkshire in "The Amalgamated Society of Telegraph and Telephone Construction Men", held a delegate conference, and representatives from the London organisation attended. At this conference it was decided to amalgamate the Manchester and London groups in one body called "The Electrical Trades Union". This new name was registered with the Registrar of Friendly Societies and the formal amalgamation ratified at a conference in Liverpool, on December 6, 1890. The Manchester group brought in 400 members with branches in Manchester, Liverpool, Leeds, Sheffield, Hanley and Dewsbury; the London group 170 members, organised in a single London branch. Manchester contributed £222 to the funds of the new body, London £75. The original membership of 570 was increased to 1,123 in the ETU's first year, and fifteen new branches were established, including Glasgow, Belfast and Hull. The head office of the ETU was then in London.

The rules of the ETU were modelled on those of the older Amalgamated Society of Engineers (which became the AEU, now the Amalgamated Union of Engineers and Foundry Workers). Strict rules of apprenticeship, however, had to be modified, because the electrical industry was so new that many craftsmen had learned their skills as they went along, having had no chance of serving an apprenticeship.

By the beginning of the First World War the Union's membership had grown to 8,195. The war brought a rapid increase in the pace of development of electrical engineering and by 1916 the union's membership stood at 12,921. During the war another union in the industry, The Electrical Winders Society, amalgamated with the ETU and by the end of 1917 membership had increased to 20,621, and the number of branches to 165. In 1920 there were 57,292 members and 403 branches.

In common with all trade unions, the ETU suffered in the post-war slump, and by 1923 membership had fallen to 26,165. More than 100 branches had to be closed for lack of members. Electricity, however, was still a growth industry, and the union's membership soon began to rise again. By 1926 it was 29,241 and in spite of the set-back of the unemployment that followed the General Strike the ETU held its own. It continued to grow even through the long depression of the 1930s and it celebrated its fiftieth anniversary in 1939 with a membership of some 70,000. The Second World War was again a stimulus to electrical engineering, and at the ETU's diamond jubilee held in 1949 membership stood at 187,520, and the union had 625 branches throughout Britain. The 200,000 mark was passed in the early 1950s and membership at the end of 1971 was over 400,000.

From 1889 to 1907 the Union had its head office in London. From 1908 to 1931 it was Manchester-based (in the sense that the head office was in Manchester). From 1931 until its temporary return to the Manchester neighbourhood at Ollerenshaw Hall during the war it was again London-based. After the war the Union acquired Hayes Court at Hayes, Kent, on the outskirts of London, for its national headquarters, and it has been established at Hayes Court since 1949. The ETU provided the Trades Union Congress with the most famous General Secretary it has ever had in Walter (later Lord) Citrine. Walter Citrine was secretary of the Mersey District Committee of the ETU during the First World War and he was elected to the newly-created post of Assistant General Secretary of the Union in 1920. In 1924 he became Assistant General Secretary of the Trades Union Congress, and he was elected General Secretary of the TUC two years later.

From the earliest days of the electrical industry its craftsmen had to be men of some education and it is natural that as soon as they became organised as trade unionists they looked to their union for political expression as well as industrial support. The ETU has always been a strongly political union, and, in its collective personality, it has always felt itself a part of the international working-class movement. Its original subscription, sixpence ($2\frac{1}{2}$p) a week, was high at a time when agricultural wages, and the wages of many labourers, were no more than seven or eight shillings (35–40p) a week, and from the start it was ready to use its funds to support the struggles of other groups of workers. Its first year's balance sheet, for 1890, shows a donation of £10—a substantial sum in 1890—to a strike fund for workers in Australia. In 1902 its members agreed to levy themselves 1d a week to support a fund for men at the Penrhyn quarries in Wales who had been locked out by the quarry owners for having dared to form a trade union.

The Labour Representation Committee of the TUC, which led to the formation of the Labour Party in 1906, was supported by the ETU from the start. It sent a delegate to the conference which set up the Labour Representation Committee in 1900 and formally affiliated to the LRC in 1902.

With such a political history it was natural that the ETU, as a union, should be generally on the Left wing of the Labour movement. The breach between Labour and Communism after the First World War was not reflected in any such clear-cut terms on the trade union side of the movement. Membership of the Communist Party was a formal bar to membership of the Labour Party, but it has never been a bar to membership of a trade union (though in some unions, briefly, it has been a bar to office). An individual Communist may not join the Labour Party, but there is nothing to prevent a trade union with a large Communist membership from affiliating to the Labour Party. Admitted Communists may not be delegates to Labour Party conferences, but an affiliated union, however Communist its complexion, is fully entitled to send a delegation which may be Communist in all but name, and to cast a card vote in accordance with the number of members (Communist or not) for whom it has paid its affiliation fee.

Lenin made no bones about the importance of Communist infiltration of trade unions in achieving revolutionary success. Holding that all is fair in revolution as in love and war, he exhorted Communists to shrink from nothing, and to resort, if necessary, to "all sorts of stratagems, manœuvres, and illegal measures, evasions and subterfuges" to defeat those who might try to prevent their occupation of trade union positions. It being clear from its formation that the Communist Party of Great Britain had no hope whatever of securing political power by normal means, its leaders, from the outset, have regarded infiltration of the unions as their main means of exercising political influence.

The Communists have tried, with varying success, to infiltrate any and every trade union in Britain, but from the early 1930s, perhaps from earlier still, they regarded the ETU as their spearhead of industrial action. As a union, it is ideal for their purpose. There is scarcely a process in modern industry which does not depend, at least to some extent, on electricity, and national dependence on the power stations has been shown only too clearly by recent industrial disputes. Every factory, newspaper office, broadcasting and television studio in the country employs electricians—they have only to pull the fuses and life comes more or less to a stop. Another major advantage of the ETU from the point of view of political infiltration is that skilled electricians (outside large electrical engineering works) tend to work in small groups. Since trade union branches (again, outside factories big enough to have a branch of their own) were organised geographically, an ETU branch might have members from dozens of different places, who never met at work.[1] If they attended branch meetings at all, and roughly 80 per cent of trade unionists never, or hardly ever, attend branch meetings, they would know next to nothing about their fellow-members. It was, therefore, particularly easy for a handful of individuals dedicated to a particular cause to "capture" a branch, in the sense that they could get themselves voted into branch office, control the agenda of meetings, and decide who was to represent the branch at trade union conferences. The ETU, which required elections for almost everything, and whose old rule book was of such complexity that it needed textual scholarship of a high order even to begin to understand it, was an ideal union in this sense also, for its constitution made things particularly easy for an active "fraction" to get the votes it wanted.

Before the war the distinction between "militancy" for strictly trade union ends and "militancy" for political purposes was even more blurred than it is now. Throughout the 1930s the "old guard" of the union, brought up in the school of Citrine and Bevin which preferred negotiation to "militant" confrontation, remained on top, but as the decade advanced there was considerable friction between this conservative (with a small 'c') leadership and "militant" branches. The London Central Committee of the union was a particularly "militant" body, and tension between this group and the Executive was brought to a head in January 1937 by a strike of electricians at Earl's Court. The committee supported the strike; the Executive declared it "unofficial", and expelled the London Committee. At elections for the Executive later that same year the "militants" hit back,

1 See pp. 259–62 for later reforms.

and secured the defeat of a number of those who had voted to expel the London Committee.

The discrediting of the Communist Party after the Molotov–Ribbentrop Pact was a set-back to Communist infiltration of the Union, and in the early part of the war the Communists and their friends wisely kept quiet. After Hitler's invasion of Russia and the re-emergence of "Popular Front" feeling in Britain, the Communist Party renewed its efforts to capture the ETU, acting so aggressively that the National Executive called a special conference in 1943 "for the purpose of dealing with the interference of the Communist Party of Great Britain in the internal affairs of the Electrical Trades Union". The delegates carried a resolution (by 31 votes to 19) "that this conference is satisfied interference has taken place in the internal affairs of the ETU by the Communist Party of Great Britain", and Mr E. W. Bussey, then General Secretary of the Union and a member of the General Council of the TUC, moved a further resolution requiring members of the Communist Party to "be debarred from holding any office or acting as a delegate on behalf of the union". At a time when Soviet Russia and Britain were allies in the same war, this was too much even for most of the anti-Communists. The resolution was not voted upon, for after some discussion it was withdrawn.

This victory, for it was a victory, though brought about by the indecisiveness of non-Communists more than anything else, enabled the Communists to continue their campaign still more effectively. Prominent members of the Communist Party, including Frank Foulkes (National Organiser of the Union) and sympathisers like Walter Stevens[1] (Assistant General Secretary), were able to combine influential office in the ETU with active participation in CP affairs. After the war Communist victory was complete. Frank Foulkes was elected General President of the ETU in 1945, and the Union's next most important office, that of General Secretary, fell to Mr Stevens in 1947, when he was elected to replace Mr Bussey, who resigned on his appointment to the board of the newly nationalised electricity industry. Frank Haxell, another Communist, was elected Assistant General Secretary. Frank

[1] He joined the CP in 1947.

Foulkes had been a member of the Communist Party since 1931, Frank Haxell since 1935.

This, then, was the Union of whose National Executive Les Cannon became the youngest member in 1945. His ability, and his own Communist allegiance, clearly marked him for success. To have a hand on the switches in the power stations was real power. Parliament was small beer compared with this.

VI

OLGA'S STORY

J. R. L. ANDERSON WRITES:

Chapters I–V of this book have told the story of Les Cannon up to the age of twenty-five. It has been pieced together from notes made at one time and another by Les himself, from family reminiscences, school and other records—those "footsteps in the sands of time" that all of us leave behind us. They are shifting sands, and in Les's case the footsteps are often faint and hard to follow; childhood in an unemployed family half a century ago was not much documented, and it is surprising how swiftly dates, events and incidents elide and become blurred in human memory. Nevertheless, Olga and I between us have reconstructed what we believe to be an accurate picture of Les's early years. From now on, the story becomes Olga's as well as that of Les. We have pondered much on how it should be told; whether in the third person, as if presenting a detached biography of Olga as well as of her husband, or whether in the first person, as if an autobiography of Olga herself. But it is neither. It cannot be a wholly detached biography, because it is also the story of Olga's own life; it is not an autobiography of Olga, because it is the story of Les. I could contribute directly to the earlier chapters because their historical setting, though in different social circumstances, was that of my own youth. I can contribute again to the story of Les's trade union career, because it has been my job for much of my life to study trade union affairs. But I can add nothing to Olga's very personal story of her life in Czechoslovakia before her marriage and of her life with Les in England. It has, therefore, seemed to me proper that her narrative should now be written in the first person. My task has been simply to edit. Towards the end of this book, when we attempt to assess Les Cannon's life and his philosophy of trade unionism, my contribution will again be more direct, but that will be clear enough in the context.

*   *   *

My childhood was in complete contrast to Leslie's.

As an only child of rather elderly parents I grew up without the daily companionship of other children in a cottage on a hillside surrounded by orchards, pine forests and meadows.

A small village lay below.

My everyday life was blissfully free, unrestricted by conventions, and amongst grown-ups whose lives flowed slowly and who had time to talk and listen to a small child. My mother's many sisters and their husbands came to stay for short spells and occasionally I would be taken for visits to town, but I was always impatient to get back to our house on the hill and to my pets—a dog, a lamb and a red squirrel.

My early childhood memories are without hurt or scars—a kaleidoscope of crisp winters, a freshly cut Christmas tree reaching the ceiling, richly decorated with home-baked goodies one could feast on for weeks. I have memories of finding the first snowdrops under the old walnut tree in front of the house, and of the spring turning the orchard into a scented sea of blooms.

Of summers so warm that shoes and clothes were discarded and the tall grasses provided a hiding place and a playground; and later in the autumn of apple-trees with branches groaning under the weight of fruit.

During these years my father usually came home only at weekends because he was in partnership with his brother in a small building firm some distance away. My parents often talked of moving, but my mother could not bear to leave what her family called "this Paradise".

When I was six years old I had to start school, and, since there was no school near, it was necessary for us to move. I was heartbroken. I used to wake up in the middle of the night sobbing and begging to go back. As my mother held me in her arms, trying to explain, I felt her own sadness and longing and it made it somehow easier for me to accept. The first time either of us ever did return was years later, together with Les and our younger son, Martin. It was 1964 and Martin was twelve. His grandmother took him by the hand and led him to a room whose windows looked down into the valley. "Your mother was born here, Martinku," she said.

My early school years were happy. We lived on the fringe of

Karvinna, which was a Czech Wigan without the cotton industry. The town was scarred by many pits which belonged to a German count, whose walled-off private park was only minutes from our home.

We lived on the outskirts of this industrial town and our home and my primary school were in the heart of the country. Every day I walked to school with my friends, most of whose parents were employees of the count, along a winding path through the fields. In summer we would push through the tall golden corn or a field of maize, pretending that we were intrepid explorers of a tropical jungle. One had to move by stealth, for the count, who owned the whole district, had many watchmen who used to chase us—but we were too quick for them.

My grammar school years were less happy. I had to travel by a tram-car to a nearby town and walk through its dreary streets to the other side. It was an ugly town and I disliked the school.

At the age of fifteen my parents transferred me to what was called the Commercial Academy. This was a grammar school type of education with strong emphasis on international trade and business in general. We studied two or three languages and commercial correspondence in these, shorthand in Czech and German, and of course all the other general grammar-school subjects like maths, literature, history, etc., without the classical background. Looking back, I realise now that in many ways it was a forward-looking type of education, equipping the graduate with a comprehensive knowledge of the modern requirements of industrial society. The school was newly opened and was at Těšín, right on the Polish border—just across a bridge was Poland.

I had barely started at this school when Munich happened. Our world collapsed suddenly, when Mr Chamberlain signed a pact with Hitler. Munich led to the dismemberment of all Czechoslovakia; the Sudetenland was transferred to Germany; Poland took a chunk of Silesia in the Northern part of Moravia; Hungary took pieces of Slovakia.

We lived in an area that became Polish and we had to go.

We were given forty-eight hours to get out. I vaguely remember my father and uncle and a friend sharing a cattle wagon to move our furniture across the border. I was sent earlier, on my own with a little suitcase and some of my mother's jewellery hidden in my clothes, to my aunt, who lived in a lovely part of Northern Moravia in the heart of a picturesque mountain region called Bezkydy. My own school moved into the premises of a primary school in a nearby town, and we used to sit at tiny desks and have language classes in a nearby pub for the better part of four years.

Even today, after thirty-five years, I still feel the indignity of those days—the indignity of a small nation sacrificed in a badly played political power game.

The first Czechoslovak republic was built on the foundations of the noble and democratic ideals of our Czech predecessors, and had at its head not a hack politician or a megalomaniac but in Thomas Masaryk a profound thinker from whose ethics and morals the world, even today, would benefit if only it knew of them.

Only a handful in the West have read anything about this modern statesman-philosopher who became the first President of the new Czechoslovakia after the 1918 war, and under whose leadership a modern humanitarian concept of democracy was emerging, unmatched by any other in Europe.

In the midst of maniac dictatorships and corrupt political systems, a real hope shone from Czechoslovakia for all humanity.

I enjoyed equality of opportunity from my first days at school. Middle-class and working-class children sat side by side. Only the very rich had private tuition and had to look for select private education abroad. In spite of the propaganda of Hitler which was calculated to sow dissent, I met no disharmony amongst the Polish and German minorities.

When I went to the Sudetenland for holidays to stay with German families in order to learn the language, only German was spoken at all state offices and schools. There was no diktat from Prague, no discrimination. The vast majority of Sudeten Germans who had to leave Czechoslovakia after the Second World War, never felt at home in Germany, and they hanker after the liberal atmosphere of pre-war Czechoslovakia to this day.

In 1938 Hitler openly used the Sudeten Germans as a spearhead in his campaign for conquering Europe and the world.

He was perfectly candid about his plans years earlier and no one in the West could claim that Hitler's intentions were unknown.

On November 5, 1937, the Führer addressed his Commanders-in-Chief at the Chancellery in Berlin. According to a military adjutant, he said:

"For the improvement of our military/political situation it must be our first aim . . . to conquer Czechoslovakia and Austria simultaneously. . . ." The Führer believes personally that, in all probability, England and perhaps also France, have already silently written off Czechoslovakia and that they have got used to the idea that this question would one day be cleaned up by Germany. . . .

Although the population of Czechoslovakia, in the first place, is not a thin one, the embodiment of Czechoslovakia and Austria would nevertheless constitute the conquest of food for 5–6 million people, on the basis that a compulsory emigration of 2 million from Czechoslovakia and of 1 million from Austria could be carried out.

The men of Munich believed that they had saved peace. The British opposition admitted: "We have betrayed a small, courageous country and its great democratic ideals." And a desperate cry came from France: "We gave Germany ammunition for a war against us and we will pay dearly for it."

By the spring of 1939 Hitler had both Czechoslovakia and Austria under his belt and he turned his attention to Poland . . . "Poland will always be on the side of our adversaries, in spite of treaties of friendship. There is no question of sparing Poland and we will attack Poland at the first opportunity."

But Hitler had to secure a promise of non-intervention by Russia in his aggression against Poland.

On August 22, 1939, after his success with Stalin, Hitler told his commanders:

The enemy (England and France) had another hope, that Russia would become our enemy after the conquest of Poland. But our enemies are little worms; I saw them in Munich. I was convinced that Stalin would never accept the British offer. Russia has no interest in maintaining Poland and Stalin knows that it is the end of his regime no matter whether his soldiers come out of a war victorious or beaten. Russia answered yesterday that she is ready to sign. The personal contact with Stalin is established. The day after tomorrow, von Ribbentrop will conclude the treaty. Now Poland is in the position in which I wanted her.

And so Poland was over-run.

But Hitler was much bothered about Russian ambitions: it was clear to him that Russia wished to increase its influence in the Balkans and was striving towards the Persian Gulf. That was also Germany's aim. Hitler also observed that Russia had given up her idea of internationalism for the time being—"in which case she will turn to Panslavism," observed Hitler.

But one thing was clear to him above all: that the Russian Army was of little worth. That was the reason that Stalin tried to buy a year or two years of respite from German aggression.

The purges had started after the murder of Kirov in 1936. It is now believed that the murder was organised by Stalin himself because Kirov was becoming extremely popular and advocated a policy of moderation and stabilisation of the new Soviet society. Stalin unleashed a police terror, unparalleled in modern history, against his own citizens. Between seven and eight million people, mainly educated people, were arrested; a million were executed and most of the rest died in the camps of the Arctic. It deprived the Soviet Army of tens of thousands of able officers, it deprived the State of talented administrators and technicians. In 1939, both Hitler and Stalin knew the total state of military unpreparedness of Russia. One might say that Stalin had no other way but temporarily to come to terms with Hitler. He had, in fact, brought about this situation three years earlier by his "purges".

During the early months of the war, most of us in Czechoslovakia viewed Hitler's advance westwards with wary disinterest, such as the people of the West had shown during our agonising humiliations of 1938–9. Feelings became blunted, and people turned inward to think about their personal affairs. Those of us who were driven out by the Poles, when they annexed Silesia, read the news of Polish defeats without sympathy. We were caught between ever-spreading military conflicts. Possibly the worst had already happened to us. For three hundred years we had been subjected to Germanic rule; and now had returned to it after a brief respite of twenty years.

All we could do was to try to survive as best we could and wait for the battle to be over.

Soon after the German occupation, new regulations were introduced in the school curriculum. We were taught the Nazi ideology during German lessons.

We spent hours crossing out whole pages of history which in any way minimised the German achievement or referred adversely to their past. The teachers read aloud the offensive passages and, strangely enough, instead of the desired effect of removing this interpretation of history from our memory, it sank in more deeply, and we learned better than we would have done under normal tuition. We were instructed to cross out the sentences with heavy lines in black ink, but we made sure that those who would inherit the books next year, would still be able to read the text.

The most distressing events of the first months of the occupation for me was when our Jewish school friends suddenly departed. For a while after, I would encounter them in the streets, sad eyed, clutching a book or a handbag to their breast on which a great big yellow star was sewn, pathetically trying to hide it.

They would go pale when I first stopped to talk to them. They would turn away from me, stopping in front of shop windows, as if just looking at the goods. They would speak in urgent whispers: "Do not stop to talk like that in the street; don't you understand we will both be in trouble?"

"Why didn't you go away, you told me you had relatives in America?" I asked one girl with whom I was particularly friendly.

"It's too late, too late to leave now."

"Can I do anything . . . ?" I ventured.

"Too late, there is nothing anyone can do. Pray for me."

It was the last time she spoke to me. I was shattered to see her later marching in a column work-gang from work on the road somewhere, dressed in men's working clothes. I stopped and tried to catch her eyes to show her that I still cared; she turned away as if she never knew me.

One early morning a train took them all away.

Years later I read a report of the Nuremberg trials, especially the evidence of a German engineer who worked in the Ukraine and described a Jewish massacre in these words:

[The Jews from Dubno had been shot at the rate of 1,500 persons a day.] Without screaming or weeping these people undressed, stood around in family groups, kissed each other. . . . During the 15 minutes that I stood near, I heard no complaint or plea for mercy. . . . An old woman with snow-white hair was holding the one-year-old child in her arms and singing to it and tickling it. The child was cooing with delight. The couple were looking on with tears in their eyes. The father was holding the hand of a boy about 10 years old and speaking to him softly; the boy was fighting his tears. The father pointed to the sky, stroked his head, and seemed to explain something to him. . . .

[They had to descend into large pits, which were already full of dead or dying people, to be shot.]

I looked for the man who did the shooting. He was an SS man, who sat at the edge of the narrow end of the pit, his feet dangling into the pit. He had a tommygun on his knees and was smoking a cigarette.

Shortly after reading this book, I visited Germany for the first time (1961). My nightmarish thoughts of 1939 returned. I looked at every German over forty as a potential murderer of my gentle childhood friend.

During the last years of my studies, I withdrew into a very private world of books, music and nature. The Germans excluded all American and English films and I hardly ever went to a cinema. My pin-up at the age of seventeen to eighteen was not some film star but the handsome Rafael Kubelik, now a famous conductor, but at that time a young and promising pianist.

In June 1941 our form—the first graduates—matriculated and I left Bezkydy to join my parents. Like thousands of others, they had had to make a fresh start. It wasn't easy. There was an influx of people who had been driven from their homes in the Sudetenland, Silesia and Slovakia. My father acquired a small wholesale tobacco business in the southern part of Moravia. Neither he nor my mother liked the district but, in the circumstances and compared with others, they were lucky to have found security.

Our interest in the war revived when Hitler attacked Russia.

Remembering the history lesson of Napoleon, who fought a victorious battle at Austerlitz—only a few kilometres from my new home—but was later to return totally crushed from Moscow, we saw history repeating itself.

The first rays of hope that Hitler might be defeated came into our lives with his attack on Russia.

We focused our attention on the Eastern Front through the initial rapid advance of the German tank divisions, and somehow never believed that Hitler could win. If not the Red Army, the Russian winter would kill his armies off. We had seen how inadequately clothed they were when they occupied us in March 1939.

In 1942, after the assassination of the Nazi "butcher" Heydrich, who was the Third Reich's protector of Czechoslovakia, even greater reprisals of terror swept our country. Daily executions of prominent Czechoslovak citizens were carried out in the major cities. People abroad have heard of the village of Lidice, razed to the ground, all male inhabitants over fifteen shot, and women and children taken to Germany. At one point, a rumour spread that every tenth Czechoslovak citizen would be shot.

I had spent these months in Brno, where I had started studying English at an English Institute. The English studies were suddenly dropped and to save myself from being sent to Germany, I managed to take an examination in German at this Institute, which qualified me as a teacher. I never taught it—in fact, I taught commercial subjects at a Technical School in Southern Moravia right until the end of the war—but I was saved from being drafted into war work or to Germany.

When the war ended—in our small town, liberated by the Rumanians, on May 1—not a shot was fired.

Not so the rest of the country. A detachment of the retreating German Army, already defeated elsewhere, started terrorising the people of Prague, plundering and burning. The citizens rose to defend their beautiful city. General Patton halted for weeks, only a few kilometres from Prague, keeping to the Yalta Agreement line.

Day after day, hour after hour, the defenders of Prague called to the American armies to come and assist them to save Prague from the devastation being wrought by the fury of the Nazi troops. In his diaries, General Patton remarked that he felt that he should have advanced right up to the river Vltara, and if the Russians didn't like it, "to send them to the devil". He did not come. The West was keeping to the Yalta Agreement to the last dot, though they could not plead ignorance of the consequences of Yalta for the Czechoslovak and other nations.

General Dean was sent to Moscow at General Eisenhower's request in April 1945, when it was clear that the Western armies were advancing more rapidly in the wake of the retreating Germans.

They could have reached Berlin and Prague much earlier than the Russians. Dean was asked to tell the Russians that the Western armies would advance as far as Berlin and Prague and later would return to the military line as agreed at Yalta. After meeting the Soviet Chief of Staff Antonov, Dean wrote in his report that, from these discussions, he could perceive the long-term policy of the Soviet Ministry of Foreign Affairs. Czechoslovakia was to remain in the Soviet sphere of interest. The gratitude of the Czechs to the American Army for liberating Prague was not part of the Soviet plan. So it was the Russians who liberated Prague and for years the Communist Party of Czechoslovakia could repeat the slogan, "The Glorious Red Army liberated Prague." The West betrayed us once again.

The path from 1945 to the Communist take-over in February 1948 was inevitable and pre-destined at Yalta. The historical consequences of major political and military mistakes are not always immediately apparent. We shall be paying the price of Munich (and Yalta) for years to come.

Our Czech Government in exile under Dr Beneš was in

London during the war. They returned home in the wake of the Red Army; that too had political significance for us.

Dr Beneš himself expressed this feeling in the speech he made in the Old Town Square in Prague on his return to Czechoslovakia on May 16, 1945. He had been living and working in London, he knew at first hand the sacrifices of the British people, but in his speech of thanksgiving for the restoration of the Czechoslovak nation he put first his gratitude to the Russians.

Let us be grateful [he said] to the peoples of the Soviet Union for the immense sacrifices which they have made for us in this great war, let us be grateful to the Red Army for the vigorous energy and outstanding military skill which enabled it to win such magnificent victories over the German fury, victories, perhaps, without parallel in Russian history. Let us be grateful to Great Britain who displayed such valour and such determination, who at one period of the war alone withstood the gigantic onslaught of the Germans and thus saved the world from a disaster which was within an ace of befalling it. Let us be grateful to the United States for its unparalleled war effort and its surprising military feats which helped to save democracy and to bring about our present victory. We gratefully remember Stalin, Churchill, Roosevelt and all that they did for mankind in this war. . . .

And for the future let us renew our oath to remain for ever true to our great Czech and Slovak traditions . . . and to remain true to our comradeship, our collaboration, and to the ideals of our new Slavonic policy, consecrated as it is with blood shed in common with the great Russian nation and other Slavonic peoples.

A Government of National Front was formed and all Parties agreed with these sentiments. We Czechs then had no anti-Russian feelings. We felt drawn to Russia because of the Russian sacrifices in the war, and we believed—at least, we wanted to believe—that the Russians were our friends. Czech history is the record of centuries of struggle against one form and another of German invasion and oppression. We believed that if some formula for Slavonic unity could be achieved, the Germans would not dare to try again.

I write as a Czech, whose home is now in England. Although I have come to understand the British people far better than I once did, I am still saddened by what seems to me a woeful ignorance in Britain of the realities of Central Europe. The British, it seems to me, simply do not begin to comprehend the deep-seated fear of Germany among the Czechs, the Poles and other Central European peoples. There was a chance in 1938 of cementing a real alliance between the British, French and Czechoslovak peoples against German aggression. That chance was thrown away by the inept amateurishness of British and French politicans. Instead of establishing a genuine alliance which, I still believe, might have prevented the Second World War and brought about the downfall of Hitler by anti-Hitler forces in Germany, the British and French Governments preferred to give in to Hitler and sacrifice Czechoslovakia —and so made war inevitable. After the war there was again a chance, though a brief one, of creating a true East–West understanding, but the West was exhausted by the war, and turned to its own internal economic problems.

In Czechoslovakia shortly after the war ended large scale nationalisation of industry followed. Plans for this programme and for modernisation of the industries were prepared during the darkest days of the German occupation, some written in concentration camps by technicians and economists. Much of the heavy industry was in foreign hands; the German and Hungarian property was confiscated automatically.

It was interesting that the Communist Party of Czechoslovakia was not the most vocal group on the issue of legalised nationalisation. They had it in their minds to have no defined lines and gradually to nationalise everything. To the ordinary Czech, the Communist policy in post-war Czechoslovakia did not appear frightening. During the first, and last, free elections in 1946, the Communist Party walked off with over forty per cent of the votes.

In the summer of 1947, the echoes of Yalta once again became apparent; this time more forcefully. The Czechoslovak Government accepted, on July 4, 1947, an invitation to attend the Paris conference on the Marshall Plan. On the same day,

Prime Minister Gottwald (the leader of the Czechoslovak Communist Party) and Jan Masaryk (son of Thomas Masaryk) flew to Moscow where, at Stalin's personal request, they telephoned the Prague Government asking it to withdraw its acceptance of the Paris Conference. We were told that it was an entirely voluntary act on the part of Czechoslovakia. Jan Masaryk told his friends in private: "I went to Moscow as a Czechoslovak Minister and returned Stalin's lackey."

In 1945 I knew little of politics and was not interested in getting actively involved in any way. Like many others of my generation, who were deprived by the German occupation of studying at University, I wanted to get a degree. With my background of commercial studies the obvious choice was the Prague High School of Economics. I enrolled sometime in the late summer of 1945.

Prague was a fantastically interesting place then, teeming with activity both culturally and politically. The oppressions of wartime were over and everyone wanted to live more intensively. The first World Students Festival took place in the late autumn of 1945, and Prague was overflowing with young people from all over the world. Politics didn't seem to matter. I myself had friends who were Marxists studying in Leningrad and Moscow, and friends who were Roman Catholics and actively involved.

During the World Student Festival I worked with a Dutch group of students, and in rushing round the country with them I neglected my health and went down with what appeared to be a bad cold. This dragged on, until in the spring of 1946, pleurisy was diagnosed. I was ill for months, too ill to travel home to be cared for by my mother, so my many friends took turns to look after me. Though it was touch-and-go according to the doctor, I pulled through. When I was able to travel I went to stay in Switzerland where I could get the mountain air, and food required for a successful recovery.

On the way back I went by train through Linz, in Austria, which was then under Four Power occupation by the British, the Russians, the Americans and the French.

Near Linz there was suddenly a commotion in the corridor of my compartment and I saw a group of soldiers struggling with a young man who was protesting in Czech and broken

Les Cannon in 1948 (*photo C. Bernard*)

In Warsaw in 1948

Wedding photographs

German. I went to ask what the trouble was and found that the Czech student who was returning from a visit to France had only a third-class ticket. The international express train we travelled on had no third class.

I spoke German fluently and English fairly well and I told the Ticket Inspector and the soldiers that the student was prepared to pay the difference in fare. Since he had no money left I lent him some. I told them to let him be. He was immensely grateful, and later, when we were back in Prague, his mother invited me to visit their home. I did, and became quite friendly with the family. It was through this chance encounter on the train from Switzerland that I eventually met Les.

Having lost almost a year of studies and having tasted life abroad I hesitated about returning to University. I felt this the more so because by this time, after the elections of 1946, the conflicts between the various Parties were coming more into the open and affected life at Universities to a disturbing degree.

I thought of working with an export firm, which would have enabled me to travel, and when an acquaintance told me that he could get me a place at Melbourne University I was quite keen.

Whatever my decision was going to be, I knew that it was imperative that I should improve my English, preferably staying with an English family for a couple of months or so. I dropped a chance remark about my ideas to the mother of the student I had rescued on my way from Switzerland. She said she knew just the person who could help and gave me his address.

That person was Les Cannon. He had met Eva, her daughter, when he had attended the World Youth Festival and she had acted as his interpreter.

It was now 1947. I was still very undecided about what I wanted to do, and meanwhile I got a job in the cultural department at the headquarters of the Czech trade union organisation—the equivalent of the TUC. The Czech unions were involved in all sorts of cultural activities, arranging lectures for factory workers, organising holidays for them, and running holiday centres at hotels and holiday camps in the mountains. I helped in all this and also helped in the foreign section of the

D

Czech TUC. But I was still interested in the possibility of going to Australia with a Melbourne scholarship, so I wrote to Les, partly with the idea of trying to arrange a visit to England, partly just to write to somebody in English. He replied that he was shortly going to a conference in Warsaw, and would be travelling through Prague on the way back.

A tour of holiday centres and other showplaces was arranged for him, and in my job in the cultural department of the TUC I was able to go round with him. I remember vividly our first meeting, when he called at my flat—he seemed nice, boyish, overflowing with life, and slightly untidy. He could speak very little Czech, but he had picked up a few sentences, and he had taken so much trouble to get the accent right that people thought he knew far more Czech than he did.

After that visit we corresponded at intervals throughout 1948. He came back to Czechoslovakia at Christmas time. By then I had been transferred to the Mineworkers' Union, and with some other young people we had a marvellous Christmas holiday in the mountains at one of the union's holiday hotels. I think it was then that Les began to be seriously interested in me. I was not then in love with him—it was certainly not love at first sight. But I respected him, and was attracted by his tremendous sense of fun and boyishness.

Back in England he began to write me much more affectionate letters, and from time to time he would telephone me. Then he asked me to marry him. I was very undecided. I certainly liked him very much, but I was not at all sure that I wanted to marry him, or anyone else, for that matter. But he was persistent and I vaguely said "Yes".

Before Les came to Prague I had changed my mind and told him so in a letter. Nevertheless he arrived in the middle of July, a smart new wedding suit in his case, obviously confident that with his powers of persuasion he would change my mind.

We spent some weeks in a spa and then two weeks hiking in the Bohemian mountains with Eva and her brother, and on and off the question of marriage was touched upon gingerly. One beautiful sunny afternoon Les and I sat on a mountainside looking down into the distant valley below and Les once again, swallowing his pride, repeated earnestly his offer of marriage.

I do not quite know if it was his tenacity or his obvious fondness for me, but my feeble resistance was rapidly eroding. I did not say "No", but I did not say "Yes" very eagerly either.

A few days later on a train returning to Prague Les said with pointed casualness: "Well, it's no point my staying in Prague. You obviously will not marry me. I will spend a few days with Eva's family and then return to England."

I suddenly felt that I might never see him again.

"Let's have dinner tomorrow and settle it once and for all," I suggested, already knowing that he had won.

On Tuesday, August 22, I told Les: "Let's get married next Friday, or not at all."

It was like tempting Fate: if it could be done against all odds —then it's meant to happen. It was a frantic rush. All sorts of "dispensations" had to be obtained. I sent a telegram to my mother, who was "standing by" because I knew she would like to be present. I had several new outfits and decided to wear a pale silver two-piece à la Dior's "New Look".

As we drove to collect my mother from the station on Thursday afternoon I remembered that she would never forgive me if I had no flowers. We stopped at the florist's. There was a bunch of red roses in a bucket: "There, you must have those—for Lancashire."—What Lancashire was I hadn't a clue but I asked the florist to have the lot ready for next day.

"Have you arranged a wedding reception?" inquired Mother.

And so, on from the station to a hotel where I managed to book a small room.

"A very special luncheon party for friends going abroad, please," I told the manager, who knew me.

"A cake?" he asked.

"Well, not a cake perhaps, but an interesting sweet— something rather special.

"But keep the main meal simple and tasty. *They* are English."

He promised to do his best.

For the life of me I cannot remember what that meal consisted of, but I do remember the look the manager gave me when he realised it was my wedding day.

The wedding was fixed for 11 a.m. at Prague Town Hall, on August 25, 1949. It is a beautiful old building, which dates back to 1338, and it still bears the scars of Czech national tragedy during the Counter-Reformation and the beginnings of the Thirty Years War. Twenty-seven fighters for the Reformation, sons of the old Czech nobility, were put to death in Prague Town Hall, and in 1945, during the Prague uprising against the Germans, the Nazis tried to destroy the building by setting fire to it. They failed, because the people of Prague, risking their lives to carry buckets of water, put the fire out, and although the building was severely damaged much of the beautiful façade was saved. By 1949 it had been restored, and the lofty Wedding Hall stood again in all its old splendour.

Les as a foreigner had to have an interpreter. The young lawyer arrived in his best tweed jacket and smart plus-fours all ready to dash off to catch a train for a weekend in the mountains. His English must have been rather incomprehensible, for intermittently a prolonged consultation ensued between him and Les, Les frequently whispering to him, "I beg your pardon?" rather exasperatingly. I thought it all great fun and giggled, hiding my face in my "Lancashire roses".

Les used to say all his life that he wasn't sure if he was legally married to me since he didn't comprehend a single coherent passage of the wedding ceremony.

Because of the short notice, Harry Pollitt, who should have been our best man, was unable to be present, and William Gallacher, the Communist MP, and his wife Jean officiated instead.

In the afternoon a handful of friends called at the house where we were staying with my mother. Les had discovered a couple of English records and so we danced and he sang "South of the Border" until the record became worn out. My mother danced with Les most and they obviously liked one another very much. In the evening we took Mother to an opera and next day we set off for a short honeymoon not very far from Prague. Les had to go back to England to attend the TUC, we had only a week left.

We arrived at the hotel rather late in the evening. There was some sort of electricity failure and the place was in total darkness. It had been a hot day and Les found that right outside the hotel was a lake. Never one to miss a swim, he was in the water within minutes of our arrival.

When we looked out of the window in the morning, we saw broken bottles and tins in the water.

"It reminds me of Wigan Pier," remarked Les.

VII

MARRIAGE

I wrote in the previous chapter of my childhood and youth in Czechoslovakia, and of meeting and marrying Les. I must now return to the political events of that period, which had an important bearing on the development of Les's own political thought.

His first visit to Czechoslovakia was in the summer of 1947, as leader of the British delegation to the International Youth Festival that was held in Czechoslovakia that year. The Youth Festival was largely a Communist affair, but Czechoslovakia itself was not then under a Communist regime. The Communist Party was very strong, particularly in the trade unions, but the Government was still nominally a democratic coalition under Dr Beneš. Les was a passionate believer in Communism, but he had not then seen the hard-faced men of the Party in action. It was still a time of hope, of the rebuilding of our shattered nation after the war. Much that the Communists were doing in Czechoslovakia was good; their cultural work in the trade unions was well organised and of great benefit to working people, and their general social work—the organisation of holiday centres, and of special trade union hotels where members and their families could stay at very low cost—was equally valuable. It was an inspiring visit for Les. He believed that he was witnessing the manifestation of all the ideas he had dreamed of as a youth —he saw a new society emerging, and it was winning the enthusiastic support of thousands of visitors to Czechoslovakia as well as of the Czech people themselves. The enthusiasm of Czech youth was intense and infectious. There was dancing and singing in the streets of Prague and at weekends lorries carried loads of singing youngsters to voluntary work on the railways, roads, farms and in the mines. The Communist and Social Democratic Ministers in the Czechoslovak Government gave receptions in the Prague palaces, there were concerts and operas, and an exciting exchange of ideas at meetings arranged between the various visiting delegations. The Russians were out to impress visitors, and meetings with members of the Russian delegation to the Festival were always spectacularly well arranged. There would not be many Russians at such meetings, perhaps a dozen or so assembled to meet a party of, say, two hundred young British people, but the Russians would be all outstanding members of the cultural élite—a composer, ballet dancer, concert pianist, singer in the Boshoi, and so on. Their leader was Alexander Shelepin, later an important member of the Soviet Presidium. In the course of discussion at one of these meetings it was discovered that the British Labour Party was not represented at the Festival. "Never mind the Labourites," said Shelepin; "they are not important." (One hopes that his knowledge of the British political scene has improved somewhat since those days.)

In 1948 there was a Communist *coup d'état* in Prague and when Les next visited Czechoslovakia it was under Communist control. Outwardly, however, nothing much had happened to change the life of the ordinary citizen—the years of disillusionment and terror in the 1950s were still ahead. I have described how, as an officer in the cultural department of the trade unions, I helped to take Les on a tour of our showplaces. Such tours were always arranged for foreign visitors considered important enough, and they were always impressive. Les saw the Miners' Rest Home in Ostrava, which had been built by the Miners' Union before the war, and was far superior to any trade union home in Britain—in developing this sort of work the Social Democrats and Communists in Czechoslovakia had a long tradition of enlightened trade unionism to build upon. Les attended miners' meetings where they pledged support for the Communist Government in the most moving fashion—miner after miner would go to the rostrum to announce the setting up of voluntary "Shock Groups" to carry out their own "Fulfilment Plans". The ideas were generated by the Czech Communist Party, but the response at that time was spontaneous and genuine.

Before our wedding in 1949 Les again saw only what was good in the Communist State of Czechoslovakia—the trade union hotels in the mountains, and at the spas in our beautiful, wooded countryside, beautiful always, whatever mess man makes of his political affairs. Les introduced me to Harry Pollitt and his wife who were staying at a spa where Pollitt was undergoing treatment. We found him rather sceptical about the political line of the resurrected Comintern—reborn as the Cominform with its own journal bearing the appallingly long-winded title: *For Lasting Peace, for People's Democracy.* Les was a bit disconcerted when Pollitt suddenly remarked out of the blue: "I'll tell you what, lad—it [meaning the Communist brand of socialism] won't come in my time, and it won't come in yours, either." It was an unexpected statement from the man who could inspire Left-wing audiences with more hope of seeing ideas become realities than any other political speaker in Britain. Les reminded Pollitt of his frequent use of the phrase: "It's round the corner, comrades".

"Ah, yes," said Pollitt, "but you have to say these things. Otherwise it's impossible to go on."

He told us that once, at an official dinner given in his honour, he was somewhat indelicately asked by a Czech Communist how long it would be before the British Communist Party would be in a position to offer similar hospitality to the East European comrades. "As soon as the Red Army pays us a visit as they did you, comrade," Pollitt replied.

I don't think that Les was much shaken by this cynicism at the time. He had his own burning belief in Communism, and he was going back to England to work for it. He liked and respected Pollitt, and he could forgive him if he occasionally showed weariness after a lifetime of political struggle.

Les had to be back in England for the TUC early in September: I had known that I could not go with him because I hadn't yet got my passport, but it was sad when we had to part so soon after our marriage. Still, we could be buoyant with hopes of the future. I was excited about going to England, and settled down to wait as patiently as I could. I was not happy about leaving my parents, but I was not then afraid of Communism, and as far as I could see they were going to be all right. My father's wholesale tobacco business came to an end when the trading system of the old State monopoly was abolished by the Communists in 1948 and replaced by outright nationalisation of the whole tobacco industry. He was able, however, to keep a retail shop. I suggested that my parents should consider coming to England with me, but they didn't want to leave Czechoslovakia. And my mother was adamant that she was not going to risk being a burden upon me in any way. In her view settling down to marriage in a strange country was a hard enough task for any woman; she didn't want to risk complicating my life by any difficulties that she and my father might have if they emigrated with me.

It was three months before the formalities about my new British nationality were completed and I did not get to England until December 8. I travelled by train and boat, and Les met me at Victoria Station. It was a grey, cold evening when I arrived, with swirls of fog about the London streets—the kind of London fog that doesn't come nowadays, when so little coal is burned on open fires. In 1949 coal was rationed, but most Londoners still depended on it for heating. As we left the station on my first evening in England, I remember thinking of the incident in Galsworthy's *Forsyte Saga* when a young architect falls under a cab in a London fog; it seemed just the same sort of night.

With Les to meet me at Victoria was Frank Haxell, then Assistant General Secretary of the ETU. I could not know then what a strange part in our lives Frank Haxell was to play. He and his wife shared our first evening in London. I thought him ponderous, and rather dull. His wife was gay and cheerful enough, but she spoke quickly with an East-London accent that went right over my head. My own English was still an astonishing brand. I knew quite a lot from my years of study, but I naturally had had little practice in speaking it.

We stayed at a small hotel near Euston, where we had supper and a number of drinks. At least, the rest of the party had drinks, but I was quite unaccustomed to drinking anything but a glass of wine with a meal and was therefore a very poor drinker. Also, I was tired after my long journey across Europe, and emotionally tired after seeing from the train some of the wounds of war that were still visible in 1949. I did not enjoy the evening.

Les had planned to take me to his home in Wigan next day, but he developed a feverish cold and had to stay in bed. So we stayed on at the hotel for a few days. I was disappointed with London, partly, perhaps, because I'd expected so much of it. The war to us in Czechoslovakia had meant largely the Russian war against Germany; I hadn't realised the extent to which England had suffered. In 1949 there were still bombed-out ruins all over London, and the post-war drabness was far worse than that in Prague. The English women I saw walking about London seemed to me sloppily dressed, with scarves tied round their heads and cigarettes hanging from their lips. The shops, too, were a great disappointment to me. I had expected wonderful shops, but most of what I saw in London shop windows seemed to me to be shoddy stuff, with little attempt to display it elegantly.

The cold seeped through my fur-lined coat. It can be cold in Czechoslovakia, of course, but there it is usually a crisp cold, with sunshine sparkling on the snow. London was just grey and damp. It was a relief when we finally got on a train to Wigan, but the relief didn't last long. The main line north out of Euston runs through some of the ugliest parts of industrial England, and it seemed to get worse as we went on—Rugby, Stafford, Crewe, Warrington—I felt depressed at the sight of endless miles of ugly little houses in row after row of mean streets.

Les had made no plans for my arrival—apparently it hadn't occurred to him that we should need somewhere to live. He had been living at home and, if he thought about it at all, I suppose he thought that I could just live there, too. But I couldn't, because there simply was not room for me in his parents' tiny house. We spent one night there and then we had to move out to stay with some friends of Les's family.

If this seems curiously irresponsible of Les, I can only say that it was, but it wasn't irresponsibility in any ordinary sense. Les had deep feelings for his family, and he would criticise his father for having acted, as he thought, irresponsibly towards his wife and children.

And yet Les was rather like his father, but in a very different way. He did not live cocooned in thoughts; he was always immersed in action. At that time he was the Lancashire Divisional Representative on the Executive of the ETU, an immense job for a man not yet thirty. He was wrapped up in his trade union work, and in his mind it took precedence over everything else. He was out to right the wrongs of *his* workers. He never spared himself, he hardly ever thought of himself. In not thinking of himself, he included me, and later our sons. But it was not that Les did not think of us as *people*—he could be the tenderest of men, and he cared deeply for all of us. It was simply that we belonged to his personal life, and wherever his personal life was concerned, his work came first.

Eventually we got two partly-furnished rooms for ourselves. It wasn't much of a home, but it was vastly better than staying in someone else's spare room. I had problems with ration books, shopping and cooking—everything was so unfamiliar and strange. The first supper I prepared for my husband consisted of Russian stuffed eggs—nice enough for *hors d'œuvres*, but scarcely what a Lancashire working man would regard as a square meal! However, I became progressively better at house-keeping. My other main problem at this time was that I was pregnant, and I had to prepare for motherhood without the guidance of my own mother. Nellie Cannon—Les's mother—was very sweet and gentle, but offered no advice at all because she did not want to seem to interfere with me in any way.

Oleg, our elder son, was born in May 1950, and soon after that we moved to a furnished flat in Liverpool. It was right at the top of an old Victorian house in Prince's Road. It had been a beautiful house in its day, and still had a sort of decayed graciousness about it, but the whole area was dreadfully neglected. I love colour and brightness, but even in summer Liverpool seemed mostly dreary and grey. I missed the cultural life that I had lived so intensively in Prague before my marriage; particularly I missed the opera. But I wasn't going to give up. I had married my strange English husband, I believed in what he was trying to do for working people, and I felt that it was up to me to make the best of our lives. However, I was very lonely. Les was out most of the time, and I had no English friends. Les was really a loner himself—he had lots of acquain-tances but no close friendships.

At about this time various things were happening to Les that I didn't fully understand until much later. When we were married he was not only one of the stars of the ETU but was also regarded as having an important future in the Communist

Party. Being very much in favour with the Communists he was put on innumerable committees. He was not paid as a member of the Executive of the Union, but membership of his various committees involved much travelling to London, and entitled him to delegation fees and expenses. Under the Communist system of control, if you remained in favour with the Party you served on enough committees and delegations to be able to live on what you got without having to do a paid job as well. It was a bad system, but one not unfamiliar in unions and Labour Party organisations in Britain. English working-class leaders used to be so scared of apparently earning more than the wage-earners they represented that to earn enough to do their jobs properly they were compelled to resort to various devices to obtain "expenses". American and Continental trade unions have long regarded their officers as equivalent in status to the employers' representatives and high Civil Servants with whom they have to deal, and tried to pay them accordingly. The British tradition was that you wore a cloth cap to negotiate with a top hat—fine as a rugged expression of human equality, but hard on those forced to live on cloth-cap wages while meeting as equals men on top-hat salaries. Things are better in Britain now: trade unions have a greater awareness of the value of their own officials, and the appointment of trade unionists to the boards of nationalised industries has helped to bring out the disparity in the rewards for representing men and representing management. Of course, no one goes in for trade union work solely for financial reward, but the labourer is worthy of his hire and a good trade union official deserves to be paid adequately. Though things are better in this respect now, there are still traces in British trade unionism of the old suspicion of paying anyone a "boss's salary".

In 1950 the tradition of expecting men to do full-time jobs for trade unions while living on air was still strong, with all its attendant evils. At the start of our marriage Les made enough from his committee work for us to live on, and he didn't have to do an outside job. Gradually the committee work fell off. Les was no Yes man, and although he was a Communist he was not prepared simply to take instructions from his Communist superiors in the ETU. He used to argue when he thought that some suggested course of action was wrong. Some of his fellow-Communists didn't like this. Nothing was said openly to Les, but he was edged off committee after committee until there just wasn't enough money coming in for us to get by. This was one of the ways in which the Communist Party exerted pressure on people to make them toe the line. If Les had been a different sort of man he might have given in and restored his position by seeking favour with the Party bosses. Instead, he returned to his trade as an electrician and got a job with the English Electric Company in Liverpool. He might be thrown off committees, but he still had his seat on the Union's National Executive, from which he could not be removed until the time came for him to stand for re-election.

He was soon in trouble at English Electric. He had not been there long before he realised that the wages of the women were scandalously low. He put in a demand for higher wages for them, and when this was refused he called the employees out on strike.

The strike was wholly successful. The women got a large wage increase, but Les got the sack. He expected the union to support him in demanding his job back, if necessary by calling another strike—but it didn't. Les felt bitterly let down, but there was nothing he could do about it. He got another job at the Liverpool power station. The working conditions there were appalling and Les didn't like the job, but a man sacked as a troublemaker had to take what he could get. Les was a first-class electrician, maintaining high standards in everything he did, but his heart was in trade unionism, not in electrical work. For the moment it seemed that the union didn't want him. He gritted his teeth and bided his time, but he was not happy.

Neither was I. In 1952 Martin, our second son, was born. I still had no friends in Liverpool, and I was homesick. I wanted to take our two small boys to Czechoslovakia for a holiday to visit my parents but I could not get a visa. I applied for it again and again. Everyone at the Czech Embassy in London, including the Ambassador, was sympathetic; Harry Pollitt tried to help; but still no visa came.

In 1953 there was a second currency reform in Czechoslovakia. Existing currency became nearly valueless overnight. No cash was accepted above about £18. All savings were frozen and only released under exceptional circumstances at a 1:50 rate of exchange. Everyone had to start again from scratch. For wage-earners who were paid in the new currency it was not too bad; they lost most of their savings, but at least had an income to buy the necessities of life. For pensioners the effect was catastrophic.

During this upheaval, and as a result of a nation-wide drive against shopkeepers, who were regarded as the remnants of capitalist society, the local Communists organised a search of my parents' home. Though all they found were some old packets of tobacco and cigarettes, they charged my father with acting against the interest of the working-class and the State, confiscated all the goods and closed his shop. Father appealed to the regional courts and his appeal was upheld. He was completely cleared. But the local authorities refused to return the shop to him, offer alternative employment or give him a State pension.

In October my father telephoned me in Liverpool. He was desperate. For the last two weeks he and my mother had lived on coffee and bread. He saw no way out under the present conditions—no one would help and there was no hope of redress.

I was both appalled and incensed. I sat down and wrote a strongly-worded detailed letter addressed to A. Novotný, the then First Secretary of the Communist Party and later President of Czechoslovakia. Among other things I told him that I could not understand why I, who had left Czechoslovakia legally and was married to a leading English Communist, was unable to get a visa to visit my parents and to help them against unwarranted persecution by the local administrators. I made several copies, in my handwriting, and posted them at different times in the hope that one of them would reach Novotný. His Personal Secretary later told me that they all arrived and that he was rather puzzled about what had made me do it.

The effect of this rather unusual intervention was dramatic. A few days later, late at night, a big black car stopped outside my parents' home. After 1950, midnight arrests were not unusual and a knock on the door in the dark of the night often spelled trouble. My parents' reaction was: "This is the end." But the men were top District Officials of the Communist Party and they came to rectify the deeds of the local Communists. My father's shop would be restored to him, and would he be good enough to sign the necessary forms and send a telegram to his daughter Olga in England assuring her that all was well again?

I was delighted when I got the news, and shortly after a visa arrived for myself and the two boys.

We travelled to Czechoslovakia in April 1954. When I saw my father on the platform I nearly broke down. I scarcely recognised him, he had aged so much.

Though I was happy to see my parents and to see their delight in their two lively grandsons, it was a sad home-coming. Everything in Czechoslovakia had deteriorated. People looked weary and sullen and my former friends were reticent and evasive when I asked questions concerning their daily lives and work. The gay atmosphere of Prague which I had so loved during the few years before my marriage had vanished. The Communist "planners", following the Russian example, had thrown all the financial resources of the country into the construction of heavy industry, regardless of lack of raw materials or problems of transport. Tremendous mistakes had been made and the people were having to go short of all sorts of consumer goods, from food to housing. The old patrician houses of Prague, already neglected during the war, had been taken over by the State and were badly in need of essential decorations and repairs. Prague seemed more drab to me than Liverpool. I arrived wearing a simple softly-coloured pink coat; as I walked down Václavské Náměstí my coat seemed to scream indecently in the midst of the greyness of its surroundings. I put it away for the rest of my stay—I felt too self-conscious wearing it.

I stayed on in Czechoslovakia with the children over the May Day celebrations and Les was able to come out to join us as a member of the visiting May Day delegation from Britain. I acted as his interpreter, and he met the Executive of the Czech Energy Workers Union—the corresponding body to the ETU in Britain. Les was interested to meet members of this union, some of whom were obviously honest workers who had studied, and were trying hard to understand, the new technical problems behind the façade of Communist Party leadership. But it soon became apparent that the whole union was under the thumb of its President, an unbearably ignorant

man who was not even an electrician by trade, but a hair-
dresser! In the labour shortage during the war the Germans had
sent him to work at a power station, and after the war he had
become a minor official at the Communist Party headquarters.
After the Communist take-over in 1948 he was seconded by the
Party to run the Energy Workers Union, much to the resentment
of the leaders of the union, who argued that he was not even
familiar with the problems of their work. They were told,
however, that they must support him, and denounce any
criticism of his lack of electrical knowledge as "remnants of
craft sectarianism". Later this man came to Britain as a delegate to the ETU conference, and he was embraced and kissed
on the platform by Frank Foulkes, then President of the ETU.

Les was not happy at the state of things he found in Czechoslovakia. He had an official interpreter as well as me, and he
became intensely irritated when he heard him expressing
violently anti-Semitic sentiments. Les decided to make a formal
complaint about this, and he demanded a meeting with the
General Secretary of the Czech TUC. The night before this
meeting took place we were invited to a reception given by the
Government at the Czernin Palace. I smile still as I remember
this occasion, though the humour of it is not unmixed with
sadness. Fresh fruit in Prague then was all-but unobtainable,
and my little son Martin, who loved fruit, was reduced to raw
carrots and lemon juice—all that was to be had in the shops.
At this glittering reception there were silver dishes piled high
with beautifully polished apples. I had only a small evening
handbag with me, and I went to find Les, who was talking to a
group of people in another room, to ask him to put a few
apples in his pockets. Being less experienced than the other
guests, by the time I got back with Les the silver dishes were
empty, and the big handbags brought by the officers' wives
were bulging, as were their husbands' smart uniform pockets.

That was the comic side of the reception; for the rest it was
not a happy gathering. People were afraid to talk much to
foreigners, or even to each other. Most of the conversation
comprised hints, half-hints, and whispers—of people who had
been imprisoned, committed suicide or who had been thrown
out of jobs. By contrast, one courageous and much-decorated
miner from Kladno was surprisingly frank. He loudly com-

plained to us that the miners were sick of politics at their weekly meetings, and that what they really wanted to talk about were wages and working conditions. We thought him remarkably bold under the circumstances.

Next day I went with Les to the headquarters of the Czech TUC to meet the General Secretary to whom Les wished to complain about the behaviour of his interpreter. The Head of the Foreign Department was also present, because he knew me well and spoke good English. The General Secretary seemed to have a job to keep his eyes open, and I remembered that I had seen him having a very gay time at the reception the night before. He did his best to appear interested, but it was clear that he was a long away away from this "fool of a young Communist from Britain". Les was so intent on making his case that he didn't notice, and I was too far away from Les to give him a kick to warn him that he was wasting his time.

When the General Secretary got up to pour himself a glass of water and to take a couple of tablets, I was able to go across to Les and explain the situation to him. In the end the General Secretary promised to look into the matter and instructed the Head of the Foreign Department to report to him. When we came to Czechoslovakia two years later and asked what measures had been taken we were told that the interpreter had become a Director of a Trade Union Hotel which catered for foreign visitors.

Back in England, Les's frustration increased. He hated his job at the Liverpool power station, and he seemed more at odds than ever with the Communists in the ETU.

The Party members in Liverpool with whom Les had to work were an uncongenial lot. There was at times a curiously Puritanical streak in Les—the Puritanism of the founders of the Labour movement—and he hated those four-letter words which have become so commonplace in modern society. He wrote a furious letter of complaint to the Lancashire and Cheshire Committee of the Communist Party about the language used by a leading Communist at a meeting:

During discussion [Les wrote] Comrade —— made the remark, "I wash my hands of the whole f——ing business." This remark was made very loudly, and was heard by the comrades in the adjoining office, including two women comrades. . . . (The partition between the offices is very thin.)

Les's letter concluded:

As I made to go Comrade ——, obviously wanting to find the most degrading description he could lay his tongue to, said, "You're just a wireman . . ." The contempt with which he gave emphasis to the word "wireman" would have led one to believe that one of the best ways of insulting someone was to describe him as a member of a section of the working class that the comrade who made the remark is supposed to lead and serve.

On another occasion Les came home late at night, dreadfully upset. I was asleep, and he woke me up to tell me that right in the centre of town he had hit a Party member for calling him "a bloody liar". He was appalled at his loss of self-control. "How could I have done it?" he said. "Haven't I always preached self-control and dignity?"

Distressed as Les was, I couldn't help laughing. I disliked the victim of Les's blow. "My only criticism, darling," I said, "is that you should have done it ages ago."

Suddenly there seemed to be a way out. In the summer of 1953 the ETU had opened Esher Place as the first residential trade union college in Britain. Esher Place had been a home of many famous men. When Cardinal Wolsey fell from the favour of Henry VIII he came to Esher and entering it he remarked: "I have found a haven . . . farewell hope and fortune . . ." Towards the end of that century Richard Drake, brother of Sir Francis Drake, came to Esher Estate where a number of Grandees captured from the Spanish Armada were held in custody. Another famous resident was Lord Henry Pelham, the Prime Minister from 1743 to 1754. During the late Victorian and Edwardian times the present house became a great social centre—the residents then were the D'Abernon family.

The establishment of this trade union college was one of the really good achievements of the Communist leadership of the ETU, which followed here one of the best features of Soviet trade unionism. The first head of the College was John Vickers, a Cambridge graduate and member of the engineering family. John Vickers had become a Communist in his Cambridge days and he had joined the research department of the ETU before the College came into being; its conception, and the syllabus for the courses followed there, were largely his work.

Before he took the job with the ETU, Vickers had been warned by a friend of Harry Pollitt: "Be very careful before you work for these people. They are not very nice, and the top people at King Street [the headquarters of the Communist Party] don't like them, and don't trust them." But Vickers had a mind of his own, and he was determined to seize what seemed to him a unique chance of helping full-time workers' education. By the end of 1953 he was disillusioned and over-worked. He was responsible for all the educational work of the college, and conducted most of the tutorials himself. Since each batch of students arrived on Sunday afternoon and left on Saturday morning, he was on duty seven days a week. He badly needed an assistant, and the ETU Executive agreed.

Les was still a member of the Executive, and of the National Advisory Committee of the Communist Party at which this question was discussed. One evening he telephoned Vickers and said, "Look, I have some news for you. They want to put —— in as your assistant. What do you think about that?"

"Not much," Vickers replied.

"Let's meet then," Les said, "because I don't think much of the idea, either."

The Communist Party, as usual keeping a close eye on the day-to-day affairs of the ETU, had decided to recommend —— as Vickers's assistant because the Party did not altogether trust Vickers as politically reliable. Their nominee was supposed to see that Vickers kept in step—as the Party saw it, the assistant's job would be far more to watch his chief than to do educational work himself. It was not a very clever choice, however, for Vickers could scarcely be expected not to know that the man in question was completely unfitted for an ostensibly educational appointment.

Les went to London to talk over things with John Vickers,

and after discussing the problems of the college for a bit Les asked, "How would you feel about my working with you?" Vickers replied that he would be absolutely delighted. That was the beginning of a happy partnership and a friendship which lasted until Les's death.

Les was, in fact, ideally fitted for the post. He had all his father's academic brilliance, but where his father had been content with pure theory, Les was intensely practical. As far back as 1950, when I was expecting Oleg, Les had attended a course on work-study arranged by ICI for trade union representatives, and he had shown such extraordinary ability that ICI offered him a job on its own staff, with the additional temptations of rapid promotion and financial assistance in buying a house and payment of moving expenses. Les laughed off the idea of joining one of the inner citadels of capitalism, but he retained his interest in work-study, and became a brilliant exponent of it. In every other way, too, Les was cut out for educational work; his wide reading and deep understanding of the history of working-class movements made him a sympathetic lecturer and tutor, quick to respond to a student's needs and capable of inspiring a genuine eagerness for knowledge. But suitability for the job was one thing; the politics of getting it was quite another matter. Les and John Vickers between them concocted a plan.

Vickers went to see Walter Stevens, then General Secretary of the ETU, and told him that he had heard a rumour that —— was to be appointed as his assistant, adding that if the rumour was true he himself would be compelled to resign, because he felt that he could not work with the man. Stevens was considerably taken aback. Only an inner group of four or five Communists were supposed to know anything of the proposed recommendation. How had Vickers heard of it? John Vickers was suitably vague—it was just a rumour that had come to him, he said. Stevens, without denying or confirming the rumour (though it was obviously true, and both men knew it) promised to consider Vickers's views.

The next step was taken by Les. When the matter came up at the next meeting of the Communist Advisory Committee concerned with ETU affairs, Les rather casually suggested himself for the job, adding: "Of course, I don't know what

John Vickers would feel about it, and whether he'd agree to work with me." The Committee jumped at the suggestion—here, it seemed, was a splendid opportunity of getting rid of the troublesome Les Cannon from the ETU Executive. Given a paid educational post within the union he would have to resign from the Executive, and would no longer be able to take part in policy planning. Moreover, the suggestion had come from Les himself—he could be got rid of without bother or fuss. Well, whatever the reasons, it was a good idea. Would Les give an undertaking that he would not stand for elective office in the Union while he was working at the College?

It was an insult to a man who had served the Lancashire and Cheshire Division of the union devotedly for nine years; he had been elected and re-elected to the National Executive unopposed. Could he give up all this, deliberately cut himself off from the main stream of trade union life? Yes, he could. Privately, Les was sick of endless rows with Communist Party members on the Executive, he was sick of his work at the Liverpool power station, and he knew that I hated Liverpool. To be asked for an undertaking not to stand for elective office while working at the College seemed gratuitously provocative—but it could also be construed as rather a compliment, suggesting that the men at the top of the ETU were distinctly afraid of Les's personal standing in the union. Reluctantly he gave the undertaking. At any rate he would be going to a worthwhile job, in which he could pass on to others something of his vast practical experience as a shop steward and officer of the ETU.

Walter Stevens put the proposition to John Vickers. If Vickers wouldn't work with ——, would he accept Les Cannon? Vickers (deliberately) was not enthusiastic. At least his objections to —— had been met. If the Executive wished to appoint Les Cannon, well, he was prepared to have a go at working with him.

So things were fixed up. The Communists were still much concerned to know how the news of their earlier decision had reached John Vickers. They suspected all sorts of people, they suspected one another. Oddly, no one ever seemed to suspect Les.

In the late autumn of 1954 we moved to a Union-owned

semi-detached house at Chessington, within comfortable reach of the ETU College at Esher. The move transformed all our lives. The house was an ordinary little suburban "semi", but it was big enough for us and we turned it into a very pleasant home. At last the cultural life of London—the theatres, opera, art galleries and museums—was within reach. For the children there were expeditions to Hampton Court, Kew Gardens and Richmond Park, and visits to the lovely Surrey countryside. It meant a vastly happier life for me. For Les . . . ?

VIII

THE BREAK WITH COMMUNISM

LES LIKED HIS work at the ETU College, he enjoyed working with John Vickers, and he put everything he had into the job. He found the constant flow of students for the weekly courses a great stimulus—he liked meeting new people, he responded to the eagerness of those who really came to learn, and he poured out his own knowledge and experience of trade unionism in lectures, seminars and tutorials. He was a popular teacher, and he was also an extremely good one; he never talked down to his pupils and he had a wonderful gift of presenting issues simply without missing the essentials. He could combine theory and practice in the most fruitful way, making the history of the Labour movement a living study, directly relevant to trade unionists in their daily tasks. He lectured on the duties of shop stewards, on how to conduct negotiations and on the practical applications of work-study for improving working conditions. The students—all rank-and-file members of the Union—who passed through the college went back to their jobs refreshed and stimulated, far better equipped for their trade union work than they were before they came, and often more complete as human beings. The ETU College was a fine conception, and John Vickers and Les between them made it uniquely valuable.

And yet he did not feel fully stretched. He missed the policy-making. However, at least half of Les could be completely happy in an academic world. When he was particularly un-happy he could find relief in books—he turned to study as some men might turn to drink. In 1953, during his unhappy period in Liverpool, he joined a Group Study course organised by the Central Educational Department of the Communist Party. It was a tough course, a detailed, critical analysis of Marx's *Das Kapital*. About thirty people started on the course, and as far as I remember, Les was the only one to finish it. Not only that—he studied Marx's text so thoroughly that he found a misprint in a mathematical equation that nobody else had noticed. It was a complex equation developed by Marx to illustrate a particular concept of his theory of the employment of capital. Les noticed that one term of the equation given in the English edition of *Das Kapital* that he was using was a mathematical impossibility. He wrote to the Party's experts about this, they went into it, and found that Les was right—the printed text was wrong!

There is an interesting report on Les after another Communist Party school that he attended. This says:

> Made a very good contribution to the school, both in his group and in the class discussion. It was a big asset to have him there, as he was able to introduce a whole number of important problems relating to our work in industry and in the broad Labour Movement. He revealed a very good grasp of theory, and is a deep-thinking comrade, always aiming to get beneath the surface of a problem.
>
> A minor weakness is a certain tendency to dominate discussion, and not to listen sufficiently to what other comrades have to say. He tends to be a bit impatient in his attitude to people.
>
> He should be used very much more for our education work among leading Party trade unionists.

In a note accompanying the report, Peter Kerrigan, the Party's Industrial Organiser and one of the major powers at King Street, wrote to Les in a rather schoolmasterish way:

> I am sure you will pay attention to the criticism made. On the very last point, we shall have to look at this in the light of your further development.

Well, the Party had looked at Les, and for reasons by no means wholly to do with education it had sent him to the ETU College. Les was often impatient in discussion in the Communist Party, but he was never impatient with his students. He was still—as he remained to his death—a convinced Marxist, but he was becoming more and more disturbed by what seemed to him so often to be a cynical betrayal of socialism by the Com-

munist Party in practice. Les was capable of the utmost loyalty
to a cause, but it could never be a blindly unquestioning loyalty.
As far back as 1946 he had complained to Harry Pollitt about
some resolutions put up by a District Congress of the Party
which seemed to him to conflict with what the Party stood for.
Pollitt's letter in reply is worth quoting. On December 13,
1946, he wrote:

Dear Comrade,
    I have read your letter of the 10th December with interest
and can understand very well the point that is worrying you.
First I want to make it clear that no District Congress has
the right to change the National Party policy. This is the
prerogative only of the National Congress of the Party, or of
any special conference that might be called in accordance
with rule. However, that does not debar District Congresses
from discussing party policy, even of disagreeing with policy,
provided that the final decision is referred to the Executive
and to the Party Congress and the District continues to
operate the policy of the Party.
    You see, the District Congresses must make a contribution
to the preparation and formulation of Party policy at the
National Congress, and the views of the Districts have to be
taken into account. That is why it would be wrong to debar
such resolutions as you mention from discussion, although
I agree with you that both are politically incorrect resolutions.
It is part of the democracy of our Party that people with a
viewpoint like this should be permitted to express it, provided
that when it is thrashed out and a decision is taken they
follow Party policy.
    I hope you appreciate the point I have raised.
                              Yours fraternally,
                              Harry Pollitt

It was significant of Pollitt's regard for Les that he should
have replied to his angry young complaint so promptly and
so gently. It was typical of Les that he should have believed
what Pollitt said about "the democracy of our Party". What he
saw of the Communist Party at work over the next ten years,
both in England and in Czechoslovakia, came first as a shock,

and then as a gradually increasing disillusionment. The more he saw of the dominance of his own trade union by a clique, the less he liked it. Les was a politican to his fingertips, but he was a trade unionist first; politics were in his brain, but trade unionism was in his blood. As an eager young Communist it was flattering to feel that he was "in" on the secret Party conclaves that determined policy in the ETU. It was flattering to attend a national committee meeting at the Communist Party headquarters in King Street, Covent Garden, and to feel that it was the proceedings here that mattered, not what went on at meetings of the National Executive of the union. If King Street decided that a particular job in the Union should go to X, then it wasn't much use for Y to stand for election.

The Communists could rely on a full turn-out of members and sympathisers at any ETU branch meeting when an important matter was coming up. Fair enough; when 80–90 per cent of the members of a union seldom bother to attend branch meetings, those who do take the trouble to attend can expect to make their weight felt. The keen ones can expect to become branch officers, and once in control of the agenda they can run things very much as they like. If dangerous opposition is expected on some matter, that particular item can be put right at the end of the agenda and the earlier proceedings dragged on and on until all but the faithful feel that they simply must go home to eat or sleep. In an election where there are several candidates, a minority which wants its own man elected can make sure that its vote is solid and not split: if there are not enough candidates to split the opposition vote, others can be nominated—not, of course, to be voted for by the Communist faithful, but simply to attract some votes away from the candidate considered dangerous. An organised minority is always in an immensely strong position against an unorganised and largely apathetic majority. This is the weakness of all democratic systems, and since the Communist Party has never been numerically strong it has thrived by exploiting this weakness. Les understood this well enough, and since he was part of the determined, organised minority, and believed in what it was doing, he was content to play his part.

As time went on, however, he saw that the ETU was often deflected from its true purpose of representing the interests of its members by being manipulated by a clique. And he saw how personal rivalries and animosities could determine union policy, to the detriment of everything that it was supposed to stand for. His own experience in the English Electric strike in Liverpool was a shattering blow—not so much to his own self-esteem as to his confidence in the integrity of his union's Communist leadership. It was an overt act to cut Les down to size by leading Communists on the National Executive who disliked his readiness to argue with them and who were becoming more than a little afraid of him. It says much for Les that he did not break with the Party then, and leave the Union in disgust. He had already been offered one good job by ICI; there were plenty of other managements ready enough to use his knowledge of work-study and understanding of labour relations. He could have promoted himself from being an electrician to a managerial job at four times an electrician's pay. And given his ability (of which he was perfectly well aware) he could have expected to end up on some big company's board of directors.

Such thoughts hardly ever entered his head. I have said that Les was loyal—he was loyal in no ordinary sense. He was loyal to the very core of his being to what he regarded as the cause of the working-class. This loyalty made him swallow his pride when he was disowned by the Union after the Liverpool strike and carry on, determined to continue with trade union work as well as he could.

His decision to resign from the Union's Executive for a staff job at the ETU College was reached only after much bitter heart-searching. He was being allowed less and less say in the shaping of ETU policy. He could be reasonably confident of remaining on the Executive: he was immensely popular with the rank and file in the Lancashire and Cheshire District of the Union, and even if the Communists decided to oppose him when the time came for him to stand for re-election it was doubtful if he could be defeated. I have written of the methods— the more or less legitimate methods—by which an organised minority can secure the election of a candidate, but there are limits to the effectiveness of those methods. With a man as well known and popular locally as Les standing for election in his own local division, the most concerted efforts by a minority might fail to unseat him. And probably the Communists would not have tried to oppose him openly: after all, Les was still a Communist himself, and although he was on bad terms with some of the Communist henchmen in the Union, he was still on good terms with a number of the Party leaders at King Street. There were other methods of dealing with him—he could simply be frozen out. The process of denying him membership of committees and delegations could be continued until he himself might be expected to give up in despair.

To side-step from the Executive of the Union to an educational post at the ETU College seemed to Les a sort of step back. I tried to be as understanding and as gentle as I could but at the same time I wanted Les to go to the College so that we could leave Liverpool, where I was lonely and unhappy. The College seemed to offer a chance of new influence in the Union, and perhaps a spring-board to other opportunities within the trade union movement.

We remained on reasonably friendly terms with Harry Pollitt and many other leading Communists. We had stayed with the Pollitts earlier, and Harry had written us a number of friendly letters. In one note to me (towards the end of 1950) he had written:

> Glad to hear about the world's most wonderful baby. I shall see another in Manchester this weekend, that of my niece, who has written in those exact words about her new baby. But I forgive all fond mothers, they will learn the truth all in good time. Regards to you and Les from all the family.

It was difficult to feel that relationships like that could ever be wholly sundered.

When Les had been appointed to the College, he had understood that he was to have the status of a National Officer in the Union, and the salary that went with it. Instead, he was paid only an assistant's salary of £672 a year. Les was never grasping—he thought, if anything, too little about money—but he resented what he felt to have been a mean trick played on him. I'm sure that this was not the Communist Party's doing, but a piece of private vindictiveness. Later, when Les was Acting Head of the ETU College, Peter Kerrigan of the Communist Party supported his claim for higher pay. But earlier Les had been put off with excuses and half-promises; he was strung along in a most exasperating fashion. To treat any man of Les's intelligence and standing in the Union in this way was insulting. Les withdrew increasingly from Communist Party activities.

In May of 1956 I took the children for a long holiday in Czechoslovakia. I was again worried about my parents, for the local bureaucrats were once more trying to make things difficult for them. We stayed mainly in Prague, but I visited my parents as often as I could. Oleg, who was just six, was soon speaking Czech quite fluently. Martin was four and he developed a brand of Czech which only a few understood. Les and I needed to earn more money, and I wanted to try to find a job that I could do. I thought of making a film about Prague, walking about the city and seeing it through Oleg's eyes—a child's eyes. That project fell through. Then I thought of translating children's books, and I did quite a lot of work on this with another woman. There is a splendid Czech literature for children, far too little known in Britain.

We stayed in Czechoslovakia then for about five months. They were vital months in the development of many people's political thinking, and they were crucial months for Les. It was the summer of Khruschev's famous speech to the Twentieth Congress of the Soviet Union, the speech which seemed to replace the tyranny of Stalin with something at least a little more human. It was not printed at the time in Czech newspapers and two copies of reports of the speech in English newspapers which Les sent to me by post were never delivered. But everybody knew about the speech and the fact that it was not published in Prague intensified the general feeling of depression.

Les had been invited to lecture at the Prague School of Economics in July, which would give him an opportunity to join us for a few weeks. In a fit of depression in June I wrote to him:

You simply cannot imagine what is going on. It is like a deep well, dark—with just a ripple of light at the bottom . . . To allow the police to infiltrate organisations, to interfere with people, to take over in many cases . . . to create consciously a terrific gap between intellectuals and workers . . . So much so that the question which determines results (often in courts) is "What is your origin?" . . . people being ashamed of being the children of a teacher or a small clerk etc. Who wants to call it mistakes? It is vulgarisation of Marxism, first class distortion of what Marx taught, teaching for which thousands have fought and died.

Les, in England, was thinking deeply about the same political problems. On June 18 he wrote to me:

. . . I must accept what you say, and the whole business disturbs me.

It is perfectly clear that not only must all the mess be cleared up but that there must be important theoretical generalisations as to how these events occurred and what is required in each separate country, according to its specific characteristics, to prevent its happening again.

Take for example Nationalisation. In USSR there is clearly over-centralisation to the point that the workers in a particular factory, though they know it is "theirs" in the sense that the state owns it on their behalf, nevertheless cannot feel as intimately as they should that they are "running the show". On the other hand there is almost complete decentralisation in Yugoslavia. . . .

I therefore agree with you about the problems of nationalisation that there is clearly a need to end all *unnecessary* centralisation and stimulate maximum initiative at the level of production *including choice of management personnel*.

But somehow this ending of centralisation must be replaced by necessary economic co-ordination. This general aim needs very considerable elaboration based on experiences in PDs [People's Democracies].

I have now made up my mind that if I don't go to Czechoslovakia while you are still there I won't go at all. Really, I must confess, my main desire now, apart from some firsthand experiences of what is going on, is to see K and V (friends I was staying with at the time) and your parents. I most certainly have the feeling now that work-study, at least certain features of it (e.g. establishment of norms), could be really harmful in the hands of some of the people you describe.

Les did come to Prague in July, and had discussions at the School of Economics with the idea of returning in autumn to give a series of lectures on modern techniques of management. He was able to stay on for a bit, and we talked to all sorts of people. Nobody seemed happy, or to have much hope for the future. Communism had turned sour. We found Czechoslovakia, once so bright with promise, a country that had become a jungle of hatreds. The old Party members hated the young, because they had not lived up to what they themselves had fought for. The young were jealous, or contemptuous of the old. The workers were jealous of each other's privileges, the miners and steelworkers were envied by the railwaymen, and by everyone employed in the neglected sphere of making consumer goods. Intellectuals were insulted, because many of the best political jobs were held by people who called themselves intellectuals but who were often barely half-educated. Careerism and back-stabbing were rampant. The trade unions were regarded as useless for helping their members because wages and conditions of work were simply dictated by the Government. There was inefficiency and bungling everywhere, and shortages of practically everything that people wanted.

Les and I had endless discussions. We tried hard to be fair, to look beyond the immediate present, to assess the good that had been achieved under the Communist regime in Czechoslovakia. In spite of all the shortages of consumer goods, the basic living standards of the poor had undoubtedly improved since pre-war days. But would this not have happened anyway? It happened far more rapidly throughout the whole Western world. Czech inventiveness, if it had been left to itself and not strangled by bureaucracy, would have accomplished far more without the straitjacket of Communist doctrines. Socially, there had been a general levelling process, but this had not made for contentment—ironically, the struggle to keep up with the Joneses seemed to have become more intense because there were fewer differences in people's social setting. When everyone was forced to have the same furniture, the same table, the same bookcase, there seemed an almost desperate compulsion to express human individuality in other ways. Working people could have cheap holidays, but the same people went to the same places over and over again. The trade union hotels were showplaces; certainly the Communists had kept them up, but the *idea* of trade union hotels and rest centres in Czechoslovakia was not Communist—the Czech miners' union, in particular, had had them long before the war.

In one of his letters before he was able to join me in Prague, Les had written:

> I must tell you that my thoughts are wandering into "dangerous" political channels. I keep asking myself what specific functions should a Communist Party carry out in the particular historical conditions in Britain, and is it possible to fulfil them in any other way than in this state of enforced isolation? Indeed, I am beginning to wonder which way can the thousands of Marxists in Britain be most effective— inside the Communisty Party, or how else? The thing that is turning my thoughts in this direction is that in many cases [he gave examples of two ETU officials in the provinces who joined the Communist Party to get their jobs] we prove an obstacle to the workers getting better leaders for themselves.

What had kept Les in the Communist Party for so long was the belief that although the Communist Party in England had made no visible headway, Communism was succeeding in creating a better and a more just society for the peoples of Eastern Europe and China, and could still succeed in doing so in other countries that were politically and economically backward. What he saw and heard in Czechoslovakia in 1956 convinced him that the idea had failed. And there was Khrushchev's speech. Here was the new leader of the Soviet Union telling the world that Josef Stalin, whose every utterance was once reverently repeated throughout the Communist world, had been guilty of crimes similar to Hitler's. The leaders of the British Communist Party claimed innocence of all these events. But could unquestioning support of Stalin over all those years be construed as innocence? They had access to information

The first morning
of the Ramsgate
Conference, 1948

Far right:
On the way home
from Uganda

Wigan: Olga and Les Cannon with Oleg

1950: The Trade Union Conference in Switzerland

THE BREAK WITH COMMUNISM 129

and could not have been dismally ignorant of the sinister happenings behind the façade.

Les came to Prague that July with his mind already made up that he was going to resign from the Party. By the time we went home in August he was even more determined, and he told several of our friends in Prague that he was going home to resign. Some tried to argue him out of resignation, urging that those who thought like Les should stay in the Party and try to change it. But there was no shaking him. He had reached his decision after years of hard thought and torturing doubts, argued away in his own mind but only to return. Now his mind was resolved. Les was among the most intellectually honest of men I ever knew. Once he had reasoned things to a conclusion he would stick to that conclusion through thick and thin.

But Les was also a politican. Merely writing a letter of resignation to King Street was not enough. He wanted his resignation to have as much impact as possible, and he wanted to try to combine it with constructive proposals for alternative political action by Marxists. As Education Officer of the ETU he was entitled to attend the Trades Union Congress as an observer, and he went to that year's TUC to do a little private canvassing. He found that Jack Grahl, another prominent Communist trade unionist, then Assistant General Secretary of the Fire Brigades Union, had been thinking on much the same lines. With Jack Grahl and one or two other Communists who had decided to leave the Party, Les drew up a document explaining their reasons for resignation and inviting the Party to consider adapting itself to an entirely new role. Their proposals were by no means merely negative anti-Communism. They suggested that the British Communist Party was out of date, and that winding it up would end the conflict of loyalties that had bedevilled Marxists in Britain ever since the Communist Party had been formed as a political party and separated them from the rest of the Labour movement. There was no reason, they argued, to continue the separate existence of a Communist Party in Britain; the proper place for Marxists was within the traditional British Labour Party, where they could work constitutionally to influence Labour thinking. In their view the *Daily Worker* (now the *Morning Star*, the organ of the Communist Party) and other Marxist journals could continue publication even if the Communist Party itself were wound up. All these journals were nominally independent, with their own editorial boards—they could continue to give Marxist direction to the progressive forces within the Labour movement. Moreover, with no Communist Party to complicate the political scene, able people whose membership of the Communist Party effectively debarred them from the main stream of British political life would stand a much better chance of making their influence felt in Parliament.

It took some weeks for this document to be drawn up, agreed upon, and signed, and by the time it was submitted to John Gollan, who had succeeded Harry Pollitt as Secretary of the Communist Party, the Russian invasion of Hungary had taken place. A number of other Communist Party members, who had nothing to do with Les's group, were announcing their resignations over Hungary, and since Les and his friends' resignation coincided with these events, the issue became confused, and many people thought that Les was also resigning because of Hungary. This meant that the constructive proposals of Les and his group were never seriously discussed. Gollan did not even reply to their letter.

In November 1956, a few days after Les's resignation from the Communist Party, we went to a reception at the Soviet Embassy to mark the anniversary of the October Revolution which overthrew the Czars. (The anniversary always falls in November by the Western Calendar because the Cyrillic Calendar used in Russia was not reformed in the eighteenth century as our Julian Calendar was.) The invitations had been sent out before news of Les's resignation was received at King Street, and although we knew that all the top brass of the British Communist Party would be present we decided to attend for the devilment of it. They were all there, Pollitt, Gollan, Matthews and the rest, and they obviously knew of Les's document. They ignored us completely, passing without a glance in our direction. Marjorie Pollitt, who clearly did not know about Les, came up and talked to me for a bit. Harry Pollitt, after watching us from a distance for a while, walked up to his wife rather uneasily and whispered a few words in her ear. She froze in front of me, unable to speak or move away. To save her further embarrassment I said a friendly "goodbye".

Les in the meantime was talking to the Czech Ambassador to Britain, Jiří Hájek,[1] whom he had known from the days of the International Youth Conference in Prague ten years before. Les was just explaining to Hájek why he had decided to leave the Communist Party when along came Peter Kerrigan, the Party's Industrial Organiser. He intervened roughly, pushing the Czech Ambassador aside with a brusque "Excuse me, Comrade, I want to speak to this Comrade." Kerrigan demanded to know the reasons for Les's resignation. Les explained his feelings briefly and Kerrigan suggested that he should come and talk over things in the Party office. When Les assured him that his decision to leave the Party was final and that nothing could change it, Kerrigan described how painful it had been to him to learn that some of his old comrades of the International Brigade had been put in Polish prisons after the strikes that year in Poland.

"What did you say? What are you going to do about it?" Les asked.

"What could I do? It is our duty to fight these things inside the Communist Party," Kerrigan replied.

Les said, "You should have denounced it, the betrayal of everything you have ever believed in, and you can do what I am now doing, leave the Communist Party."

Kerrigan decided that there was no point in continuing the conversation, and like all the other Party leaders never spoke to Les again.

After his resignation from the Party Les continued to be influenced by the Marxist thinking which had governed his actions from the formative years of his youth and throughout his adult life. Early in the New Year (1957) he described his feelings in a long letter to Maurice Cornforth:

I must say, Maurice [he wrote], that my decision was not a snap one, and would have been taken (perhaps a little

[1] Later to become a Minister of Foreign Affairs under Dubček.

later) irrespective of the K. report or Poznan or Hungary. As I wrote in the document to the E.C., it is not sufficient to rethink the *British Road to Socialism* and inner Party democracy because this confines our thinking to "what should be the programme and role of the C.P.". This is an automatic acceptance of the need of that type of party in the specific conditions in which we live and work.

The question I have been examining for some time is *"What is a Marxist programme for Britain and what is the role of Marxists in achieving that programme?"* When I say what is the role of Marxists, I don't mean just those who are assembled in the ranks of the C.P. and thereby cut off from participating in the life of the Labour Party. I mean also those Marxists who never thought it correct to isolate themselves from the mass party of the workers, and who, rightly or wrongly, always thought it correct to fight for socialism as a member of the Labour Party. This last sentence represents new thinking on my part, because until recently I, like almost all members of the Communist Party, never accepted the idea that a person could be a Marxist unless he also recognised the imperative need for all Marxists to belong to a single party as an "organised, advanced detachment of the working class". You will forgive my immodesty if I now tell you I think it is possible to be a Marxist in Britain without being a member of the C.P.

Not only am I absolutely convinced that there is no place for the Communist Party now, my studies of Lenin on Britain have led me to seriously doubt if it should ever have been born.

It is claimed that the reasons for the Party's existence, not only here, but in every country are:

to achieve power
to consolidate the power and defeat reaction
to build a socialist superstructure on the basis of socialist nationalisation of the main industries and agrarian reform.

(Just a point of interest in passing, without any intention to generalise, the Hungarian and Polish Parties:

did not achieve power
they did not consolidate gains but threatened them, they

did not defeat reaction, but in fact created conditions favourable to a return of reaction

though the basis of a Socialist society existed, and still exists, and though elements of socialist superstructure were created, in general, it could not be said that the socialist superstructure was being built.)

Actually power has been achieved in many different ways:

Russia 1917: A revolutionary coup d'etat by the Bolsheviks, power being handed over to workers' and soldiers' soviets.

China: By classical military methods (enriched during the course of the struggle itself). The fact that the Marxists led the Chinese Peoples' Army only indicates the different purpose of the revolution, not the method by which power was achieved.

Yugoslavia: Mainly by national liberation struggle with a final liberating blow by the Red Army. (Again the same remarks apply about the purposes as distinct from method.)

Countries of Eastern Europe: Mainly by virtue of liberation from the East instead of the West (as in the case of Greece).

It is not borne out by history that man, in his long struggle, from the days of primitive society, to transform old society (whatever it was) into a new society, needs the type of party we have said that he needs in all circumstances. I do believe that in those countries where the bourgeois revolution is passing over speedily into the socialist revolution, then a party having the main characteristics of the Bolshevik Party is necessary. I have, however, come most firmly to think that such a party has no place in the specific political conditions in Britain at the present time.

It is time we heeded the voice of the workers. For fifty years they have made it clear to us that the Labour Party is the instrument by which we shall achieve Socialism in Britain. Of course they have often been disappointed, disillusioned and betrayed. And, of course, they will be disappointed, disillusioned and betrayed again. But one day the British workers will make the Labour Party do the job they want it to do.

Every conceivable situation making for this famous "break through" for the Party which we have boasted about (more to convince ourselves than others) has occurred. War and peace, slump and boom, depression and recovery, mass unemployment and full employment, high tide and ebb tide of Labour's popularity: never, not even at the time of the greatest betrayal in 1931, have British workers ever given a sign that they are going to turn to an alternative Party.

So much for the role of the C.P. in the achievement of power.

Our experiences of the role of the Party in the exercise of power have shown that even in the countries concerned, there require to be serious modifications in the organisation and role of the Party.

Not only was there little democracy in the parties, but the methods and principles of so-called "democratic centralisation" were transposed into the Trade Unions, the social, cultural, and economic organisation of the people, as well as the state organs, leaving them too bereft of real democracy.

Much has been said about mistakes and crimes. I believe that serious mistakes were made at the beginning. Terribly wrong economic policies were carried out (a statement I am prepared to support by argument) which cut right across the economic base of the various "National Fronts", turning, in some cases overnight, the friends of the People's Democracy into its opponents. It was this process which was accompanied by the corollary of power passing out of the hands of the National Front led by the working class into the hands of the Communist Party, and increasingly into the hands of a few members of the hierarchy. The Party then became, instead of the best means of reflecting the desires of the people, the means by which the protests of the people, against the effects of these wrong policies, were suppressed. Thus we get, in addition to other influences (e.g. Beria) the beginning of crimes to cover up the mistakes.

I had many experiences whilst in the Party which showed me that the same mentality exists among many prominent leaders of the Party; that in embryonic form we have the makings of it all here.

I have had a number of experiences since I left which confirm this; two of which are typical:

1. When I resigned I was naturally offered many facilities to "explain" my point of view—ITV and one or two mass circulation newspapers. I refused. Later I was repeatedly contacted by Woodrow Wyatt and pressed to appear in *Panorama* with Gollan and others. I refused. I can well understand the sneers of some people if I had accepted these offers. This would not have perturbed me, but I would have been sad because of the misunderstanding it would have caused among so many, the overwhelming majority, of Communists I have known and worked with. I did, however, write a letter to the *Daily Worker*, of which I am a shareholder, to reply to attacks of "cowardice" and "escapism" which appeared in a letter from one of our very wealthy comrades who also accused people like myself of refusing to face up to the realities of the class struggle. However, even though I refused the platform of the mass circulation papers and a few million televiewers (which Gollan accepted), I cannot get a letter in the *Daily* [*Worker*]. This is the freedom of expression I am sure Campbell[1] would want to introduce into a socialist Britain.

2. A second experience was at the close of the *Daily Worker* Conference (shareholders) in the Holborn Hall.

A motion and an amendment were before the meeting. I preferred the amendment, but naturally if the amendment were to be defeated I would then vote for the motion. I raised a point of order but Arthur Horner told me I could not raise it while the vote was being taken—actually the point of order was concerned with the way the vote was being taken. I gave way and then raised my point of order after the vote, making it clear that in the event of the amendment being defeated, I wanted the opportunity to vote for the motion. Arthur accepted the point of order. *But* from the time I rose to my feet to the time when I could make my voice heard there were literally screams of "shut up", "sit down", "throw him out". I turned round to the meeting, and it struck me like a blow that if I had been in Hungary there would have been two AVH men waiting at the door, and what is more,

[1] Then editor of the *Daily Worker*.

that the attitude of mind of people such as did the screaming at that meeting would have permitted it—indeed, been glad of it.

The attitude of the remaining members of the Communist Party to an ex-Communist is that of members of some harsh religious sect to an apostate. Les was either ignored, or openly insulted. He described one such incident, in Wigan, to a woman member of the Communist Party, who had written him a long letter criticising him for leaving the Party. At least she wasn't insulting. When Les showed me his reply to her I felt that it would certainly not convince her, but that it was too good a letter to be wasted, so I kept it myself instead.

He began with a defence of me. "In case the idea again occurs to you that I am unduly influenced by Olga's ideas," he wrote, "I should say that we discuss political questions on the basis of mutual respect, without any domination." Describing the incident in Wigan, he wrote: "I tried my best to be civil to him, but he clearly didn't want that. . . . I regret that I ever counted among my friends one who calls me disgusting names, which bring distress to those near me, and yet fails to gather the courage to argue his point of view with me."

The woman who had written to Les had mentioned sacrifices made by the secretaries of Communist Party organisations, and how poor they were. Les continued:

The problems of —— and —— were the economic problems of being full-time organisers of a Party which has no mass basis of support among the people. Those who decide to do that work must recognise that in general the workers are not prepared to sustain them in that work. My experiences were not of that kind, although it can be said that in our respective lives I have suffered an equal degree of poverty. Whether you believe it or not, my experiences at the hands of Allison,[1] Pollitt, Abbott[2] and others have been enough to convince me that whatever they are attempting to build for the future is not what I have been dreaming about since I was a young boy. The perversion of working-

[1] George Allison, a prominent member of the Communist Party.
[2] A District Secretary of the Communist Party.

class power by the Rakosis exists in embryonic form in the British Communist Party, and I shudder to think what they would do if they had more power.

. . . I haven't joined Gaitskell. I have joined the Labour Party, which also consists of tens of thousands of genuine, ardent socialists, as ardent as you, or I, or *any other Communist* ever was, except that we have always, in our masochistic devotion to the Party, been too immodest to admit it.

You may say, "Ha! Ha! But they are not Marxists!" But then, you tell me how many members of the Wigan branch of the Party are real Marxists? Indeed, you send me a letter to justify the need of a so-called Marxist Party, consisting of the most advanced, politicially conscious workers, and you preface all your remarks with the words, "As you know, politically I am uneducated."

I am proud of twenty years of consistent study of Marxism, but I should hardly have the confidence to say the final word on this question, as you seem to have done in your letter. You say, "We in Britain will have to wait much longer for our Socialism through the Labour Party than if we fight for it through 'our Party'." . . . What on earth makes you feel that the British workers will ever proceed to socialism through the Communist Party? What historical evidence is there of this?

Les went on to make the same points which he had made in his letter to Maurice Cornforth, that in the thirty-seven years since the formation of the Communist Party in Britain working people had been through every conceivable form of the sort of crisis that might be expected to make them turn away from Labour to an alternative party without the slightest sign of doing so. He concluded:

What kind of situation do you expect to occur which has not yet taken place in which the workers will turn to the Communist Party. . . ?

I beg of you to understand that I am in no need of sympathy. I have never been more sure of the correctness of a decision than of the one I took last year. . . .

One final point. You should not think that those who

leave the Communist Party have feet of clay. I assure you that after seventeen years of membership it cost me many months of serious thought, reflection and loss of sleep. The coming months will show you whether I have feet of clay. I've never felt in better fighting trim than I do now. What is more I have never been more clear of my way forward.

Les's mood and thoughts at this time are best expressed in his own words. I take these passages from some notes he began making for a book which, alas, he did not live to write.

Until 1956 most of the C.P. members believed that they belonged to a British Party fighting for Socialism in accordance with British traditions and institutions. Their support and admiration for the Soviet Union was explained by the belief that the C.P. in the USSR, had, in an historically record space of time, lifted a backward, overwhelmingly illiterate group of nations, once dominated by a Tsarist Greater Russia autocracy, from extreme poverty and abysmal ignorance to a proud place among the world's greatest powers. Until 1956 they could find sustenance for this belief from the utterances over the years of some of the world's leading statesmen and men of letters. The fact that many of these people retracted later was not convincing, and, indeed, in the minds of most Communists, did not measure up to fresh evidence from workers' delegations that everything in the Soviet garden was blooming.

History, as always, decided who was right. In 1956 Mr Khruschev told the Soviet Party Congress, and later the world, that Josef Stalin, hitherto the Leader and Teacher of all mankind, etc, had in fact been a perpetrator of some of the worst crimes in the history of man. The leaders of the British C.P. claim innocence of all these events. Thousands of us, however, regarded them as being as guilty as Stalin, because, if only by their silences, they condoned his deeds inside the Soviet Union.

Since that time the Polish workers struck at Poznan in mid-1956, and again all over Poland in October 1956. The Hungarian people rose against the terror of Rakosi and his gang in November 1956. Later the world was horrified at the secret trial of Imre Nagy and his summary execution, and filled with loathing for those narrow-minded bigots who are still persecuting one of the Soviet Union's poets because he dared to write his impressions of Soviet life up to the middle 1930s [Pasternak].

All this, and much more, is now known to the new generation of Communists. Those who have remained members can never say, "We didn't know". They are now consciously members of a Party which has no other purpose to serve in Britain than providing apologists for every twist and turn of Soviet home and foreign policy, according to which gang happens to have gained the upper hand in the struggle for power.

Les made notes also of a discussion he had with a Communist Party member. He (Les) had referred to Yugoslavia, observing:

In 1948 we are told they have strayed from the path of socialist construction. Not a single word in the vocabulary of political slander was omitted in describing the activities of Tito and his fellow-lackeys of imperialism. Pollitt and Co. joined in, Klugman[1] theorised it all in his book *Trotsky to Tito*.

In 1955 Khruschev exonerated Tito. Mistakes yes, but nothing more. Unqualified apologies accompany the explanation that the charges against Beria were that he engineered the whole thing.

Later, Pollitt withdrew his remarks. The Executive Committee of the C.P. withdrew unreservedly Klugman's book.

Les continued his conversation,

Suppose that Khruschev had been defeated by the so-called anti-Party group led by Malenkov—wasn't it just touch and go? Would the C.P. and the *Daily Worker* have supported the anti-Party group and derided Khruschev and his pals

[1] James Klugman of the Central Educational Department of the Communist Party.

as they now support Khruschev and deride Malenkov and his pals?

His notes add,

> He [the C.P. member] ruefully admitted that the Party could only support whoever happened to be the victors, however temporary, in the struggle for power in the Kremlin. He left me a little angry, but he was really angry with himself. He wanted there to be an answer to what I had said, but he could not think of one.
>
> One day his anger will turn against the leaders of the Party because he will one day realise that it isn't just that he doesn't know the answer but that there is *no* honest answer.

IX

THE CONSEQUENCES

WE KNEW THAT Les's resignation from the Communist Party would make his position in the ETU very insecure. As Education Officer[1] of the Union he was a paid official, subject to dismissal by the National Executive Committee. With the Executive under Communist control, Les was obviously extremely vulnerable. But the Communists had to go a little carefully. After Hungary, and the resignation of many leading members of the Party, Les among them, newspapers were alert to Communist Party affairs, and anything that looked too glaringly like persecution of an ex-Communist by a Communist-controlled trade union was to be avoided if possible.

The first attack on Les was subtle. In the spring of 1956 he had started to learn to drive a car, and sometimes used a Bedford van belonging to the College. As an L-driver he had to be accompanied by a driver with a full licence, and one of the College staff often went with him. One day a porter accompanying him wanted to go to a shop a little way before they got back to the College, so Les dropped him and drove on alone. On the way he slightly scraped a parked car. This was awkward, but the damage was slight and nobody was hurt, and when Les got back to the College he asked a member of the Executive who happened to be there if he would "cover" him by saying that he had been in the van. The man agreed, and Les reported the accident by telephone.

When it came to filling in the insurance forms, for some reason Les changed his mind. He asked the man who had originally been with him if he could say that he had been there at the time of the mishap, and, with his consent, Les entered this man's name on the form. The claim was small and settled

[1] Formally, Acting Education Officer, for although he had been Head of the ETU College since John Vickers left, his position was never confirmed and he was still Assistant Education Officer acting as Head.

without fuss. Nothing more was heard of the incident for nine months. Then, shortly after Les had left the Communist Party he got a memo from Frank Haxell, General Secretary of the Union, saying he had mislaid his copy of the statement by the man who said he had been accompanying Les and adding: "In appreciation of the possibility that Mr —— might find some difficulty in remembering precisely what he had written in the statement, I have decided to interview him in my office." Mr —— was duly summoned to Head Office, but he stuck to what he had said, and no pressure succeeded in shaking him. When he returned from Head Office Les thanked him: "That's all right, Mr Cannon," the porter replied. "I have been in the Communist Party myself. I know only too well about their methods."

Les was in the wrong, of course. He *had* made a false statement, although it was a trivial affair. Had his witness been less loyal to Les, it is easy to see what would have happened. Les would have been convicted by the Executive of conduct unbecoming to an official of the Union, and he would have been sacked—not for leaving the Communist Party, but for having made a false statement about a road accident. This could have been blown up to quite serious proportions giving the Executive an excuse to say that a man guilty of such conduct could not be considered a desirable person to remain in charge of education in the Union. People might know well enough that Les's real crime was leaving the Communist Party, but he could not have denied the van incident, and it would have been difficult to protest at his sacking. But this scheme failed.

The next attempt was much more elaborate. On the evening of April 17, 1957, the telephone rang in our house. The caller was a reporter on the *Daily Express*, and Les later wrote down the conversation which took place:

Reporter: Does Mr Cannon live there?
Les: Speaking.
Reporter: Could you tell me, Mr Cannon, if the closing of the Union's College and your being sacked has anything to do with your having left the Communist Party last November?
Les: I think you've made some mistake. I know nothing at

all about the College being closed, and certainly nothing about being sacked.

Reporter: Are you pulling my leg, Mr Cannon?

Les: On the contrary, I think somebody is pulling yours. I don't know what the source of your information is . . .

Reporter: I can assure you that it is a good source. Do you know that the Union's Convalescent Home is also to be closed?

Les: No.

Reporter: Well, there's a circular to all branches announcing the closing of the College and the Home.

Les: When was that sent out?

Reporter: Today.

Les: Well, all I can say is that I know nothing at all about it.

That telephone call was a bit of a shock. We had been expecting trouble, but we had not expected that the Communist leadership of the ETU would go to such lengths, hurting so many innocent people, and undoing so much of the really good work that had been achieved by the College and the Convalescent Home. Les tried to telephone Frank Haxell. He was not in. He then rang the Assistant General Secretary, Robert McClennan. He wasn't in either, but Les managed to speak to his wife, who promised to ask her husband to call back as soon as he got home. Then Les rang a man called John Hendy, who had been his assistant at the College for about six months, and who had recently been elected to the National Executive. He wasn't in, either.

Finally Les succeeded in getting hold of Tom Vetterlein, a good friend of his, who had just attended his last meeting of the Executive, having been elected an Area Officer of the Union.

Tom confirmed that branch secretaries had just received a letter informing them that the College and Convalescent Home were to be closed.

Les: Did the E.C. decide to give everybody the sack without consultation?

Tom: Well, no, not just like that. They agreed that the G.S. [General Secretary] should consult you.

Les: What is the likelihood, then?

Tom: Well, you know that they are after you. It wouldn't have done for me to have said anything, don't you think?

Les: No, I don't suppose it would, Tom.

And it wouldn't have done any good. Tom is a very nice person, stolid and human, but the attitude of Communists towards friendship is interesting. To speak up for a friend whom one thinks is being subjected to unprincipled criticism is condemned as "displaying a lack of objectivity". To suggest that "a friend in need is a friend indeed" is "bourgeois sentimentalism".

No, it would have done no good for Tom to speak up for Les.

McClennan did not ring back that night, but he did telephone Les at home in the morning. He greeted Les cheerfully and asked what the trouble was.

Les told him of his conversation with the *Daily Express* reporter.

McClennan said that he'd written a letter to Les at the same time as the circulars had gone out to the branches. It had gone to Les's office at the College, and would presumably be there that morning.

Les asked what the letter said.

McClennan replied rather airily that it just explained that the Union had had to close the College for financial reasons, and that he, Les, should come to a meeting at Head Office on Wednesday next week to discuss the matter.

Les observed that that was only half of what the reporter had told him. What about his own sacking?

McClennan said that he couldn't discuss things like that over the telephone. All could be discussed at next week's meeting.

Les insisted that McClennan could at least say whether the proposed sacking was true or not, but McClennan refused to commit himself.

Les went to the College, where he found that a letter from Head Office had, in fact, arrived. He called together the staff

and opened the letter in their presence. He told them that
he had been given no prior knowledge of the proposal to close
the College, and that he knew no more than what was in the
letter. He arranged to meet the staff again immediately after
next week's discussions at Head Office.

That week-end was Easter weekend, which partly explains
the week-long delay by the Executive of the ETU between
announcing the closure of the College and saying anything
to Les about his future. More probably, the announcement
was made before Easter to have an excuse for keeping Les
in suspense and so giving him a bit of additional punishment.

Les spent the Easter weekend in Wigan, with his parents.
While there he met two area officials of the union, both long-
time members of the Communist Party, but both also able administrators and good negotiators. They were full of complaints
against the leadership for what they regarded as incompetence
in handling the Union's finances. The financial crisis, which was
the ostensible reason for closing the College, had been brought
about entirely by Communist policy as interpreted by the
Communists on the Executive Council. Early in 1957, after the
failure of negotiations between the Confederation of Shipbuilding and Engineering Unions and the Shipbuilding Industry
and the Engineering Employers two significant strikes took
place. Later on further sporadic strikes were called by the ETU.
The cost of these strikes was something in the region of £200,000
and it amounted to a figure greater than the liquid assets of the
Union. This relatively minor skirmish brought a financial
crisis to the Union because the total reserves of the Union,
both in liquid and fixed assets, were no more than £750,000,
which was roughly a little more than £3 per member—the
lowest per capita figure of any major union inside the
TUC.

In reality, there was no need for a crisis of any sort. Union
dues were still averaging only about one shilling (5p) a week,
a ridiculous contribution in relation to post-war wages. After
a series of strikes in 1954 requiring heavy expenditure on strike-
pay it was estimated that the Union had spent about £1 8s 6d
(£1·42½) more that year per member than it had got from each

member in contributions. Even the Communist Party was bothered by this financial recklessness, and many Communist members of the Union urged that contributions should be raised in order to restore the union's finances. But this policy was always opposed by the top leadership of the ETU which held—without the slightest evidence—that ridiculously low contributions would attract membership.

Membership of the ETU was growing because the electrical engineering industry was growing, and although there might have been a few grumbles, there could have been no serious objection to a substantial increase in contributions.

The Area officials Les met in Wigan strongly supported this view, as, of course, did Les himself.

Instead, the Executive Council had passively accepted a report, presented on April 13, calling for economies, including the closure of the College, to save £57,000 a year. To sweeten the pill those Communists who were paid officers of the Union agreed to a reduction in their own salaries.

On the afternoon of Wednesday, April 24, Les attended at the Union's Head Office for the promised "discussions".

In addition to Haxell, the General Secretary, and Robert McClennan, the Assistant Secretary, the head of the Union's Convalescent Home, and the staff supervisor at the College, were also present.

Haxell confirmed that the Union's precarious financial position had compelled the closure of the College and Convalescent Home, and said that the staff were to be given a month's notice.

The two men were invited to stay on as caretakers of the Convalescent Home and College respectively. The terms of compensation for those to be dismissed were discussed and agreed, and Haxell then indicated that there was nothing more to be discussed.

Les asked if he might raise one or two matters privately. McClennan replied that anything Les wanted to say should be said in front of all present.

Les had no objection to this, and said that he wanted to ask how all these proposals affected the Education Officer of the Union.

"You'll have to find a fresh job, mate," Haxell replied curtly.

At this point the other two became embarrassed and withdrew. Les was left alone with Haxell and McClennan, two of the top Communists in the Union. In telling me about it afterwards Les clearly felt the dramatic quality of the situation. Here were the men with whom he had not seen eye to eye for many years, and it now seemed to him that he had delivered himself into their hands. In resigning from the Executive Council to go to the College, Les had lost the protection of holding an elected position in the Union.

But Les had always been a fighter, and was not to be put down easily.

He reminded Haxell and McClennan that many unions had Education Officers without having colleges, and he argued that to close the College and dismiss the Education Officer meant abandoning all organised education within the Union. There was still, he pointed out, much that he could do. He could maintain an educational programme and carry it out in the form of branch lectures.

Les told me that McClennan then asked who would do the lecturing. Les replied that the lecturers could include national officers and members of the Union's Executive Council and that he would be glad to give lectures himself.

"*You* lecture!" they said, as if they could scarcely believe what Les was saying. Haxell added that he had gone into the matter, and did not agree with Les's argument.

There was no point in continuing the discussion. Les asked: "Is that your final word?" and when they said that it was final he got up and walked out. "I shall fight you in the branches," he said as he left the building which had become so familiar to him, knowing that it would be a long time before he returned.

This summary dismissal after having served the ETU for over seventeen years hurt Les deeply. I wanted him to leave the Union altogether and start a new life in some completely different kind of work. I never doubted his talent and ability, and many jobs would have been open to him. But I knew also how much the Union meant to him, and that he could never be happy, no matter how successful in his own life, if he knew that his beloved ETU was still in the hands of the Communists. Les was, perhaps, the only man living who knew enough, and understood enough, to be able to clear them out. Britain was still a democratic country, no matter how imperfect its democracy. We had seen in Czechoslovakia what happens once democratic institutions are destroyed and power usurped by a political clique. It was not too far-fetched to imagine that this could happen in Britain; and Communist control of the ETU was precisely the kind of lever to be used in the trade union movement to bring it about.

It was early evening when Les had come home from his meeting with Haxell and McClennan. We talked far into that April night and agreed that Les was not going to give up the fight. We did not under-estimate the difficulties, which were formidable. Our two sons, Oleg and Martin, were six and a half and four respectively, which meant that I could not take a job. Les would have to return to his old trade as an electrician, and spend all his evenings visiting union branches. It would be a tough struggle.

What the Communists in their eagerness to get rid of Les had failed to realise was that they had timed his dismissal (from their point of view) extremely badly, for in June elections for the whole Executive Council were coming up. Having ceased to be a paid official of the Union, Les was free to stand for election to the Executive Council, and he decided to oppose the sitting member in Division No. 9. This was a division from South-West London through the Home Counties to Bournemouth, Portsmouth and the Isle of Wight. It was a Communist stronghold, having been held by a Communist since 1938. Had the Communists waited until the end of 1957 before dismissing Les, it would have been much more difficult for him to fight back. The elections for the Executive Council would have been over and he would have had to wait for a suitable opportunity to make his challenge. Memories evaporate, and time soon deposits a kind of sludge over human feelings. As it was, Les was able to throw himself into his election campaign in a white heat of anger. The Communists' rather hasty timing of his dismissal proved a blessing in disguise.

It was about the only thing that did help for we soon began

to feel that the odds against us were pretty well overwhelming. Our financial reserves did not amount to much. Les got a job in an electrical engineering works at Kingston, and he bought an old car—a venerable Rover—to travel the country on his campaign.

The first step of his campaign was to go to Folkestone, where the Union's annual policy conference was being held, just before the elections for the Executive Council. Les was not, of course, a delegate to the conference, but nothing could stop him visiting Folkestone while the conference was taking place. He was able to meet a number of the delegates from branches in Divison No. 9, to discover whether they would accept him at forthcoming quarterly branch meetings as a nominee for the Executive Council and, if so, what measure of support he could expect.

In many ways Les was surprised at his reception in Folkestone. As was to be expected, the Communists gave him a rough time —they thought he had a cheek to be in town. More surprising was the reaction of some of the anti-Communist delegates. Les knew many of them well—often they had been among his students at the College—but when he stopped to speak to them in the street he would find them looking over their shoulders to see if anyone was watching. This was a reaction that was to become increasingly familiar—sinister evidence of a spreading atmosphere of intimidation. However, there were also many who were less timid, who received Les well and offered their full support in the fight he was about to undertake.

A significant event at this conference was the debate on Hungary. If it had been held at the end of 1956, immediately after the Soviet oppression of Hungarian workers, it is quite possible that a resolution condemning the Russian action would have been carried all-but unanimously. By June 1957 feelings had cooled to some extent. Even so, a resolution condemning the Soviet action was carried, although not by any great majority. Still, it was a formal resolution by the conference, and as such it had to be accepted by the Executive Council. Haxell, in commenting on the resolution for the Executive, did his best to minimise it, saying that he felt that the conference had made a big mistake in voting for it. Nevertheless, he accepted the will of the conference, and it was assumed that he would write a letter to the Soviet Embassy indicating the terms of the resolution. Whether this letter was ever sent, or what it said, we were never able to discover. After the court case in 1961, which we shall come to in due course, the defeated Communists in the ETU burned a great mass of papers which they felt, perhaps, might have incriminated them in various ways. We looked for a copy of Haxell's letter to the Soviet Embassy, but were unable to find one.

In Chapter V we have given a brief account of the history of the ETU and of its steady infiltration by the Communist Party before, during and just after the Second World War. It may be helpful here—and it will help to explain some of the technicalities of Les's fight—to continue the story of Communist carpet-bagging in the Union into the 1950s.

In the 1930s and during the war of 1939–45 Communist influence in the ETU was strong, but the Communists were not effectively in control. The special conference called in 1943 to consider Communist interference in the Union's internal affairs was a temporary setback to the Communist Party. It was called because a number of Party documents which came into the hands of E. W. Bussey, then General Secretary of the Union, indicated that the Communist Party's so-called "Advisory Committee" concerned with ETU affairs was actively trying to determine ETU policy. That conference (as we have recorded) decided overwhelmingly that there *was* Communist interference in the Union, but it did not go on, as E. W. Bussey proposed, to ban Communists from office. This was because of the war situation, and it is known that Bussey later regretted having allowed his proposal to be withdrawn. Although the Union took no action, the calling of the special conference alarmed the Communists, who realised how close they had come to losing ground in the Union. Harry Pollitt, having reprimanded certain leading members who were deeply involved, decided that the Communist Party's "Advisory Committee" should go into cold storage for a time. From then on only occasional consultations between individuals took place. The Advisory Committee came into being once more in 1947 after E. W. Bussey, who was a rugged anti-Communist trade unionist, accepted a job on the Board of the newly-nationalised

Electricity Authority and the way was opened for a rapid Communist advance.

A comparison of the political allegiance of the Union's chief officers in 1945 and 1955 is illuminating:

	January 1945	*January 1955*
General Secretary	Anti-Communist	Vacant
President	Anti-Communist	Communist
Assistant General Secretary	"Progressive" (i.e near-Communist. He joined the Communist Party in 1947)	Communist
National Officers	1 Anti-Communist	1 Anti-Communist
	1 Communist	4 Communists
Executive Council	7 Non-Communists	5 Non-Communists
	4 Communists	6 Communists
Area Officials	14 Non-Communists	18 Non-Communists
	9 Communists	19 Communists
Total Membership	110,000	220,000

The descriptions "non-Communist" and "anti-Communist" call for some clarification. "Non-Communist" means simply that the man concerned was not at the time a member of the Communist Party. "Anti-Communist" means that he was known to take a firm line in opposing Communist Party policy. Among the "non-Communists", however, were a number whose attitude in all but name was indistinguishable from the Communist Party line. This was a problem not confined to the ETU: the trade unions and Labour movement generally were bedevilled throughout the decade by the actitivities of so called "fellow-travellers"—those who insisted that they were not themselves Communists, but who consistently supported whatever might happen to be Communist policy at any given moment. These "fellow-travellers" were invaluable to the

Communist Party. Their passive acquiescence largely defeated the efforts that were made in some unions, notably the Transport and General Workers Union under Arthur Deakin, to ban Communists from union office.

Analysing the ETU table more closely, it should be noted that among the seven members of the Executive in 1945 listed as "non-Communists" there was a majority of genuine anti-Communists. Of the five "non-Communist" members of the Executive in 1955 only one could fairly be called "anti-Communist", and even that is using the term in a sectarian rather than a strictly political sense.

In 1945 most of the fourteen "non-Communist" Area officials in the Union were "anti-Communist". In 1955 most of the eighteen "non-Communist" officials were friendly to the Communist Party. The total national membership of the Communist Party of Great Britain during the decade was around 40,000—the total Communist poll in the General Election of 1955 was 33,144. At no time can there have been more than about 700 Party members in the total membership of the ETU—700 out of 220,000 in 1955. Yet by 1955 Communist influence was dominant. In 1945 only a handful of delegates to the Union's annual conference were ready to argue a militant Communist Party case. In 1955 there was barely enough speaking time for the delegates queueing up at the rostrum to express Communist policy. Many of them were briefed by Communist Party organisers, who supplied them with figures and dates and prepared their speeches for them.

How was it done? The decisive years in transforming Communist influence into Communist control were 1947 and 1948. In 1947, after E. W. Bussey's appointment to the Electricity Authority, there was an election to replace him as General Secretary of the Union. There were two candidates, Walter Stevens, who had been Assistant General Secretary, and John Byrne. Stevens, who was not then a Communist but who joined the Party shortly afterwards, was the Communist Party's nominee. He was also in a strong position as being already Assistant General Secretary—in all trade union elections there is a natural tendency to favour those who are already doing a job. Byrne was an ETU official in Scotland, and a stalwart supporter of the Labour Party. In his election address he referred to his membership of the Labour Party and called for an end to Communist interference in a union the vast majority of whose members supported Labour and not the Communist Party.

Stevens won the election, but the size of the vote for Byrne was a shock to the Communists. They hastened to use their power on the Executive of the ETU to make a rule that no future candidate for full-time national office should be allowed to mention his political allegiance.

Walter Stevens's election as General Secretary meant an election for the post of Assistant General Secretary. This took place in 1948, and there were three candidates. John Byrne stood again, and he was opposed by Frank Haxell, the Communist Party's nominee, and a Mr Lowden. Byrne topped the poll, with 27,587 votes against some 25,000 for Haxell. With a third candidate standing, however, Byrne missed an absolute majority by just over 200. This necessitated a second ballot between Byrne and Haxell. In this ballot Byrne's vote was returned as 28,732 but Haxell's went up to the remarkable figure of 33,399.

Woodrow Wyatt, who made a close study of the vote for his pamphlet *The Peril in our Midst* (1955), found that in the first ballot the votes of the Blackpool branch of the Union had been returned as Byrne 1, Haxell 595. In the second ballot the Blackpool figures were Byrne 5, Haxell 695—a total of 700 votes. The total of paid-up members[1] of the Blackpool branch entitled to vote at that time was 559. He found that ten other branches of the Union had returned a larger number of votes than the total of their members qualified to vote.

There are two points to note specially about these figures. First, the voting at some branches was *prima facie* fraudulent; secondly, the total (including unexplained votes) of votes cast in the ballot as a whole, 62,131, represented only about one-third of the then membership of the union. (And a poll of even 33 per cent is high by the standards of many trade union elections.) It is this apathy of the majority of trade unionists that gives the Communists—or any other minority intent on

---

[1] I.e. less than thirteen weeks in arrears with contributions.

capturing a trade union—their chance. As long as it remains certain that the majority of those entitled to vote in an election are not going to bother to use their votes, there will be opportunities for a determined minority to fiddle the voting.

Along with the use of blank ballot papers, the Communists had another technique for controlling returns in ETU elections. This could be done very simply by disqualifying branches with a high anti-Communist vote for some breach, or alleged breach, of election procedure. Since the Executive assumed power to decide whether or not a branch was in breach of rules of procedure, the Executive was both judge and jury in such cases, and a Communist-controlled Executive could favour Communist candidates as it pleased. Trade union rules, like written constitutions generally, tend to be excessively complicated. Generations of rule-making and rules-revision had left the ETU with a rule-book almost as incomprehensible to the ordinary member as an Inland Revenue form, or the small print on the back of an insurance policy. An expert in the rule-book could find breaches of procedure to meet almost any occasion. And here again the Executive was all-powerful. A Communist branch found to be in breach of procedure could be let off with a warning, and its vote allowed to count; a non-Communist branch in breach of the same rule could be disqualified. True, there was provision for appeal, but since the Executive controlled appeals as well as everything else, this was no safeguard against ballot-rigging.

In 1947 the "Advisory Committees" at Communist Party headquarters for dealing with the affairs of the ETU were revived. This seems to have come about not so much from a decision by the Party as from demands by the Communist members of the ETU themselves. The Party would probably have remained content to stay a little in the background, and to exercise control of the ETU informally. The Communist leadership of the Union, however, seems to have felt that its own status in the Party required more direct links with King Street, so the committees were back in business. Les knew all about them, because he had attended committee meetings. Control over every aspect of the union's policy was close. Before any ETU conference, or an important meeting of the Executive, the "Advisory Committee" would meet to discuss the agenda, and to lay down the appropriate Party line. Whenever there was a vacancy for office in the Union, the Communist committee would decide which candidate to support.

One of the most important tasks of the Communist Party's ETU committee was to consider resolutions put before it by the Political Committee of the Communist Party itself for placing on the agenda of the TUC, the Labour Party Conference, or the annual meeting of the Confederation of Shipbuilding and Engineering Unions. This was the way in which the Communist Party, itself ineligible for association with the Labour Party, was able to interfere directly in Labour policymaking. As far as the strictly political resolutions were concerned, these would always be related to the current Soviet line on foreign policy. Indeed, it was invariably the practice of the Advisory Committee when it met at Communist Party Headquarters to begin its discussion with a report of the current Moscow line on world affairs. Some members of the committee —perhaps to show their own erudition—would try to relate even the remotest happenings in the ETU to some aspect of Soviet policy. Sometimes there would be criticism both of union policy and of the Communist leaders of the Union. Such criticism, however valid, was unlikely to produce results because the Party would always stand by the leaders of the ETU. Anyone who persisted with criticism was likely to find himself isolated, or even ostracised. This happened to Les as time went on and he became more and more weary of the whole business. It was always evident that the Party, above all, must be right; to ensure that they always got their way the Party chiefs established a kind of cell within a cell, an even closer liaison between themselves and the three top leaders—President, General Secretary and Assistant General Secretary—of the ETU. This was a guarantee of possessing supreme power at the top of the ETU, and enabled the Communist Party to use this important union as a vehicle for carrying out its political line throughout the Labour movement, and in industry. A typical example was the ETU's wages policy during the period when Mr Attlee's Labour Government, with the help of the General Council of the TUC, was asking trade unions to accept a policy of wage restraint. The Communists compelled the

ETU to lead the fight against wage restraint, primarily to embarrass the Labour Government and to undermine the economic base of its foreign policy, which was then under particularly severe attack from Moscow. This attack on wage restraint was first decided at an ETU Advisory Committee meeting in King Street. It was rubber stamped by the ETU Executive at its next meeting, and the Union machine then went into action throughout the country. Branches were told to put resolutions on the agendas of local Trades Councils and constituency Labour Parties, protesting against the Labour Government's policy of wage restraint. This was only one incident, though a vital one, in the manipulation of the ETU to serve Communist political ends. And in this case the Communists won, for although the policy of wage restraint was at first supported by the General Council of the TUC, it came under such increasing pressure from the ETU and other unions in which Communist influence was strong that a resolution supporting wage restraint was finally defeated at the Trades Union Congress of 1950, and the policy had to be abandoned. This defeat of a General Council of the TUC anxious to help a Labour Government to create a rational policy for wages has had untold effects on all attempts at national economic planning ever since.

Perhaps only those with fairly intimate knowledge of the top level administration of a trade union can appreciate the full effect of the Communist capture of the ETU in 1947–8. The Union's membership did not change; it remained solidly Social Democratic, giving traditional support to the Labour Party. But almost overnight, with the change of General Secretary from E. W. Bussey to Walter Stevens, the personality of the Union seemed to change. The personal influence of the men at the top of a trade union is enormous. For other examples one has only to look at the role of the Transport and General Workers Union under Frank Cousins and Jack Jones compared with the role of the same union under Arthur Deakin, and at the sharpening of left direction in the Amalgamated Union of Engineering and Foundry Workers after Hugh Scanlon took over from Lord Carron.

Ernie Bussey was no theorist—anything but. Yet in spite of his pragmatism, and often without a single note, he could put a remarkable case in negotiations. He was a formidable opponent of the Communists, and disliked by them as long as he lived. With Bussey went Walter Lewis, who had been exceptionally able as the Birmingham Area official; Lewis was among the most feared of anti-Communist speakers at the ETU conference. The capture of the Union by the Communist Party was almost too complete—it actually caused the Party some embarrassment. Harry Pollitt, always sensitive to British working-class feeling, tried to get the ETU Advisory Committee to soft-pedal on the election of Communist candidates to Union office and to work for the election of more "progressive" Labour Party men. This might have been cynical, but it was shrewd political sense. It was a policy, however, that could not be carried out very far, for the Communist members of the ETU wanted the rewards of Party membership. When Frank Haxell was elected General Secretary in 1955, after the death of Walter Stevens, Robert McClennan, a Party member since 1926, wanted the job of Assistant General Secretary. In terms of political strategy it would have been wise for a "fellow-traveller" rather than a known Communist to have the job, but it was argued that in view of the political offensive then being conducted by the Labour Party against Communism, it would be a fine gesture of defiance for a Communist to be elected to yet one more of the top jobs in the ETU. McClennan was duly elected. Thus it came about that at the time of Hungary, the Communists in the ETU held the positions of President, General Secretary, Assistant General Secretary, 4 national officers out of 5, 6 Executive positions out of 11, and 20 Area officials out of 39. Of the remainder of that 39, all but a handful were as compliant fellow-travellers as anyone could wish for.

This was the formidable fortress that Les set out to storm single-handed. The first thing he had to do, to have any chance at all of winning the election of Division 9, was to secure the maximum possible number of branch nominations for his candidature. This was extremely important, partly because a long list of branch nominations looked well on the ballot paper, the more so because a member of the Union with no corrupt interest in the voting, and with no personal knowledge of the candidates, would tend to vote for the man nominated by his

own branch. The lengths to which the Communists were prepared to go in ballot-rigging were not then as apparent as
they became later. And even the most elaborate ballot-rigging
cannot completely cloud all honest voting, particularly if the
honest vote is too massive to be ignored. In standing for
Division 9 Les was not only opposing a Communist candidate
supported by the whole Communist organisation; he was
opposing a sitting member of the Executive, who had all the
advantages of being established at Head Office. Les knew
exactly what he was taking on. But if he could get a sufficient
number of branch nominations he could attract an honest vote
sufficiently big to win.

There were sixty-one branches in the Division, and he had to
try to visit them all during the last two weeks of June, when the
quarterly meetings were held—it was at these meetings that
the nominations of candidates for the forthcoming election
were made. He used to leave work at 5.30 and set off at once
in our ancient Rover to go on his rounds. He drove to places
as far afield as Southampton, Portsmouth, Newbury, Basing-
stoke, Reading, as well as visiting all the branches in the Division
nearer London. He planned these journeys like a military
campaign, managing sometimes to fit in visits to two branches
in one evening. He was seldom home before midnight, and he
had to set off again early in the morning to go to work. His
determination was at once wonderful and deeply worrying.
I was filled with admiration for the single-minded way in which
he fought, but I also worried about how tired he looked.

The Communists, of course, were out to secure the nomination
of only one candidate, their own man. Les sometimes got a
lot of amusement out of the ineptitude with which the Communist Party candidate was put forward. Some Communist
member of a branch would take a piece of paper from his pocket,
read out the name of the candidate, add a few biographical
details from his note, and usually end with the parrot-phrase,
"And he is doing a great job for members of the Union."
Sometimes the biographical details were wrong, and Les
would throw the nominator into a state of confusion by showing
that he didn't really know the person he was nominating, and
perhaps had never even met him. The sad thing was that this
farce of nominations was going on in hundreds of branches of

the Union, with seldom a challenge to the proposer about the source of his information, or how much he really knew about the supposed qualities of the man whose candidature he was urging the branch to support.

By the end of June Les succeeded in getting sufficient nominations to make a respectable showing on the ballot-paper. He had then to make all his journeys over again, to try to secure the maximum vote from those branches which had nominated him, and also to see if he could win votes in those branches which had nominated his Communist opponent. This nightly journeying went on from the beginning of July to the end of the balloting in September. We hardly saw Les, except at weekends, and even then he would go out again, often taking us with him, to visit the homes of shop stewards, branch secretaries, or other active members of the Union.

In making all these visits Les was not just asking for votes. He took the opportunity of raising many other issues of direct concern to members of the Union, particularly the state of the Union's finances, and the neglect of this problem over many years. He made his own position perfectly clear: he explained that he had been a Communist, and he described the working of the Communist Party's Advisory Committees, and how they governed Executive decisions in the ETU. He explained his reasons for leaving the Communist Party, and why it was imperative that Communist power in the Union should be broken. He described the manner in which the ETU College had been closed, and stressed that no educational work of any sort, even on a basis of minimum cost, was then being carried out by the Union. He found a large number of members eager to have a chance of discussing matters that had been worrying them for some time.

As the time for the September elections drew near the Communists in the Division grew seriously alarmed, and they mounted a substantial campaign against Les. At least five Area officials—all Communists—visited branches in the Division to assist the sitting candidate. The candidate himself found Executive Council reasons for visiting the Isle of Wight twice, Reading twice, Porstmouth twice, etc.—all with full delegation fees paid. The General Secretary actually *instructed* one branch to accept a visit from the Communist candidate; at the same time he wrote to Les, accusing him of a breach of rule simply for writing to a few branches saying that he would like to attend their meetings. Every conceivable attempt was made to blacken Les—he was accused of being in the pay of Roman Catholics, the Economic League, and the capitalist press.

The system of balloting in the ETU at that time was roughly this (it was changed after the court case in 1961). Every member who was not in arrears was entitled to receive a ballot paper at his home address. He could vote in one of several ways, by post to the branch secretary, by bringing the ballot paper in a sealed envelope to the branch secretary, or by handing it to a shop steward at his place of work. These people would then bring the sealed envelopes to the quarterly branch meeting, and hand them over to the scrutineers.

Two scrutineers were appointed to receive and sort the votes, and to declare the result of the ballot, which had to close within one hour of the start of the branch meeting. The result of the ballot in each branch was recorded on a form, with the number of votes cast for each candidate. This form was signed by the scrutineers, by the chairman and branch secretary, and then posted to the Head Office of the union.

It was absolutely imperative for Les to know the result of the voting by the branches as the results were declared in each branch, for he knew well enough that if he won the Communists would do everything they could to upset the result by invalidating votes. By various means, through friends, or by being present personally at the September meetings of branches, Les learned the results of fifty-six out of the total of sixty-one branch ballots. The five branch returns he didn't know included Cowes and Newport in the Isle of Wight, and Gosport in the Portsmouth area. Allowing all unknown results as majorities for his opponent—based on previous election figures for the branches concerned—Les calculated that the final total showed a victory for him. He went over his arithmetic again and again, but there was no doubt about it: he had won, and by an unmistakeable majority.

He was absolutely elated—the results meant that at his very first try, against tremendous odds, he had defeated the whole

In Liverpool with Oleg

In Liverpool with Martin

1953: Les and his father with Oleg, in Wigan

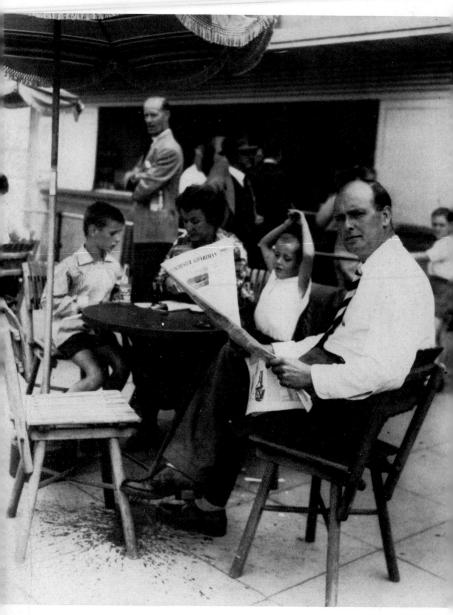

With the family at Bournemouth just before the 1958 conference

Communist Party machine, without any organisation behind him. True, he had had the help of some good friends, and branch secretaries who had made special efforts to persuade people to vote, but this was all. He had had no organised campaign, and had been given no publicity at that time. His victory, Les felt, would have a devastating effect on the Communist leadership of the Union. Then, as he noted in his diary, "things began to happen".

FIGHTING BACK

INSTEAD OF DECLARING the result of the ballot, as was the normal practice, at a meeting of the Executive Council on October 19, the General Secretary reported that inquiries were being made "into the way in which a number of branches had conducted the ballot held at the September quarterly meetings,"[1] and that meanwhile the results could not be announced.

This in itself was a breach of the ETU's complex rules, for according to the Rule Book the General Secretary had no power to conduct investigations of such a kind, the rules specifying that only the *Executive Council* could order an investigation, and then only if the Executive Council were satisfied that the alleged breach of rule in conducting a ballot had been such "as would materially affect the result of the ballot". In this case, however, the members of the Executive Council mutely accepted Haxell's ruling and simply agreed "that the report be accepted".

An unprecedented investigation into the affairs of two branches which had supported Les was then set on foot.

It was at this point that Les realised that he would have to overcome his antipathy to publicity and invoke the help of what he still regarded as "the capitalist Press" to carry his campaign to a wider audience. Les's distaste for personal publicity was real; it derived partly from something in himself, which regarded a cause as of far more importance than the personal affairs of individuals, partly from an ingrained suspicion of the Press, deriving from his long membership of the Communist Party. He never lost his repugnance for the way in which newspapers too often trivialise events and falsify important issues by omissions, or reporting out of context, but he came to

---

[1] Minute 142, p. 391 of ETU Executive Council reports.

have great respect for many of the journalists who write for "capitalist" papers.

Our first encounter with the Press was arranged through me. I got in touch with Geoffrey Goodman of the *News Chronicle* (now defunct) and Len Jackson of the *Daily Mirror*, a charming and able journalist, who, to our deep sorrow, died suddenly in 1962. On a dismal October Sunday afternoon, accompanied by Dennis Kingston and Harry Marshall—the Secretary of Mitcham Electronics branch, which was being "investigated" —we met these two amiable representatives of the "capitalist" Press in a dingy café near Raynes Park station. The next day these two papers reported the delay in announcing the result of Les's election, and the "investigation" of the Mitcham branch. Under the heading "ETU Election Row—*Communist Didn't Win*" (the *News Chronicle*'s underlining) Geoffrey Goodman wrote:

A powerful branch of the Electrical Trades Union is asking for a thorough inquiry into all election ballots inside the union. This follows a reported probe by the union's Communist leaders into how the branch voted in a recent key election.

The branch is the 1,100 strong Mitcham Electronic Engineers. It supported 37-year-old Leslie Cannon, an ex-Communist, for a seat on the union Executive against the sitting candidate, 35-year-old Communist Jack Frazer.

Cannon and Frazer have been contesting the ETU's No. 9 division, which covers one in ten of the 230,000 members in South-West London, Surrey, Berkshire, Hampshire, the Isle of Wight and the Channel Isles.

And despite the efforts of the ETU leaders, Cannon is believed to have won—by more than 300 votes.

The Executive has not yet announced the result. The union chiefs met at the weekend but no statement has been issued.

If they invalidate the returns from the Mitcham Electronic Engineers, the effect could be to snatch victory from Cannon.

His election would be a big blow to the Communist chiefs of the union as he quit the Communist Party over Hungary, called for the dissolution of the British Communists and was later dismissed from the ETU's full-time payroll.

One of the Mitcham members, 28-year-old Dennis Kingston, said last night that Cannon polled 410 against Frazer's 35 in the branch.

Mr Kingston, a TV electrician in a big Croydon electrical factory, is a former president of Mitcham branch. He is still an active member. But now he risks expulsion from the ETU by disclosing:

1. What happened on the night of the ballot in the Cannon–Frazer contest.

2. That last Thursday his branch passed a resolution saying it would welcome an inquiry into the whole question of ETU ballots and adding that it could only regard the selective investigation of the ballots of certain branches as a move to keep Jack Frazer in office.

Mr Kingston explained last night that the Mitcham votes came in from the members in sealed envelopes. They were checked by scrutineers.

"But", says Mr Kingston, "when the Communist branch president, Mr Eric Chesterfield, was asked to sign he refused, claiming there had been a technical infringement of rule. He said he had been advised to do this by a national officer, Mr Bert Batchelor, who was also a party member.

"The national officer, without prior notice, attended the branch on the night of the ballot.

"The branch has never in its 15 years' experience seen a national officer.

"The ballot was conducted exactly as all ballots in the past —and the president has never before refused his signature."

Mr Kingston said that the branch had asked for an explanation from Union headquarters.

But the only reply was a demand from the ETU chiefs for the branch's books, ledgers and ballot papers, plus members' names and addresses.

Mr Kingston added that he believed a similar probe had been ordered by ETU leaders into at least two other branches which had backed Cannon, one in London and another in Southampton.

Our next meeting with the Press, about a month later, was on a beautiful afternoon in November when we met Geoffrey

Goodman in Richmond Park. We brought our sons and Geoffrey brought his wife and family. I was delighted to discover that Mrs Goodman also came from Czechoslovakia. Les told Geoffrey that he had learned that several of the ETU branches which had voted for him were to be disqualified and that he expected to be fiddled out of his victory in the election for Division 9. It was a credit to his courage as a journalist and also a measure of his trust in Les that he printed the story the following day. He had to wait nearly four years for his report to be proved true and completely accurate. One of Leslie's happy moments on the day when Mr Justice Wynn delivered his judgement of the ETU trial was to see Geoffrey in court and hear his story vindicated.

It was one of those stories in anticipation of an event. If those eight branches had been included in the results, then Leslie would have been the elected candidate; as it was, with the invalidation of those eight branches, his opponent was declared elected.

Geoffrey Goodman's story had alerted the Press, radio and television to ETU affairs and when the Communist whom in fact Les had defeated was declared elected, there was a wave of questioning publicity. This led up to a remarkable broadcast on Les's election and ETU affairs in general presented by Woodrow Wyatt[1] in the BBC television programme *Panorama* on December 9, 1957. This was hard-hitting stuff. It was also a programme of historical importance, for it was one of the early demonstrations of the tremendous impact of a television interview on public opinion. Television was then still fairly new in Britain; it was only four years since the magnificent pictures of the Coronation had opened people's eyes to the power of this new medium. Woodrow Wyatt, John Freeman,[2] and a handful of other journalists were turning to television with imaginative insight, giving the picture-interview an immediacy and dramatic effect that were new in mass communications. Wyatt's *Panorama* programme about the ETU was a landmark in this new field.

[1] Author and journalist, Labour MP for Aston (Birmingham) 1944–55; Labour MP for Bosworth (Leicestershire) 1959–66.

[2] Editor of the *New Statesman*. Later British Ambassador to India and the United States.

The programme consisted of interviews with a number of members and branch officers of the ETU. Because some of them were afraid of being "disciplined" or even expelled from the Union for taking part they were not all identified—their backs only were screened. This was intensely dramatic, but some of the things said were even more dramatic. One interview went like this:

Q. How long have you been a member of the Union?

A. Twenty-three years.

Q. Do you think that the Executive Council has behaved correctly over the business of the election of Cannon and Frazer?

A. I don't think so. They seem to have put bias in favour of Frazer. They don't seem to want Cannon there for some reason or other, and I think under the circumstances and the way the whole ballot has been conducted they should have called a fresh ballot and given the members the right to vote. It has been done in the past, why not this time?

Q. Apart from elections, do you think that the Executive Council behaves reasonably and fairly towards members?

A. Not entirely so because if a member does something which doesn't appear in favour with them, they can take action against the member and withdraw his card, whereby he can lose his livelihood.

Q. Do you think many members are afraid of the officials in the ETU?

A. They don't say so openly, but I think in their minds they are.

Q. Are you?

A. No, but I am afraid of my livelihood, because my wife and family depend on the week's wages.

Q. And that is why you are not appearing with your face on the screen?

A. That is correct.

Asked what he found disturbing about Communist influence in the ETU another member said:

Well, the fact is that the majority of the people in the

ETU are non-Communist. But of course the muck of Communism rubs off on the rest of us. After all, it's supposed to be a trade society, but at present it's just a political platform for the Communist Party.

The programme was also useful in bringing out the extent to which the Communists thrived on the apathy of the non-Communists. A telling set of questions and answers was:

Q. How long have you been a Branch officer.
A. Four years now.
Q. And how many people usually vote in your branch?
A. Well it will be something like fifty out of a thousand.
Q. Do you think that is the average for most ETU branches where the votes aren't fiddled?
A. I should say, knowing what I do now about apathy, it is just about the correct percentage.
Q. Do you think that the members of the union want to have a Communist-controlled Executive?
A. Oh, no. They certainly don't want to have a Communist-controlled Executive Council at all.
Q. Well, why do they have it now?
A. Well, as I said before, it is just general apathy, that is all. They won't vote.
Q. But what is the guarantee that their votes will be honestly dealt with when they have recorded them?
A. Well I couldn't give any guarantee where that is concerned at all. But I would say that if the majority of the members did vote it would be useless to even try to fiddle it.

The effect of all this on television was profound. Unfortunately the over-dramatisation of some of the programmes offended a good many non-Communist members of the Union, who felt that the Union's affairs were just being "blown up" to make a good TV show. You don't have to be a Communist to distrust the way in which many newspapers and radio programmes deal with trade unionism; much of the history of

British trade unionism has been a battle against misrepresentation and abuse. The *Panorama* broadcast antagonised a number of people who might otherwise have been on Les's side, and it left a great many others feeling bewildered and perplexed.

We suffered also from an unhappy error in the Press reporting. For some reason only *seven* out of the *eight* branches invalidated after Les's election were mentioned in the newspapers and on radio. Journalists have to work against the clock and this was probably no more than a genuine mistake, but it became a serious embarrassment to us, for it enabled Haxell to circulate a statement that if all the invalidated branches *mentioned in the Press and on radio and television* were included, the *result* of the ballot would not have been affected. If, however, the *eighth* invalidated branch (Walton and Hersham, which had voted heavily in Les's favour) had been included, the result would have been vitally different—Les would undeniably have won. The Communists exploited this omission to the full. In the mass of arguments and facts which they produced to counter Press criticism, the statement—that even if the votes of all disqualified branches *mentioned in the Press* had been counted the result of the election would have been unchanged—served to convince a lot of ETU members that the Press really was making a fuss about nothing, and that the anti-Communist campaign was precisely as alleged—a smear campaign designed simply to injure a militant trade union.

Les decided to fight back by sending out a circular of his own to 675 branches of the Union. He took the offensive by demanding a general inquiry into the affairs and electoral practices of the Union:

Dear Sir and Brother,

Because of the circular sent to branches by the General Secretary, and which has been delivered to the Press, we find it necessary to correct the thoroughly distorted and incomplete version of recent events. Bro. Haxell says that everything that has happened is merely a repetition of what has often occurred before. This is not true. Many things happened which are quite unprecedented, not only in the ETU but in trade union history. The only charge which he has attempted to answer is that of the cancellation of the Mitcham and LSE 14 (London Station Engineers) votes. We shall deal with this first. . . .

Les went on to refute in detail the allegations against these two branches, and then turned to the astonishing difference in the treatment meted out by the Executive Council to branches which had shown majorities for Les and those which had voted for the Communist. As an illustration of this we took the outcome of the inquiry into the voting performance of two branches at Reading. One, known as Reading Branch, had returned 50 votes for Les against 12 for the Communist. This branch was disqualified, the General Secretary observing in a letter to the branch: "though your difficulties are appreciated, your branch return cannot be accepted". The other, known as Reading Supply Branch, had returned 80 votes for Les against 137 for his opponent. Although this branch had sent in its election returns two days late, its breach of rule was dismissed with a mild reprimand: "Your ballot returns will be accepted on this occasion but they must be returned in accordance with rule in future."

The circular concluded:

Is this how the General Secretary interprets his powers under the rule? No previous General Secretary would have dared to be so presumptuous. When the General Secretary himself breaks the rules we are asked to overlook this. For example Rule 10, Clause 2F, requires the two National Scrutineers to report in writing to the Executive Council the result of any ballot within 14 days of the close of such ballot. Yet the General Secretary only called the National Scrutineers together on the 17th October, twenty days after the close of the ballot. While dealing with the National Scrutineers it should be mentioned that Bro. —— of Chatham branch signed the National Scrutineers' returns invalidating many branches' votes for electing their scrutineers at the quarterly meeting despite the fact that he was present at his own branch quarterly meeting where the same thing occurred under his very eyes. You will notice, however, that Chatham branch votes were not invalidated.

The concluding sentence of the General Secretary's circular says that had the Mitcham and LSE 14 votes been included the result would not have been different. He could not say this about the *total ballot returns*. He knew and the Sub-Executive Council knew (even if the full Executive Council didn't) what the result of the ballot was before the National Scrutineers met. When they did meet they were confronted with the invalidated branch returns and the fact that an investigation was being conducted into other branches over the heads of the officers of those branches asking members everything, except precisely who they voted for.

These are but some of the features of the ballot. . . . They present a *prima facie* case for a full-scale enquiry within our Union. If these facts and others are substantiated—as they can and will be—it means that Bro. Haxell . . . has proved himself unfitted for the honoured position of General Secretary of the ETU. In the meantime we appeal to all those who are feeling dismayed not to leave the Union but to stay on and fight to put these matters right.

You will easily understand why we cannot sign our names to this document.

I addressed all 675 envelopes myself, and Les and I drove round Surrey posting them in different places in batches of ten to twenty.

I should like now to replace that last sentence with: "We are delighted to sign, Les and Olga."

Neither of us liked sending out an anonymous letter, but it seemed the only thing to do. At least the facts were as straight as we could make them, and we hoped that facts would speak for themselves.

The facts were on our side, but the Communists had powerful allies, some of them deliberate fellow-travellers, some merely victims of half-truths and propaganda. An example of the way in which efforts were made to turn the Labour Party against the anti-Communist campaign is a letter sent out to members at the end of December 1957 by the secretary of the St Pancras South Constituency Labour Party. This said:

Dear Member,

The following resolution is to be moved at the January meeting of the General Management Committee on January 16 at 53/54 Doughty Street at 7.30 p.m. I was instructed to advise you of this in case you would like to be present.

"Holborn and St Pancras South Labour Party completely disassociates itself from the anti-working-class activities of one of its members, Mr Woodrow Whyatt [*sic*], who has sought to villify [*sic*] and bring into disrepute the Electrical Trades Union by an unscrupulous use of TV. Mr Wyatt has previously sold himself to papers and radio for the purpose of witch-hunting good trade unionists in Briggs Motor Bodies at a time when those workers were engaged in a fight with the Ford Motor Company against unemployment and short time.[1] For this activity Mr Wyatt has been well praised by the capitalist Press but we, the members of his own Party, condemn him for it. We ask the NEC to remove Mr Wyatt's name from the lists of prospective Parliamentary Labour candidates."[2]

This sort of thing was both personally wounding, and damaging to the anti-Communist cause. It was typical of the success the Communists had in pretending that they alone represented the true interests of the working-class against the entrenched forces of capitalism and large sections of the Labour Party itself.

To Les, with his deep loyalty to the working class and profound understanding of the realities of Communism, it was doubly hurtful—it made him feel that the very people he was fighting *for* were being enlisted against him. As always, however, Les was a fighter. Such intrigues hurt him, but they seemed simply to make him more determined to carry on the fight.

The Communists in the ETU tried to conduct an offensive

[1] A confused series of strikes in which Communist influence was undoubtedly strong.

[2] Mr Wyatt was, however, elected Labour MP for Bosworth (Leicestershire) in 1959.

against the BBC. Frank Foulkes, the Communist President of the Union, formally complained to the Director-General (then Sir Ian Jacob) of the *Panorama* programme as "a campaign of vilification" against the Union. Foulkes did not get very far with this attack. His letter of complaint was duly reported on the BBC's news services, but the Corporation firmly supported the *Panorama* programme, which it described as having been "factual" and "objective". Foulkes was on rather weak ground in that his Executive had declined an invitation to appear on the Woodrow Wyatt programme—they would have had, of course, to submit to questioning by Wyatt. So the Communists then changed their line of attack, saying that they were not prepared to be "put in the dock" by the BBC but that they would participate on a "live" programme if they were given twenty-five minutes (the time given to the *Panorama* interview) without any "questioning". This was quite good propaganda but an unrealistic request, and (not unnaturally) it came to nothing.

They also approached Independent Television. On December 14, 1957, Frank Foulkes appeared in a "live" programme on ITV, in which he was able to repeat the statement that even if all the invalidated votes in Les's election had been counted, the outcome would have been the same, and Les's Communist opponent elected.

This statement continued to hurt our cause, and was one of the lies shown up in the trial in 1961. We had no crystal ball, however, in December 1957, and could not foresee the future. We were kept going through that miserable time only by our own faith in the rightness of what we were trying to do.

If the Communists had their successes, they continued to receive some damaging blows. In January 1958 the *New Statesman* published a long article by Woodrow Wyatt called "The Case Against the ETU". This set out, point by point, the evidence of ballot-rigging and general Communist interference in the Union's affairs. This stung the leadership into vigorous (and vicious) counter-attack. First, they sent a reply of immense length to the *New Statesmen*, and protested bitterly when the Editor of the *New Statesman*[1] said that he could accommodate

[1] Then Kingsley Martin.

only 1,200 words.[1] The Union then proceeded to publish its reply in a twelve-page pamphlet, in which it called "The Case against the ETU" in the *New Statesman* "a vicious smear article". The pamphlet, signed by Frank Haxell, described the ETU as "a democratic organisation" with "the powers of the Executive Council, the General Secretary, President and other officers clearly stated and defined in the rules". Of Woodrow Wyatt he wrote:

> The problem of Mr Wyatt is his almost complete ignorance of the trade union movement, and, in particular, his sad lack of knowledge of the ETU, but perhaps it is too much to expect him to know any better.

Of Les, he wrote:

> Mr Cannon, I am given to understand, claims that from the time that his employment ceased with the Union to the end of the election, he had visited some 90-odd branches of the Union, during the course of which he criticised the policy of the leadership, dissociated himself from it, disavowed any part that he had played in framing that policy and advanced his claims as being the most suitable person to be elected. He has, indeed, since that election, continued to visit branches from Dundee to Southampton, to Birmingham, Liverpool and Manchester, in fact all over the country, advocating an appeal against the Executive Council's decisions.
>
> I am sure all honest people will agree that it could not be a fair election if it took place in circumstances in which the press had used its great influence on behalf of one candidate by suggesting that this candidate had been unfairly treated and playing on the natural feelings of the membership for fair play; by creating the utmost sympathy for their candidate; by continuously repeating a lie that he had been deprived of his victory by machination and plotting and by

[1] It should, perhaps, be pointed out that 1,200 words is a most generous allocation of space for a letter to a newspaper.

pretending that this was all because he had left the Communist Party; at the same time fostering the utmost political
bias and prejudice against the other candidate.

In the Union's view there would be nothing fair about it.
But what is more important is that it is turning over to the
press the right to determine who is elected. For what does it
mean in fact? It means that if any candidate favoured by the
national press is not elected, there has only to be a high pressure
press campaign to force a further election and in the process
create a climate most suitable to ensure the election of their
candidate. That is not acceptable to the Executive of the
ETU nor to its membership nor, I am sure, to any reasonably
honest person.

This pamphlet, *The ETU Replies to the New Statesman*, was
but one shot in the war of words by which the Communists
sought to confuse every issue, and to pretend that they were
being attacked solely by "capitalists" and their allies in a
campaign directed against the working-class. The Union's
official journal, *Electron*,[1] for January 1958 carried a long
article called "Our Reply to the Humbug and Hypocrisy of
Fleet Street", which began:

Everyone now knows that the recent election for an
Executive member to represent No 9 Division was made
the occasion for an anti-ETU stunt by the Press and the
BBC. . . . And behind the whole campaign were diehard
Tory backbenchers, pressing Iain Macleod, their Minister of
Labour, to impose shackling legislation on the trade union
movement which would put back the clock to Taff Vale.

The same tactics—and they were quite effective tactics—
were used in every case: attacks on the leadership of the ETU
were *really* directed against the whole trade union movement,
the ETU being singled out because it was such an effective
union, with a militant policy solely directed to serving the
interests of its members. Detailed accusations of ballot-rigging

[1] This name was changed to *Contact* after amalgamation with the
Plumbing Trade Union in 1968.

were wrapped in a fog of words calculated to confuse anybody who might think that there was something in them.

The other main line of the Communists' counter-offensive was that all Communists in the ETU were good trade unionists first and Communists a long way second. This had been a persistent refrain since the 1940s. An interesting example is a circular sent by a branch secretary "To All Female Members". It goes back to a time a little before Les's campaign opened, but it is worth quoting here for the state of mind it typifies. It runs:

Dear Sister,

It has been brought to my notice that some of our female members wish to withdraw their support from our Union, as they feel that it is dominated by the Communist Party. May I emphatically deny this.

First according to official figures, the membership of the Communist Party is stated to be 20,000 and the membership of the ETU is 200,000, which means that if all the members of the Communist Party were in the ETU they would be definitely outnumbered. This is only logical isn't it?

It has also been said that our General President and our General Secretary and the majority of our Executive Council are members of the Communist Party, and that I do not know as I am not a member myself and none of our branch officials are, so your guess is as good as mine.

This I do know, since 1941, when brother Foulkes General President, and brother Stevens General Secretary, became prominent in our Union, we have greatly increased our membership, also we have marched forward as an organisation to the extent that we are the only Union in the British Isles that has its own College where all members can attend to learn Trade Unionism.

We also have a Convalescent Home for our male members which is free. Our Female members can go to a Convalescent home on the same basis as the male members.

May I conclude by saying this, if Brothers Foulkes and Stevens are members of the Communist Party, they are ETU workers first and last. Their sole aim is to work for us, remember you are their employers, and pay their salaries. I trust you will read this letter with diligence and remember you are Trade Unionists and it is up to you to do your best to make things better for yourself and your fellow workers. Some of you are mothers and have children. By your actions now you will decide the future of not only yourself and your children but all of us, and all our children.

Yours Fraternally,

———

Branch Secretary

In January 1958 the ETU reopened its Educational College at Esher.

XI

THE LONG SLOG

As the excitements of December and January evaporated we began to feel that we were not getting anywhere. The *Panorama* broadcast, the *New Statesman* article and a lot of other Press publicity had caused the Communist leadership of the ETU a great deal of concern, but they had hit back with their own propaganda, and they were still firmly in control of the Union. As the publicity died down, Les and I learned a lesson that, perhaps, we ought to have understood earlier—that feelings engendered by a Press campaign about almost anything are not sustained for very long. People get angry, they may even stay angry, but they do not remain active over long periods if they have no personal stake in the matter. We had a personal stake—everything in Les's life outside his family was bound up with his campaign to free the Union which he had served since his apprenticeship from domination by a clique whose policies, he now knew, were inimical to every real interest of the working-class.

In thinking back over this period of our lives I find myself feeling angry that so much was left to Les. Communist corruption in the ETU—and not in the ETU alone—was nothing new. It had been going on in one way or another since the British Communist Party was formed in 1920, and it had been practised as a major arm of Party policy ever since the war. There is no doubt that John Byrne should have been elected as Assistant General Secretary when he stood against Haxell in 1948. Byrne was nominated by no fewer than 168 branches of the Union, against the 74 which nominated Haxell. Byrne topped the poll in the first ballot.

Everyone expected him to walk away with the election on the second ballot as he was an immensely popular figure in the Union, which he had served for twenty years. Why had

he accepted defeat, why had he not fought back then? And
there were others who could have challenged the Communists many times in the years since the war; why had no
real challenge come from anybody? There had been, of
course, the anti-Communist forces of the Old Guard of the
trade union movement, represented by men like Arthur Deakin
of the Transport and General Workers and Sam Watson of the
Mineworkers. But they fought from positions of strength, unshakeable in their own personal prestige and power. The real
danger was going on beneath them, in the undermining of the
unions by Communist intrigue. As the Old Guard died or
retired the Communists and their fellow-travelling friends
moved up. This had happened in the ETU when E. W.
Bussey left. Did no one care? How was it *possible* that a
Party with never more than 35,000 members in the whole
of Britain could control, or largely influence, great trade
unions with memberships running into hundreds of thousands?

The appalling apathy of most of those hundreds of thousands
of non-Communist trade unionists was the Communist Party's
fertile ground—if no one bothers to take active interest, anyone
can usurp power. But why were decent, solid trade unionists,
many of them loyal adherents to the Labour Party, so apathetic? Fear might explain apathy to some extent; a tight bunch
of Communist shop stewards could certainly harass any
member of their union who persistently challenged them,
perhaps even take away his livelihood. But that could happen
only in a few cases; and if enough members of any union were
prepared to stand up against the Communists, it could not
happen at all. In terms of real power, the whole Communist
edifice in Britain was never any more than a house of cards—it
needed only a few fingers lifted against it, and it would collapse.
But those fingers were not lifted.

It was certainly not by reason of properly-conducted anti-
Communist propaganda that Communism failed to make much
greater headway in Britain after the Second World War. The
reason, basically, is that the whole idea of Communism is foreign
to the vast majority of the British working-class, which
has long traditions of democracy. In his university lectures
in Prague as far back as 1901, Professor Thomas Masaryk,

the future first President of the future Czechoslovak State, had said:

> There is no home-made anarchism in England, only foreign anarchists meet there. England has political freedom.

The real danger lies in assuming that freedom can be taken for granted. Because of the British tradition of political freedom, the Communist Party was free to intrigue as it pleased. Because the vast majority of British people simply did not believe that Communism could ever seriously threaten any of their established institutions, the evidence—and it was often glaring evidence—of their fiddling and corruption in trade union elections was ignored. People did not want it to exist; therefore it was best not to think about it.

As it happened, there never was an organised opposition to the Communist Party's activities in trade unions. There were individuals, like Woodrow Wyatt, Herbert Morrison and others, who tried to open people's eyes to what was going on and there were organisations which took an anti-Communist line, but they were not effective and no co-ordination existed between them. The Roman Catholic church and its association of Catholic trade unionists were perhaps the most eloquent of the anti-Communist forces, but quite ineffective. When Les started his campaign he soon learned that Byrne, who was a Catholic, had no organisation in Scotland. There was a variety of other anti-Communist groups, but the real motives of some of them were so dubious that their activities were as likely as not to alienate non-Communists who were honest trade unionists.

Les was accused by the Communist Party at various times of being everything from a secret Roman Catholic to a crypto-Fascist. His record made all such allegations absurd, but the Communists threw mud when they could in the hope that some of it would stick.

The established political parties—Conservative, Labour and Liberal—were, of course, opposed to Communism, but their attitude to Communism in Britain was to regard it almost as if it did not exist.

There were exceptions, a notable one being Herbert Morrison, who sharply attacked the Communists and the ETU in a speech to the Colne Valley Labour Party in December 1957:

> We have (he said then) a domestic problem of our own, on what appears to be a matter of Communist dictatorship, namely, the Electrical Trades Union.
>
> It is easier to get a police state than to get rid of it. It is easier to get Communists in control of a Trade Union than to get rid of them. A livelier interest in Trade Union activities would prevent the situation from arising.
>
> But it's a pretty awful state of affairs when Trade Union rank and filers have to argue their case for British democracy before TV with their faces blacked out in case they are victimised. I should be sorry if the Government took over supervision of Trade Union organisations, but I do think that there is a case for TUC intervention.

Haxell wrote back to Morrison observing that such statements might damage friendly relations between the Union and the Labour Party. He added that this might affect the Union's readiness to assist the Labour Party. (He was alluding to financial assistance to the Labour Party—O.C.)

Morrison's reply was:

> Dear Mr. Haxell,
>
> Thank you for your letter of April 23rd 1958. I quite understand that you should disagree with the part of the speech which you quote in your letter.
>
> It is one of those matters upon which there is, I fear, bound to be disagreement between us. I am sure you will agree that I must reserve my right to express my mind on these matters, as I would willingly agree that you should express yours.
>
> I have, however, noted what you say on the point of controversy.

It is very good of you to intimate in the last paragraph that you hope for a sympathetic response to our Appeal from your Executive.

Yours sincerely,

(An additional grant of £500 was approved by the Executive Council.)

The Labour Party came nearest to recognising that there was a Communist menace to British life, but opposition to Communism within the Labour Party was constantly rendered ineffective by Labour's own Left Wing. Throughout the 1950s the Labour Party was torn by bitter battles with the so-called Bevanites, a mixed body of Left and Extreme Left wing opinion which attached itself loosely to the personality of Aneurin Bevan.

Bevan himself was never a Communist, but he was flattered by the Communists and within the Bevanite group were a number of fellow-travellers who might call themselves members of the Labour Party but whose attitude on any given issue was indistinguishable from the Communist Party line. The post-war Labour Party leadership was always so busy either fighting the Bevanites, or making uneasy compromises with them, that it had no time for dealing with such matters as the rigged trade union elections of Communism in practice.

Les's natural allies were the people for whom he was fighting —the great body of non-Communist men and women loyal to the Labour Party. It seems incredible now that the Labour Party did not take up Les's case and use it to root out the Communists who were threatening everything the Labour Party stood for. Yet the Labour Party did nothing; Les was left to go it alone.

Going it alone was becoming extremely hard. By the beginning of 1958 our savings were all gone. The campaign of the last six months of 1957 had taken every penny we had. Les's Communist opponents in the ETU had the use of union cars and could draw expenses when they went from branch to branch; Les had to pay for all his travelling himself. This was very expensive, and we also had to live. Les never really thought of giving up his fight, but he would get desperately tired, and sometimes he wondered if it was fair to Oleg and Martin and me to continue to devote all his resources to an apparently endless struggle.

I was deeply worried about him, but I could not—and I did not want to—change his fighting spirit. All I could do was to try to help in every way I could, to encourage him always, to see that at least he had proper meals and went to bed when he came home.

To earn more money Les took a job on the night shift of the Hawker Aircraft Company in Kingston. But even with Les's night job we just did not have enough money to get by and there was none coming from anywhere. I hit on the idea of asking Woodrow Wyatt if he could help. Les was reluctant, but in the end he said that, if I wished, I could go ahead. I approached Woodrow Wyatt and he responded with sufficient cash for Les to make what we called his "grand tour" of branches of the ETU, travelling up the East coast as far as Dundee and back via Glasgow and the West coast.

Unfortunately, the resources of the leadership of the ETU were far greater than ours. Officials of the Union followed in Les's wake to give their version of events, so that much of Les's work was nullified. Nonetheless he made some most valuable contacts which proved of inestimable benefit when it came to the election for the General Secretary in 1959 and later to collecting evidence for the trial in 1961. Indeed, without Leslie's tour in 1958 it is doubtful that events would have moved with the intensity and speed that they did.

We continued our campaign of sending circulars to all 675 branches of the Union. Haxell's pamphlet, *The ETU replies to the New Statesman*, appeared at the end of February 1958. Les countered with a circular which we headed: *The Skeletons Are Rattling in the Cupboard*. The circulars were duplicated sheets on cheap paper. The ETU's pamphlets were well-printed affairs, and they cost the Union a pretty penny. Les began with a reference to this:

All branches have now received the General Secretary's latest pamphlet which he calls *The ETU replies to the New Statesman*. How much more is the union going to have to pay for Bro. Haxell's defence of the Communist Party's tactics inside the ETU?

Les had many friends from his old days in the Union, and he was exceedingly well informed about what went on in various branches. He gave chapter and verse of a number of branches which had returned impossibly high votes for Communist candidates, and referred particularly to the fiddling of postal votes at a number of branches, all of which he named:

> Need it be added that all the branch secretaries mentioned are Communist Party members? Who do these people think they are kidding? When are they going to stop taking the London members for fools? At least their fiddling has now been narrowed down to the postal vote—perhaps the members will observe these phenomenal postal ballots in future elections.

Returning to the charge of Communist Party interference in the internal affairs of the ETU, Les wrote:

> A basic point that Bro. Haxell has never answered is the clear charge made that the Communist Party Special Advisory Committee for the ETU (with members sitting on it who do not even belong to the ETU) has for years met once a month to tell the Communist majority on our ETU Executive what to do. With this control of the union by the Communist Party, it ill becomes Bro. Haxell to complain of outside interference from any source.

Haxell made a great political error in sacking Les on the eve of the elections for the Executive Council in 1957 and he made still graver errors in underrating him. A more politically astute man would have encouraged Les to be re-elected to some office in the Union, and then, from his own commanding position as General Secretary, kept him under control. In such a situation it would have been impossible for Les to conduct an open fight. The fact that events turned out differently was at least partly due to Haxell's political mistakes.

In March 1958 nominations were taken for election to the

post of London Area Official in the ETU, and Les decided to stand in this election. He also sought nominations for election as one of the Union's delegates to the forthcoming Trades Union Congress. The two ballots were taken at the same time, at the June quarterly branch meetings.

The Communists, embarrassed by the number of Party members already at the London office of the ETU, decided to support a non-Communist candidate on this occasion. There were three candidates in the election, the Communists' nominee, Les, and one other man. The Communists got their man in with 3,960 votes, but Les came second with 2,860—the third candidate received only some 600 votes. In the ballot for the TUC delegates Les did extremely well. This was a union-wide vote, not confined to London, and Les handsomely won a place in the Union's delegation.

On the night of the ballot Les attended the meeting of a branch known as London Electronic Engineers No. 2, a branch which included all members of the Union working at the EMI factory at Hayes (Middlesex), and which was then Communist led. As he sat watching the scrutineers open the envelopes handed to them by individual members, it struck him how few people there were, considering the high number of votes usually recorded by that particular branch. Then, in the middle of the count, the branch secretary, a Communist Party member, came across with a hold-all bag, so filled with ballot-envelopes that he had difficulty in getting them out as he undid the zip-fastener of the bag. Eventually he piled a heap of envelopes on the table, and Les noticed that comparatively few of them bore a postmark. There and then he decided to challenge the secretary. He got up, quoted the rules, formally "cast suspicion" on whether the votes were honestly cast, and said that he was going to report the facts to Head Office and insist on an investigation similar to that carried out at the Mitcham branch after it had voted heavily for him in the election for an Executive Councillor the previous year.

Needless to say the Communist branch secretary was acquitted, and he then proceeded to charge Les with bringing discredit on a member of the Union.

In that summer of 1958 I realised that our lives were becoming so involved in the struggle against the Communist leadership of the Union that I might be prevented from visiting my parents in Czechoslovakia. After the Hungarian rising in 1956 the Communists had tightened their grip on Czechoslovakia, and I was more than ever worried about my parents. I wanted to make another attempt to persuade them to come to live with us in England. I travelled to Czechoslovakia in July taking Oleg with me—Martin was left behind with Les. A kindly old lady of seventy, who was one of our neighbours, helped Les to look after him.

We were away for nearly a month. As I should perhaps have known, I failed to persuade my parents to come and live with us. My mother was resolutely opposed to the idea, and my father, of course, supported her. She brought up all the old arguments against adding to our difficulties by imposing an elderly Czech couple on our household in England, and reinforced them by saying that nothing must be allowed to interfere with Les's fight against Communism. She was intensely proud of our challenge to the Communist Party, and insisted that Les must not be put in a position where he might feel compelled to weaken, or even to abandon, his struggle through the responsibility of providing for my father and herself. It made me desperately sad, but I could only respect it. My visit to Czechoslovakia did, however, enable my mother to have a much-needed rest. I persuaded her to go to a Spa for a short holiday while I looked after my father.

While I was away in Czechoslovakia, Les received a letter giving him one week's notice that the charge of having brought discredit on a member of the Union would be heard by the Area Sub-Committee on July 15. The letter, dated July 8, added that if he wished to attend but was unable to be present on the date fixed, the Committee would consider a written request for a postponement; otherwise, the charge would be heard in his absence.

Les, who had six-year-old Martin on his hands, wrote back to say that domestic difficulties made it impossible to attend the hearing on July 15, and he asked for a postponement. The Area Secretary of the Union replied on July 16 offering to postpone the hearing to July 24.

On July 19 Les wrote back:

> I have to tell you that the domestic difficulties referred to in my last letter arise from my wife's visit to her parents, and that I have my youngest child at home with me. As the problem of his care is one that I can only solve day by day I am not able to guarantee my attendance at the sub-committee on the date mentioned in your letter. My wife will be returning in a fortnight's time, and I will be available any time from Monday, August 4, onwards. I hope your committee can accommodate these circumstances.

There was a further complication to which Les now drew attention. The charge of having brought discredit on a member of the Union arose out of the acquittal of the then secretary of the London Electronic Engineers No. 2 branch from Les's complaint of ballot-rigging. The Kingston branch of the Union, Les's own branch, had, however, appealed against this decision. Les explained this in his letter, and added that in view of the pending appeal the complaint against himself was premature.

Les received no reply to this letter, but on the evening of July 23, the day before the date of the postponed hearing of the charge against him, he had a telegram from someone he did not know saying that the hearing would take place as notified. Since the Area Sub-Committee was not due to meet until July 24 it could not even have considered his request for a further postponement before the telegram was sent. Therefore he ignored the telegram. He heard nothing more for a whole month. On August 23 he wrote to the Area Secretary

> I received a letter from you dated July 16 informing me that my "case" would be heard on July 24. I replied on July 19 stating that I could not guarantee my attendance at the hearing on that day for domestic reasons, which I outlined. I offered to attend on any date after August 4, which is 24 days before the succeeding Area Committee Meeting, to which the sub-committee reports. This proposal, I thought, would be considered by the sub-committee as reasonable. However, before the sub-committee could con-

sider my letter of July 19 I received a telegram signed by
someone named Wood (whose identity I have failed to discover) at 7.30 p.m. on Wednesday, July 23. According to
this telegram the hearing would take place the following
morning.

As I have had no further correspondence on this subject
since the telegram signed by Wood I can only assume that
the substance of Mr (or Mrs) Wood's telegram has been
effected. The whole affair is made all the more ludicrous and
prima facie illegal by virtue of the fact that the substance of
the complaint is the subject of an appeal by the Kingston
branch against the E.C. decision on the matter, and is,
therefore, as far as the Area Committee is concerned, *sub
judice*. I have made this point before to you in this exchange
of letters, but you have chosen to ignore it.

I wish now to place on record my strongest possible
protest at this blatantly undemocratic, and, in my opinion,
illegal procedure, and to insist that the whole of our correspondence on this subject be placed before the full Area
Committee along with the sub-committee's report.

Les knew very well that in spite of the dubious legality of
the whole proceedings, his conviction on the trumped-up
charge against him was a foregone conclusion. He knew, too,
that the almost certain penalty would be suspension from
holding office in the Union, which meant that he would not be
allowed to serve as a delegate to the Trades Union Congress,
which opened at Bournemouth on the first Monday in September. It was, therefore, important that he should be able to go
to the Congress without having had any official notification of
being disqualified. So we decided to go off to Bournemouth a
week early. There was no reason why we shouldn't take a holiday to add on to the week of the Congress—many delegates did
this with their families; it was an entirely normal thing to do.
But letters from the Union would be sent to our home address. If we
were at Bournemouth on holiday, it was reasonable that we
should get them later, only after they had been re-directed.

To keep the record straight, that is precisely what happened.
On August 28, in a letter beginning with the fraternal greeting,
"Dear Sir and Brother", the Area Secretary of the Union wrote

to Les notifying him that the Area Sub-Committee had found him guilty of the charge alleged against him. The punishment decreed was:

1. That he should be disqualified from holding any office in the Union for five years.

2. That he should be fined £5.

The letter duly advised him of his right to appeal to the Executive Council by giving notice of appeal within seven days and said that if he could prove financial hardship he might be allowed time to pay the fine.

On the next day, August 29, Haxell, the General Secretary, followed up with a letter saying that because of this conviction Les could not be a delegate at the forthcoming Trades Union Congress, and that his name would be withdrawn from the list of those representing the union.

Since we were at Bournemouth, we could not know anything about these letters until they were forwarded to us. At the very soonest, that could not be until the Saturday before the TUC opened on Monday.

We had a pleasant few days' holiday at Bournemouth. The boys loved the sea. Oleg, who was eight and always one to go off by himself, splashed about on his own, but Martin, who was six, preferred to sit on Les's shoulders while the waves surged over them. For Oleg and Martin, and for me, this was a wonderful little oasis in our lives. We could hardly ever be with Les when he was completely relaxed, and in those few days at Bournemouth before the storm broke he put everything else out of his mind, determined to be nothing but a father on holiday with his family. He was such a splendid father, too. We loved every minute of that brief respite with him.

On the Saturday morning the *News Chronicle* carried a story saying that Les had been suspended from holding office in the Union.

XII

THE 1958 TUC

LATER THAT SATURDAY a registered letter, forwarded from home, arrived at the boarding house where we were staying. It contained the first of the two letters that I have already referred to, the one from the Area Secretary of the Union. This was the letter informing Les of his suspension and of his right, if he wished, to appeal against the findings of the Area Committee. It did not say anything about his position as a delegate to the TUC—that was in Haxell's letter, sent to our home address a day later. Les was, therefore, still entitled to say that he had received no communication from Haxell about the TUC. He decided for the moment to ignore the Area Secretary's letter. He knew, however, that his credentials as a delegate had been withdrawn because, in addition to the story in the *News Chronicle*, he had been told by Trevor Evans,[1] Industrial Correspondent of the *Daily Express*, that the ETU had written to the General Council of the TUC informing it that Les had been removed from the delegation.

The annual conference of the Trades Union Congress always opens on a Monday. Delegates from the constituent unions assemble over the weekend, or, as we had done, come to the resort where the Congress is being held in the week beforehand. On Sunday, the day before the Congress opens, it is customary for most of the larger delegations to hold preliminary meetings of their own, at which the agenda for the coming week is discussed. The ETU's delegation meeting took place on Sunday morning. Les went along as if nothing had happened.

Frank Foulkes, the President of the Union, was in the chair, and he and the other delegates could scarcely believe their

---

[1] Later Sir Trevor Evans, doyen of the Industrial Correspondents' Group.

eyes when Les walked in. The following conversation, recorded by Les immediately afterwards, then took place.

> *Les:* Mr Chairman, I would like to ask what has happened to my credentials.
>
> *Foulkes:* Why are you asking me?
>
> *Les:* I am asking you as the President of the Union. I have been elected as a delegate, but have received no credentials, or communication.
>
> *Foulkes:* In that case you'd better go home and find out.
>
> *Les:* Is that all you have to say?
>
> *Foulkes:* Yes.

Les then left the meeting. His sharp mind had seized a vital point about those credentials. *They had not been withdrawn—they had never been issued to him.* And that pointed to something very strange indeed, because they ought to have been sent to him several days before the Area Committee had decided to suspend him.

Every trade union affiliated to the TUC is entitled to send to each Annual Congress a number of delegates based on its affiliated membership. The TUC has to be informed of the names of delegates well in advance, in sufficient time for the names to be printed by the opening of Congress. Credentials in the name of each delegate—documents giving admission to the Congress as well as invitations to any official receptions that may be held during the week—are sent by the TUC to the head offices of the unions about a fortnight before the date of the Congress. Les knew that all the other members of the ETU delegation had duly received their credentials *before the date of the Area Committee meeting which confirmed his suspension.* His credentials, alone, had been withheld at the head office of the ETU. This meant that the decision to suspend him had been taken *before* the Area Committee had even considered his case!

Les was pondering these matters when he again ran into Trevor Evans, always friendly, and with a deep understanding of everything to do with trade unions. Trevor was interested in Les's story. "Look, dear boy,"[1] he said, "there won't be any

---

[1] This was Trevor's hallmark, followed in greeting, if he knew that one was married, by: "And how is your lovely bride?" Many journalists and trade union leaders have cause to be grateful for the kindly wisdom of Trevor Evans.

other news about the TUC tonight, and everyone will be glad of something to write for tomorrow's paper. Why don't you hold a Press Conference?"

That, certainly, was an idea. Les, from his initial horror of the Press, was becoming more accustomed to its ways, and he understood well enough how the Press could help him. But a Press Conference—single-handed, stealing the thunder, as it were, of the whole TUC! It needed thinking about. Haxell and Co. had already tried to make out that Les was no more than a tool of the capitalist Press. Nonsense as this might be, it was the kind of mud that was inclined to stick in some quarters, where Les might otherwise find friends.

The only person at hand whom Les could consult was Bill Blairford,[1] a member of the ETU's delegation and an old friend, who was staying at the same boarding house. Blairford was horrified at the idea of Les's holding a Press Conference to announce his troubles with the Union. "Leak" the story to the Press—that is, have a discreet word privately with one or two journalists—by all means. But openly and blatantly to hold a Press Conference would, in Blairford's view, do Les more harm than good. We understood this point of view. It was the natural aversion of the worker to the capitalist Press, an aversion that Les until quite recently had shared to the full, and in many ways still shared. But Les had been learning many things since his break with the Communist Party, and learning them the hard way. The Communists showed no scruples of any sort in their campaign against Les. Why should he pull any of his punches now?

If Les had been in Bournemouth alone he might have accepted Blairford's view, and abandoned the idea of a Press Conference. But I was all for it; I saw what an opportunity it was, and I didn't want Les to miss it. This was one of the occasions when I was helpful to Les in his battle. He himself was more than half in favour of the idea, anyway. I tipped the balance, and encouraged him to go ahead.

[1] William Blairford, of Edinburgh, sometime Chairman of the Edinburgh branch of the ETU. He had joined the Communist Party in 1942 but left it in 1956 after the Hungarian rising. In 1959 he stood against Frank Foulkes for election as President of the ETU and polled 15,262 votes against Foulkes's 18,051.

It was arranged to hold the Conference at a hotel at eight o'clock that evening. Our landlady gave supper to Oleg and Martin, and kindly agreed to put them to bed so that we could go off to the conference hotel well beforehand. On the way there we ran into Frank Cousins, whom, of course, Les knew, but whom I had never met. He was most jovial. He had recently come back from a visit to Yugoslavia, and was full of his experiences, which he recounted with great enthusiasm. His impressions were far more rosy than the underlying reality could possibly have been—I knew too well from my own experiences in Czechoslovakia how only the best is shown to Western trade union visitors. Nevertheless, I liked the man, and enjoyed meeting him.[1]

The Press Conference was a resounding success. Every British newspaper, radio and TV correspondent covering the TUC came along, and there were a good many representatives of foreign newspapers as well. Les started off by reading a statement which he had prepared that afternoon. This began:

> Firstly, I wish to express my regrets to Congress delegates that this unsavoury business has marred the opening proceedings of Congress. It was certainly not my wish that this should be so. I have decided to make this statement to you after eighteen months of consistent provocation, resulting from a continuous campaign by the Communist Party inside the ETU to discredit me, and ultimately to deprive me of my democratic rights inside the Union.

> Yesterday afternoon a registered letter came to hand confirming that what I had read in the *News Chronicle* that morning was substantially correct. I am in no doubt that such a vicious penalty, with the consequences which might flow from it, would not have been initiated by the Communists unless it was a well-discussed decision of the National ETU Advisory Committee of the Communist Party, of which Mr Haxell is a chairman. It would also be bound to have the approval of the Political Committee of the Communist Party.

> The significance of this will be fully appreciated when it

[1] We met Cousins again after the news of Les's Press Conference had filled the papers. This time he just said, "Oh, hallo," and brushed past. I could never quite forgive him for that.

DADDY,
            I had all my
ums   right   today.

                    MARTIN.

Daddy, I got my first Silver star
or sums I am the first one to get
a star for Sums.

                    Yours   ✳
                        Martin

Good night!

Notes from Martin
to the father he rarely saw

Dear Daddy,
miss you
every day.
please don't be
ong.
Love M
    MARTIN
nday letter (February 2ⁿᵈ 1958).

Summer 1959

Les and Olga in 1960

is known that of the sub-committee of five which decided on the penalty, three are members of the Communist Party, including the chairman and secretary. On the full Area Committee which ratified the decision of the sub-committee there are eleven Communists, a number of whom are members of the National ETU Advisory Committee of the Communist Party.

In regard to the substance of the charge of bringing discredit upon a member of the Union, arising from which this penalty has been imposed, all I can say is that this is subject to an appeal against a decision of the Executive Council. It was, therefore, in my opinion outside the power of the Area Committee to discuss the matter at all until the appeals machinery had been exhausted.

I have been asked, "Have my credentials been withdrawn?" The answer is, "No, they have not. They were never issued to me in the first place." This, despite the fact that the TUC issued credentials in my name a fortnight ago. All other delegates received their credentials before the decision of the Area Committee. Mine were withheld.

Les then turned to the question of whether, in view of what he regarded as the illegality of the whole proceedings, he would try to take his seat as a delegate when Congress opened in the morning.

He repeated his brief conversation with Frank Foulkes at the ETU's delegate meeting that Sunday morning, and continued:

I left the meeting, having learned in this peculiar way that I am no longer a delegate. I do not intend to try to take my seat.

Finally, I want to anticipate the question as to whether I intend to use the appeals machinery of the union. The experiences of the last twelve months, during which I spent a great deal of time, effort and personal savings trying to the utmost to exercise the right of appeal,[1] have convinced me

---

[1] I.e. over the disqualification of branches in the 1957 elections for the Executive Council.

that such attempts to exercise this fundamental democratic right are rendered abortive by Mr Haxell. In these circumstances I am left with little alternative but to seek legal advice.

Next day, on Monday, Les also had his first personal experience of TV. An outside broadcast team took him up on the roof of a building and he was interviewed with traffic roaring past on the road beneath and an aeroplane flying overhead. TV producers always strike me as being slightly mad. These were no exception. Technicians with earphones surged about the roof, apparently acting on instructions from five different voices simultaneously. One of the technicians nearly fell off the parapet. The interviewer, a pleasantly-freckled young man (now a Tory MP), kept up a stream of largely irrelevant questions, most of which Les couldn't hear, but to which he replied as well as he could. It was interesting, but exhausting. "I'll never go through such a circus again," Les said at the end of it. (Well, not many years later, he was almost a TV personality!)

Trevor Evans, brilliant journalist that he is, had counselled Les shrewdly. The timing of his Press Conference was exactly right. There was not much other Home News that weekend, and Les's story got wonderful coverage in the morning papers on Monday. It was a sensational opening for the TUC. Walter Padley, of the Union of Shop, Distributive and Allied Workers, raised the matter of Les's exclusion at the opening session of Congress. This was a courageous thing to do, for he laid himself open to the charge of interfering in the domestic affairs of another union. There is no doubt, however, that the sympathy of many of the delegates was with Les; they were shocked not only by the fact that the Communists had barred a properly elected delegate, but by the manner of Les's exclusion—the arrogant withholding of his credentials, and the announcement of his removal from the delegation at the very last moment. But there was nothing that Congress could do. The selection of delegates is a matter for individual unions, carried out according to their own rules, and all that concerns Congress is to know that only properly affiliated unions are represented. In certain circumstances the behaviour of an individual union can be inquired into by the General Council of the TUC, and Padley was invited to refer his complaint to the General Council. This he did. It was one incident in the complex and contorted story of the relations between the TUC and the Communist leadership of the ETU, a story that dragged on for years. It had no immediate effect.

Les's Press Conference on the eve of that 1958 Congress brought about a qualitative change in his whole campaign against the Communists. It was a declaration of open war, and made it impossible for his campaign to be regarded as a domestic squabble within the ETU. Nevertheless, there were large sections of the Labour movement, and of the TUC, which were not at all anxious to take sides, and really hoped that Les would soon go away and shut up. There were many reasons for this faint-heartedness, some fairly valid, some wholly discreditable. The Labour movement generally—as evidenced by Bill Blairford's attitude to Les's proposed Press Conference and, indeed, by Les's own feelings—has always had a deep suspicion of the Press, particularly when it criticises anything to do with trade unionism. It is a feeling that might be summed up like this: Yes, trade unions are sometimes pretty rough organisations, and not everything is always done according to the Queensberry Rules. It's a pity, but there it is. But the unions are the main defence of the working-class against capitalist exploitation. Newspapers may *say* that they are on our side, but most newspapers are owned by big business, and anything they can do to weaken the unions is obviously in the interests of employers. We may not like a good many of the things that this or that union does, but we like newspaper attacks on it a great deal less.

In the light of working-class history, that feeling is understandable, if often misguided, for it takes no account of the genuine integrity of many editors and journalists, who, though they may work for capitalist employers, have high standards of objectivity in what they write.

Then Les was an ex-Communist. He had been a Communist for many years, he had himself been on the Executive Council of the ETU. If what he was now saying was true, he himself must have been guilty of the same malpractices in his Communist days. Was his quarrel with the ETU now anything more than a personal row between Commies and ex-Commies? Let them fight it out.

That feeling, too, is understandable.

Wholly discreditable, however, was the reluctance of so many in the Labour movement to look beyond personalities, to ask questions and try to find out what all this was about. If it was to Les's discredit that he had acquiesced in Communist Party machinations in the past, surely it was infinitely more to his credit that he had thrown away his trade union career and was now risking his very livelihood to expose the evils of Communism? It is all right to pour scorn on those who see Communists under every bed; it is equally all wrong to refuse to see Communists when they walk in with bags of forged ballot papers. It may make for a comfortable Left-wing political life to pretend that Communists do not exist, or that they are all good fellows at heart, doing a grand job in the unions; it is a comfort that will not long survive a Communist take-over—of a trade union, a government, or any other human institution. The Labour Party and the General Council of the TUC were incredibly slow in taking notice of Les's charges. They were reluctant to help him, slow even to admit that he was the victim of monstrous injustice at Communist hands. Walter Padley and Vic Feather were notable exceptions. Vic befriended us in those years and remains a friend to this day.

One or two of the Industrial Correspondents were stalwart friends to Les, but the Press, as a whole, was only half-helpful to him. It would take him up eagerly whenever he made a story, and then more or less ignore him. This irritated us, but that was largely because we didn't yet understand the Press all that well. Most journalists *were* interested in Les simply as a story—that was their job. They were not particularly concerned to crusade with him. We were living our story, day after day, week after week, month after month; the Press would get excited about one incident, and then turn to something else.

There were other reasons why Les did not always get the publicity that we thought he deserved. There were plenty of people ready to dismiss him as a troublemaker, and reporters were naturally worried about the possibility of libel actions if they published Les's statements about the Union.

Looking back, I am astonished that journalists had the courage to print as much as they did. Les knew that he could prove the things he said, but it was expecting a lot of journalists that they should take everything he said on trust. It was remarkable how often they did so.

In fact, the ETU never brought an action for libel—that became an issue later in its long wrangle with the General Council of the TUC. The leadership of the Union was obviously reluctant to face the cross-examination that a libel action would involve. The last thing that the Communists wanted was to have to defend themselves in court—they were not going to invite a court hearing of Les's charges against them. In the end they had to be forced to court in a different way.

After the Bournemouth TUC we were left with a sense of anti-climax. With a great flourish of publicity Les had thrown down the gauntlet—and nobody had picked it up. Nothing seemed to be happening. Les took legal advice about the fine of £5 imposed on him, but he was advised that as the rules of the Union stood he would have to pay it. So on September 9 he did, handing in the money to his own Kingston branch of the Union. He wrote to tell the Area Secretary that he had done so, adding:

> I informed the branch, as I wish to inform the Area Committee, that I paid the fine under protest, and without any admission that the Area Committee had the right to either fine me or suspend me from holding office in the circumstances of the case.

The five-year suspension from holding office in the Union was much more serious to Les than the £5 fine. Suspension meant that he could not fight any more elections, that he could not challenge any of the Communists in the Union at the polls. Les's contention that both fine and suspension were illegal because his branch's appeal against the Executive Council's dismissal of the charge of ballot-rigging was still unheard, was lost in the complexity of the Union's rules. In a letter to the Kingston branch Haxell simply stated flatly that the decision was taken in connection with the scrutineer's report, "and such decisions are not subject to the appeals procedure within the union".

It was a weird interpretation of the rules. Les, apparently, could be suspended for "bringing discredit" on a member of the Union cleared by the Executive Council of his charge and Les, it will be recalled from the Area Secretary's letter to him, had been told that he could appeal, if he wished, against his own sentence. But there could be no appeal against the Executive Council's findings which led to the charge on which he had been sentenced! It seemed a total denial of natural justice, but the complexities and ambiguities in the ETU's Rule-Book were going to cause everybody a lot more trouble. Les had already decided that his only hope of redress was to bring a High Court action against the Union for the restitution of his rights. But he was earning £16 a week, and was told by a solicitor that he would not be eligible for legal aid.

Les might be unable to stand in elections, but he was far from powerless in other ways. He returned to his circulars. He had another strong weapon that he now decided to use—the question of the Union's finances. A little earlier, when the Communists were digging up everything they could to try to discredit Les, the accounts of the ETU College for 1957 were examined, and Haxell had written to him asking him to account for eighteen telephone calls, which appeared to include some personal calls. Two were to Les's parents. Les wrote back freely admitting that the calls were his, but adding that they were made in accordance with normal practice and that he had no intention of divulging their contents.

This brought a stern lecture from Haxell, accusing Les of having grossly abused the facilities of the Union by using them for his private business, and asking what he intended to do about it. Les replied that he would gladly pay for the telephone calls that had been personal if every National Officer and Executive Councillor of the Union would do the same. This drew another long-winded rebuke, and Les wound up the correspondence by saying: "Even though I know it is not customary, I nevertheless will make the payment." The sum involved was £2 4s 3d (£2·21).

Les got a wry amusement out of this. It was a game, he felt, that two could play. Exercising his rights under Rule 12 Clause 14 of the Union's rules, he wrote to the General Secretary asking for the Union's account books to be made available for his inspection.

Three months later there was still no reply, so Les wrote again. This time Haxell did reply to him, saying that he could trace no previous correspondence about finances. It was now November 1958.

In December, after still more correspondence, he extracted a promise to the effect that arrangements were being made for him to see the accounts. Nothing more happened until February 1959, when Les lost patience and sent copies of his correspondence to the Registrar of Trade Unions.

As the law then stood, the Registrar of Trade Unions had great responsibilities with virtually no powers, but Les's approach to the Registrar did, apparently, stir up things at the Union's head office, for on February 19 Haxell wrote offering a date in March for Les to inspect the books.

Les replied acidly, accepting the date, and adding: "It seems perfectly clear to me that had I not sought the assistance of the Registrar I should not have had an opportunity of seeing the books even as 'early' as March." This drew a sharp note from Haxell remonstrating with Les for his "irresponsible attitude".

By this time the campaign against Les was such that I worried about his going to Head Office alone, particularly since Haxell wrote that he should come to see the books after office hours. I begged Les to take a witness with him and he asked Bill Sullivan to join him. After their very first visit they realised that they would need to come again several times, particularly since no co-operation was offered from the National officer present. On the contrary, some of their questions were repeatedly ignored.

As the outcome of his study of the Union's accounts Les compiled a series of financial circulars which he sent to all branches of the Union. These asked a number of questions about disbursements which had apparently been made without the kind of authority required by the rules. The questions drew official answers at the Union's next policy conference, but Les proceeded to question several of the answers. It was hard work, for he had to be extremely careful to get his facts right. There was no immediate outcome to all this questioning, but it helped to keep the campaign against the Communist leadership of the Union active, and it certainly contributed to their later overthrow.

XIII

WHILE ALL THIS was going on, battles were being fought simultaneously on a number of other fronts. All were confused by side-issues and irrelevancies, some deliberately fostered by the Communists in order to cloud the reality of the evidence against them, some more or less inevitable in a body as amorphous as the trade union movement. The two main fronts at this time were the TUC and a private inquiry ordered by the Communist leadership of the ETU. These overlapped considerably. In addition, there was occasional sniping in Parliament to try to persuade the Government to order an inquiry into the ETU—efforts which consistently failed.

Before attempting to discuss events on these various confused fronts I must try to explain the rather loose confederation of allies which gradually grouped itself around Les. The alliance was united in opposing the leadership of the ETU, but individual aims and motives differed widely. Moreover, as time went on, more and more of the abler people were, like Les, disqualified from holding office in the Union, so that they could not themselves contest elections. To find anti-Communist candidates to fight elections tended to become a matter of choosing whoever happened to be available rather than of putting up the best and ablest man for the job. Some of our allies were doughty fighters and staunch, unshakeable friends— no praise can be too high for them. Others were less able, or had less heart in the fight. Nevertheless, most of them did their best according to their lights, and Les was always conscious of his debt to them.

One of Les's first and most active supporters was Harry Marshall, the Secretary of Mitcham Electricians' branch, which voted heavily for Les in the 1957 election. He was a tough little fellow, who was a paratrooper during the war and proved a fearless activist, going to branches at short notice and helping Les whenever he was approached. He was among the first to be charged by the Communist Executive.

Another was Frank Chapple,[1] whom Les first met at the Prague Youth Festival in 1946. Like Les he had been an active Communist for many years. Before he joined the Army in 1942 he was a full-time paid organiser for the Young Communist League. After the war he became active in the ETU and from 1948 to 1956 he was a member of both the "London Advisory Committee" and of the "National Advisory Committee", through which the Communist Party exercised its influence in ETU affairs. Thus, again like Les, he knew at first-hand precisely what went on. He became disillusioned with the Communist Party in 1956 and was suspended from the Party's "advisory committees" for advocating that disillusioned Communists should stay in the Party to try to democratise it and change the leadership. In spite of this breach he stayed in the Party and was elected to the Executive Council of the ETU in 1957, against the wishes of both Haxell and the "National Advisory Committee" of the Communist Party. His membership of the Executive Council was useful to Les, who, through Frank, obtained information about the goings-on at the meetings.

Two men thrown together as closely was were Les and Frank Chapple could scarcely have been more different. I have always felt that Frank Chapple was not naturally a political animal, as Les was. Les thrived on argument, on the cut and thrust of debate. Frank Chapple, I think, by nature much preferred privacy. He loves animals, and has often said that he would have liked to be a farmer. In the middle of our fight with the leadership of the ETU he toyed with the idea of going out to join a friend who was farming in Australia. He changed his mind and agreed to join John Byrne in the court action to strengthen his case.

In some ways Frank Chapple was, perhaps, more realistic than Les. He knew, as well as Les did, how strong was the Communist grip on the ETU, and I think he felt that the Communists could not be beaten by direct assault. Certainly, until Les's open challenge, every attempt at opposition came to nothing. Les would often be impatient at his cautious

[1] Now General President of the EETU/PTU.

approach to the battle, and I think Frank Chapple sometimes did things against his own judgment because he was unable to resist Les's persuasive enthusiasm. That Les's faith in the outcome of the struggle was in the end justified was a kind of miracle, brought about by Les's own tenacity. It was an outcome against all realistic assessment at the time.

We first met Mark Young at Frank Chapple's house. Mark, then Chairman of the Finchley branch of the Union, was about ten years younger than Les. He, too, was a disillusioned Communist. His own break with the Party had been an angry affair, during which he had published in the *New Statesman* extracts from a long letter which he wrote to the Communist Party. He had been charged with disagreement with Party policy. In his letter, published in the summer of 1958, he wrote,

> I fail to see how you can make these charges on the basis of conversational fragments of which your committee members' report consists, such as "He has not read the *Daily Worker* for 12 months", "refuses to work for Party candidates", "alleges corruption of the Party leadership in the ETU". . . . I am hostile to those elements within the Communist leadership of the ETU who take and maintain power by forging ballots, and to those members of both the London and National membership of the Party who actively help and condone these practices. It is now four years since I raised this issue . . . I have raised it at all levels in the Party.

The Communist Party's attitude to Les was one of his specific complaints. He wrote of a meeting of the Communist ETU "Advisory" at which, he said, "the only topic of discussion" had been how to defeat ex-comrade Cannon in the 1957 election for the Executive Council. He went on,

> We were directed to visit every branch that had nominated Cannon and to try to undermine him, principally by describing him as the candidate of the Press. I challenged that meeting. I challenge you now to show me what evidence there is for labelling Cannon the candidate of the Press. . . . No efforts were spared on behalf of the Party candidate. The

whole union machine was placed at his disposal, unprecedented activity around the branches by union officials took place, smear and defamation raised the atmosphere to fever pitch. . . . The result of machine against individual was not too successful; when the complete list of nominations became known Cannon emerged as a real challenge.

Mark Young concluded his letter: "These are my views, and if they merit my expulsion from the Party the decision will be entirely yours." The District Committee of the Communist Party obliged, and expelled him "for political activity incompatible with Party membership". The letter telling him of his expulsion added that he had the right to appeal, and helpfully gave the address of the Appeals Committee at King Street. By then, however, he was beyond that stage.

Mark's letter had been written without any consultation with Les, because at that time there was no co-ordination of anti-Communist policy. Later, Mark became an active member of the small group opposing the ETU leadership.

Others who allied themselves with Les included Bill Sullivan, a long-standing opponent of the ETU leadership. Bill Sullivan had been bitterly hostile to Les when Les was on the Executive Council, but in spite of their differences in the past they came together now and fought together. Bill was an important partner in analysing the Union's financial affairs. Les was always sorry that he left the Union to take private employment, for he would have made a fine ETU official.

This loose group that gathered around Les was referred to collectively, both in the Press and by the ETU leadership, as "the rebels". In the winter of 1958 one of the most colourful of the "rebels" returned from South Africa, where he had been working as an electrician with a British film company. This was Richard Odlin, always known to us as Dick Reno. His father was a well-known comedian, whose professional name was Reno, and Dick commonly used his father's professional name. He was a talented comic himself, and could keep an audience laughing until tears ran down their faces—I remember particularly his acting of a telephone conversation between his foreman and his boss, the foreman always taking off his cap when he spoke to the boss on the telephone. But Dick, urbane and mild as he looked, would explode with anger when he met Communist chicanery, and he could be a formidable opponent. It was Dick who stood in the next Executive Council election when Les was barred; he challenged Haxell at an ETU Conference about certain expenditure of union funds, and was severely punished for his pains. He was later barred from holding office in the Union for ten years (later still he received a public apology). Les was very fond of him, and they often played tennis together. When Les was very ill in hospital, a few weeks before his death, he asked specially to see Dick Reno.

To explain the long wrangle between the General Council of the TUC and the ETU I must return for a moment to 1956. On September 10, 1956, Woodrow Wyatt, who had been collecting details of Communist malpractice for his pamphlet *The Peril in Our Midst*, wrote the following letter to Sir Vincent Tewson, then General Secretary of the TUC:

Dear Sir Vincent,
Recently I have had occasion to acquire material about election methods for National offices in the Electrical Trades Union. The evidence I have obtained shows beyond any reasonable doubt that elections in this union have been manipulated by falsification of the voting in order to secure the victory of Communist and Communist supported candidates.
Feeling that the General Council would wish to investigate the situation I enclose a memorandum in order that the General Council may take what action it thinks fit.
I can supply further evidence if the General Council require it.

On September 14, 1956, Sir Vincent replied:

Dear Woodrow Wyatt,
I am most grateful to you for your letter of September 10, together with enclosures.
I would like you to leave the matter with me for the time being, but I think it would be inadvisable for the General Council to act as you suggest. The next time I see you I

would like us to have a brief chat, when I can explain certain
matters which lead me to the above conclusion.

Nevertheless, I am very grateful to you for the trouble
you have taken. I would not like you to think that the effort
is wasted so far as I am concerned. There are alternative
methods.

This cautious—one might say timid—attitude was maintained by Sir Vincent and the General Council for the next
three years. Woodrow Wyatt got nowhere in his attempt to
stir the TUC to action. Had the General Council shown even
a modicum of political courage during those three years much
damage could have been prevented, to the lasting good of the
whole trade union movement. Why was the General Council
so reluctant to act? It was not for lack of power, for the General
Council has formidable powers. Rule 13 of the constitution of
the TUC specifically empowers the General Council to investigate activities which may be "detrimental to the interest of
the trade union movement". An individual union may be summoned to send representatives to explain any matter which
the General Council may think requires explanation. If the
General Council considers that any activities by an individual
union are detrimental to the interests of the movement as a
whole, that union may be required to desist, and to give
undertakings for the future. If such undertakings are not given,
or if they are given and ignored, the General Council may
suspend a union from membership of the TUC, and invite the
next annual Congress to expel it. This was the course ultimately
taken with the ETU, but the process, from Woodrow Wyatt's
first letter in 1956 to expulsion of the Union in 1961, took five
years, and came too late.

It is a story in which the TUC can take no pride, and it
holds many lessons for the trade union movement. Here was an
affiliated union, flagrantly defying every principle of democratic
administration, and for years the TUC, the supreme trade
union authority in Britain, did nothing about it.

Woodrow Wyatt's approach, in spite of all the evidence of
ballot-rigging that he could produce, and that he published
in *The Peril in Our Midst*, accomplished nothing. The *Panorama*
broadcast in 1957 and all the publicity then given to the rigging

of the Executive Council election against Les left the General
Council unstirred. The withdrawal of Les's credentials as a
delegate to the 1958 Trades Union Congress compelled the
General Council to take some notice of the fact that things were
going on in the ETU which were not exactly helpful to the
good name of trade unionism, because Walter Padley had
specifically referred the matter to the General Council. Even
so, it did not hurry. The Trades Union Congress was at the
beginning of September. On December 17 the General Council
asked the ETU for its observations on the publicity about
Communist influence and ballot-rigging in the Union. Over a
month later (on January 23, 1959) the ETU replied that its
affairs were not controlled by the Communist Party but by its
own Annual Conference and Rules Revision Conference. The
rest was all the fault of the Press, which wanted to discredit
trade unionism, and the ETU proposed to do all it could to
"nullify and minimise" such criticism.

On February 18 Les himself wrote to Sir Vincent Tewson.
He took this step after much thought, for in the ordinary way
the General Council of the TUC does not deal with individuals,
but only with the authorised representatives of affiliated
unions. In the circumstances, however, since the question of
the withdrawal of his credentials as a delegate to Congress had
been formally referred to the General Council, it seemed reasonable that his own case should be heard. He began with an
apology,

> I am writing to you regarding the continuing state of
> affairs in the Electrical Trades Union. I apologise for taking
> this unorthodox step, but, having tried to use the constitu-
> tional machinery of the ETU and found it wrongfully blocked
> at every turn, the only course left open to me seems to be to
> appeal to the General Council of the TUC, which I now do.

He went on,

> You may remember that I made a statement at Bourne-
> mouth following the cancellation of my credentials as a
> delegate to the Bournemouth TUC during which I said that
> I proposed to take legal advice. This I did. I was informed

that, taking the events of the past eighteen months into account, I had an excellent case against the leaders of the ETU for conspiracy. I have hesitated to take this step without exhausting all the possibilities of resolving the question within the trade union movement because I was afraid such a case might be followed by legislation, some of which might be aimed at restricting the proper functions of the trade union movement. The advocates of such legislation already argue that the machinery does not exist for the just resolution of such problems as at present exist within the ETU. Another reason is that there are many ethical as well as legal aspects to this case which the TUC could decide upon, whereas the Courts are not so fitted, and in any case refuse to decide upon them.

ETU members, including some holding very responsible positions in the Union, are prepared to substantiate the following allegations at any inquiry which the General Council may decide to hold:

1. Conspiracy on the part of Communist Party members to alter the results of ballots.
2. The deliberate obstruction of the appeals machinery of the Union by Mr F. L. Haxell, General Secretary.
3. The abuse by Mr Haxell of the proper function of the General Secretary by concealing from the ETU Executive Council over very long periods of time (eighteen months in the case of my branch) correspondence sent by the Branches disagreeing with the actions of the General Secretary, also of usurping important functions of the Executive Council, particularly its power to interpret the rules of the Union.
4. Use of the Union's machinery to discredit critics of the Union's chief officials and the use of blatant discrimination by communist union officials in exercising the Union's disciplinary powers against critics.

The reason for my statement at Bournemouth was the fact that after 22 years' membership, for 17 of which I held office including 9 years as an Executive Councillor and nearly 3 years as an education officer, the first opportunity was taken to impose the vicious penalty of 5 years' suspension from holding office as well as a fine of £5. My Branch has been trying to have its complaints concerning the whole circumstances leading up to this suspension placed before the Executive Council since last October. Again this attempt has been deliberately obstructed by the General Secretary. Branches writing in to complain of this penalty, are being told half-truths which in their context are worse than lies.

He then referred to the possibility of further disciplinary measures against him as a result of his Bournemouth Press Conference for having disclosed union business outside the Union, and commented:

The irony of this and other similar charges is that the great majority of the Executive Council including the three chief officials of the Union have been consistently, continuously, and with impunity in breach of this same rule for more than 20 years, by divulging ETU business inside the advisory committees of the Communist Party.

He concluded,

It is not just a question of wrong things happening. The problem is that the machinery for putting matters right, which exists within the constitution whatever its inadequacies, is palpably obstructed, particularly by the General Secretary. My branch placed a motion on the policy conference agenda calling for an inquiry committee of lay members of the ETU. It was ruled out of order by the E.C. So it seems the only hope is an inquiry by the General Council of the TUC.

As I appreciate your difficulty as the General Secretary of Congress in regard to letters addressed to you from individual members of affiliated unions, I hope you will not mind my having addressed a copy of this letter to members of the General Council.

This letter was not even acknowledged, but it was not without effect, for on February 25 the General Council wrote to the ETU to inquire what, precisely, was being done to refute criticism of its affairs. There was nearly another month of silence, and then, on March 20, the ETU returned with a complaint that it could not get newspaper editors to publish letters. It referred to its own pamphlets allegedly "answering" Press charges, and added that it had considered libel actions, but that legal action was expensive and, in the ETU's view, "not in the best interests of the trade union movement".

The General Council was now getting a little fed up with this evasive correspondence, for within a week (on March 26) it wrote back to say it considered these replies unsatisfactory and that the Union ought to arrange an official inquiry into the allegations made against it. To this the ETU responded (on April 16) that it was asking those of its members who were making charges against its conduct of affairs for proof of their various allegations, and on April 29 the Executive Council decided to appoint an internal Committee of Inquiry to investigate things.

The setting up of this inquiry kept the TUC at bay until the autumn, but the whole operation was just eyewash. It was not, and was never intended to be, a far-ranging inquiry into charges against the Union; it was simply another attempt to discredit Les. The inquiry itself, although it served to keep the TUC quiet, was not the outcome of correspondence with the General Council. It arose from the new action against Les referred to in his letter to Sir Vincent Tewson.

In December 1958, the Executive Council, still smarting from Les's Bournemouth Press Conference, decided to pursue him for the unauthorised disclosure of union business. Haxell's first move was to ask Les to give an undertaking that he would abide by the rules of the Union in future. Les could not reply at once because of the death of his mother, which came as a severe shock to him. She had meant much in his life, and he was vividly aware of how much he—and the whole family—owed to her devotion and patient self-sacrifice. Her death made him feel bitterly that he had done little for her in return—an unnecessary pain, for he was always a devoted son. He was deeply upset by her passing, and for a time had no heart to think of anything else.

In January 1959, however, he replied to Haxell's letter. After explaining that his delay in writing had been due to his bereavement he denied that he was in breach of any union rule and declined to give the undertaking asked for. On April 4 he was summoned before the Executive Council to answer the charge of unauthorised disclosure of union business. Mark Young was similarly charged—for his letter to the *New Statesman*—and summoned with Les to appear before the Executive Council.

At this hearing Les and Mark counter-attacked vigorously, accusing their accusers of all the malpractices that had been going on for years. Specifically, they charged the Executive Council with disclosing union business to the Communist Party and with permitting Communist interference in ETU affairs, and they charged Haxell with habitually acting outside his powers in not bringing complaints from branches before the Executive, in not allowing appeals against Executive Council decisions, and in usurping the functions of the Executive Council. Les also brought up his more personal complaints— ballot-rigging against him when he was a candidate for election to the Executive, the circumstances of his suspension from holding office in the Union, and his sacking from the post of Education Officer, which he held, had been due to Communist influence.

The counter-attack was so effectively pressed home that the Executive Council was not at all sure what to do next. The Committee of Inquiry was set up to try to find an answer to the accusations.

No independent person was invited to serve on the inquiry— the committee consisted of two members of the Executive Council and one National Officer of the Union. Les and Mark naturally refused to produce evidence to the inquiry on the ground that it was not impartial. On June 9 the committee produced its report, a long document dismissing all the charges brought by Les and Mark and completely whitewashing the Union leadership. On Communist interference the committee reported:

> No evidence has been produced to show that the Communist Party has interfered in the affairs of our union; nor was there any evidence to show that even if there had been

such interference it would or could have affected the democratic processes by which our union elects its officers and officials and carries out its business, including the important internal matter of conducting appeals.

The report concluded with a vicious swipe at Les and Mark:

The committee considers it necessary to express their unanimous view that the Executive Council have been excessively lenient in connection with the continued activities of those members who, in our opinion, have abused their democratic rights.

We wish to impress upon the Executive Council our fear that if they continue to act with such leniency there is a grave danger that considerable harm will be done to the union. It is our view that the E.C. have displayed this leniency in an attempt to effect the greatest possible unity, but a continuation of the present undesirable atmosphere will make this laudable intention impossible.

The report was published in the *Minutes* of the Executive Council on July 18, and a copy was sent to the General Council of the TUC.

Slow as it had been in nerving itself to act against the ETU the General Council was not prepared to submit to having wool pulled over its eyes for ever. A résumé of its correspondence with the Union was published in its annual report for 1959, and having received the findings of the Committee of Inquiry it invited representatives of the ETU to meet it in order to "clarify" the various issues involved. The meeting was to take place after the annual Congress in September. To remind the General Council of just what were the issues involved—and to prod it a little—Les, Mark Young and Dick Reno all wrote letters to Sir Vincent Tewson, on different dates.

After listing a number of detailed complaints, Mark Young wrote:

I would say that this report [of the Committee of Inquiry] is an attempt to deceive the General Council of the true nature of the state of affairs in the ETU. Therefore, if at any stage the General Council require my appearance or evidence before them, I wish to assure them of my co-operation.

Les wrote:

Mr Haxell denies any interference by the Communist Party in the affairs of the union and challenges anyone to give proof to the contrary. This calls to my mind the occasions when General Council spokesmen have accused the Communist Party of holding fraction meetings of Congress delegates. The General Council spokesman, whilst stating what everyone knew to be an obvious truth, would nevertheless have had difficulty in proving it. Even if evidence had been available he would not have submitted it to a sub-committee of the Communist Party set up to inquire into the validity of the allegation.

One can well understand Mr Haxell's denial of this allegation. The consequence of admitting it would be to acknowledge that a direct majority of the Executive Council and seven of its eight National Officials have been over a period of many years in serious breach of the Union's rules. . . . It is because of the certain knowledge that Mr Haxell is denying the truth of this matter that I and others refuse to recognise this committee as anything but a mockery of an investigation. I don't know what would have been said if instead of the Lynskey[1] Tribunal, Sidney Stanley had appointed a committee to investigate corruption. . . .

I note from the General Council's report that the Executive Council has been invited to appear before the General Council to clarify the issues involved. I sincerely hope, in the interests of the Electrical Trades Union, of the trade union movement in general, and the speediest possible resolution of this matter, that I too shall be invited in the near future to present my evidence and to name my witnesses, to the

[1] A tribunal under Mr Justice Lynskey appointed by the Government in 1949 to investigate allegations that a certain Mr Sidney Stanley had corrupted various members of the Government and trade union leaders.

General Council or to any impartial committee it may care to appoint.

Dick Reno wrote as a member of the Fulham branch of the ETU, urging the General Council's intervention to clear up a situation which, as he put it, "is making a mockery of democracy written into the union's constitution".

Nothing came directly from any of this. As before, the "private" letters to Sir Vincent Tewson were not acknowledged, and neither Les nor Mark Young were invited to appear before the General Council. However, neither did anything come of the attempts by Haxell and Co. to clear themselves in the eyes of the TUC. The "Committee of Inquiry" was a transparent whitewash, and the General Council could not swallow that one. In its view, the ETU had the choice of two simple and straightforward courses of action to clear its name. These were:

1. To sue for libel newspapers or individuals making charges of irregularities against the Union.
2. To agree to submit to a "judicial inquiry" into the various allegations.

Haxell and the other Communists had no wish to do either. After a further exchange of correspondence, which dragged on until November, the General Council wrote (on November 25) saying bluntly that "the majority of the present leadership of the ETU" seemed more concerned to evade than to deal adequately with questions. The letter concluded:

In view of the evasive nature of the replies sent by your union's leadership in answer to the comparatively simple questions put to them, and their persistent habit of seeking to delay the General Council in reaching a conclusion, the General Council do not propose to engage in any further abortive discussions of this character with the present ETU leadership.

What the General Council meant by this letter is far from clear. It reads like the preliminary to some decisive action, such as suspension of the ETU from Congress. In the Byzantine politics of the TUC, however, immediate, decisive action was about the last thing probable. Haxell managed to delay things a little longer by suggesting that the ETU would bring a libel action against its accusers *if the TUC would pay for it!* The General Council dismissed this proposal, adding the uncompromising statement:

> The General Council have come quite firmly to the conclusion that the principal reason why the present ETU leadership has consistently sought to evade and delay dealing with the charges publicly made against them and which the General Council brought to their notice is because the present ETU leadership, who are in a position to know, are aware that there is so much substance in these charges that they are unwilling to have them thoroughly investigated and unable specifically and unequivocally to deny them.

In December 1959 Haxell had to stand for re-election as General Secretary, his term of office having expired. He was opposed by John Byrne. On February 7, 1960, the result of the poll was announced, giving Haxell a slim majority of 1,034 votes (Haxell 19,611, Byrne 18,577). So many branches were disqualified that there was an immediate outcry, with further accusations of ballot-rigging. The General Council of the TUC, now showing a spirit of collective anger, instructed the leaders of the ETU to appear before a committee of the Council to explain the situation. By this time the writs in Les's action for the restoration of his rights had been served on the Union and Haxell was able to secure another delay by pleading that everything was now *sub judice*. Les instructed his solicitor, however, to write to the ETU, sending a copy of his letter to the TUC, offering to forgo legal action if the ETU would accept the TUC's proposal for a judicial inquiry.

The General Council then issued an ultimatum to the ETU, giving the leadership until May 18 either to agree to a judicial inquiry, or to institute proceedings for libel against its accusers. Failure to do either of these things would result in the Union's suspension from the TUC.

On May 9, however, John Byrne and Frank Chapple issued the following joint statement:

> We have decided to institute proceedings in an attempt to redress the very serious grievances of the members of the union. We are mindful of the difficulties of the General Council of the TUC in the protracted exchanges with the ETU and appreciate that in the light of the lack of co-operation from the leaders of the ETU they might have no alternative but to suspend the union, leading to disaffiliation from the TUC in September.
>
> Unfortunately, this would deprive our members of the prestige and privileges of affiliation to Congress and would still leave all questions unresolved. We are proceeding at this stage because we believe that the very considerable and important issues involved can only be resolved in the High Court. We feel that the membership will understand that we are left with no alternative but to act in this way.

This was the opening move that led to the great trial in 1961. It put the TUC's activities against the ETU temporarily into cold storage.

XIV

JUSTICE

SEVERAL BOOKS COULD be written—and in time, maybe, will be written—about the events leading up to that statement issued by Jock Byrne and Frank Chapple on May 9, 1960. A detailed study of these events will concern social and political historians because they crystallise the countless individual actions of ordinary men and women that are necessary to preserve democracy. All such individual actions are based on the hopes, fears, ambitions, timidities, resentments and jealousies that are common to humanity; their sum is the preservation, or destruction, of society. It is a fascinating study, to be explored in detail when time has permitted that historical assessment of the motives for human action which cannot be attempted when many of the actors are still living. Here I cannot do more than sketch briefly the outcome of events which, thanks largely to Les's organisation and driving force and tireless sense of purpose, brought about the overthrow of the Communist conspiracy within the ETU.

Les knew all along that the chicanery and malpractice that kept the Communists in power in the Union could be defeated only by the Courts. With the Communists in control of the constitutional machinery, there was nothing to be gained from appeals within the Union, whatever safeguards there might appear to be on paper. Les had worked hard to try to secure the intervention of the TUC, but he had little confidence in its effectiveness. He explained his doubts in a long letter to his father. What good, he asked, would it have been to members of the Union for the TUC to suspend the ETU with all its problems unresolved, and with the Communists still in control? "This," he observed, "would almost certainly have been followed by a migration outwards of a fed-up membership, thus reducing our support, and an immigration of members from other unions sent in by the Party to rescue the Party from its difficulties. . . . This was not the road we wished to travel." And suppose the Communists had accepted, or seemed to accept, some form of inquiry that would have satisfied the General Council of the TUC? Les went on to answer his own question:

> The General Council would have had to clarify the terms of reference—whether the inquiry should affect other unions, would witnesses be sub-poenaed, would they give evidence on oath, could witnesses be cross-examined, could people whose interests might be affected by the outcome of the inquiry be represented by Counsel? These are just some of the questions that would arise. With the General Council meeting once a month and the ETU executive meeting once every two months, it is not difficult to imagine just how long these exchanges would take. . . .

To explain the ineffectiveness of the TUC, however, was one thing; to justify recourse to the law, which he had been brought up to regard as an arm of capitalist exploitation, was something else. As in his earlier relations with the Press, Les had to convince himself as well as others that the working class could properly turn to the law when its own institutions failed. In his letter to his father he put it like this:

> It is also necessary to take into account that all this has been a terribly unequal battle. Even the Press campaign, which has exposed a great deal of their [the Communists'] activities has often rebounded in their favour. . . . Individuals can't go on for ever battling against a machine with £1 million at its disposal, to say nothing of a fleet of cars and well-paid cadres all over the country. It has become absolutely necessary to face them on equal terms, and that can be done only by the action taken. Who are they to complain? Haven't the critics been brought up on a diet of Lenin which says (among so many things which I have found useful in this combat) that one must resort to legal and illegal methods.

Paradoxically, recourse to law in this context is the extra (ETU) constitutional (illegal) method.

It had not been easy to persuade the others in the "rebel group"—the loose Reform Committee that had gathered around Les—that writs should be issued against the Union to force an examination of their grievances in the Courts. Dick Reno was an unwavering supporter, but some of the others needed much persuading. Les had his own claim for restitution of his rights in the Union on the file—the claim which he had offered to withdraw if the ETU would agree to a judicial inquiry. But his own claim was not going to be enough. If it could succeed it would do no more than permit Les to stand again for election to union office but it would leave Haxell and Co. still in power. What was needed was a much more direct challenge to the whole ETU leadership. The election for the General Secretaryship in 1959 offered such a challenge.

But before this, in June 1959, nominations were taken for the post of the President. It became a straight fight between F. Foulkes and Bill Blairford—the Executive Councillor for Scotland. The result of the October voting surprised everyone: Blairford 15,261; Foulkes 18,000.

This was an honest ballot and only twelve branches were disqualified. It shook the ETU leadership to find that their most popular man, opposed by a virtual unknown, came so close to losing. They knew what to expect in the forthcoming election for the General Secretary, and prepared for it. For us it was good news and fine encouragement for the next and final stage of the battle.

Haxell had been elected General Secretary after Walter Stevens's death in 1954. The term of office was five years, so he was compelled to stand for re-election in December 1959. Had Les been free to stand he would have fought Haxell himself, but he was barred from standing, so his group had to find someone else. By this time the anti-Communists had learnt a thing or two—not least the experience that Les and his fellow ex-Communists had brought from their own days in the Party. They were determined that the anti-Communist vote should not be split—that there should be only one candidate to oppose

Haxell. There was much discussion on who this candidate should be. Les favoured Jock Byrne, partly because he felt that Byrne deserved the secretaryship after having been denied it in 1948, partly because he recognised in Byrne a dour Scots fighter, with a strong nucleus of anti-Communist support in Scotland. But not all the "rebel group" favoured Byrne. However, Byrne was a national figure in the Union, and Les's arguments won the day.

Once Byrne's candidature had been decided, Les and his friends went to work, visiting branches to secure nominations for Byrne and enlisting support for him in every way possible. Again Les went on his intensive travels, often covering two branches in one night.

The election campaign went well, and as soon as we began to get the first results of the ballots from the branches we felt that we were going to win—I mean, of course, we felt that Byrne was going to win, but Byrne's victory would equally be ours. Within two or three days of the opening of the ballot we had some fifty results reported to our home by telephone from friendly branch secretaries, "rebels" on the road, and other well-wishers. It was my job to record all these branch returns, for it was vitally important to know precisely how each branch had voted. By Christmas we knew that Haxell had been defeated. That gave us a very happy Christmas, and we took the children to a pantomime at Richmond.

Then we began to get news of odd happenings at various branches—of batches of ballot-papers, all voting for Haxell, being returned to branch secretaries before the members to whom they were supposed to have been sent could have received them. After Christmas we began to hear of branches being disqualified for alleged late posting of returns to Head Office, or other alleged breaches of the Union's excruciatingly complex rules. It was obvious that the Communists were beginning to see the situation as a desperate one, and it certainly appeared as though they intended to remedy it by taking desperate measures.

The result of the election was declared after a meeting of the Executive Council of the Union on February 7, 1960. Even the "official" figures were close—they gave Haxell 19,611 votes against 18,577 for Byrne. No fewer than 109 branches were dis-

qualified—the highest number of disqualifications in any
ETU election.

There was a scream of protest from the disqualified branches,
which maintained that their returns had been posted in good
time, and that they had otherwise complied with the rules. It
was this outcry which stirred the General Council of the TUC
to demand an explanation from the Union. The cynical merely
observed "The Communist Party has done it again". And, but
for Les and his "rebel group", the cynics would have been
right; the outcry would have died down, the ETU Executive
would have gone on stalling with the TUC, and the Communists would have remained in power. Les, however, had gone
into action, and although they did not yet realise it, the Communists were no longer in control of events. On February 8
our solicitor, Ben Hooberman, was instructed to go ahead with
the issue of writs against the Union. On February 10 he telephoned to say that he had submitted the papers to Mr Gerald
Gardiner, QC (now Lord Gardiner), to apply for an injunction. It was still to be some time before the machinery of the
law began to roll—as recorded in the previous chapter, the
Byrne-Chapple statement announcing the institution of
proceedings against the ETU was not made until May. But the
inexorable process that led to the downfall of the Communists
had begun.

I must now digress again to discuss our personal circumstances, which continued to be difficult. As 1959 went on Les
found it more and more of a problem to combine full-time
night-work for Hawker-Siddeley with his campaign against the
Communists. He was desperately tired, and inevitably he
sometimes missed his shifts. He was not sacked, but he was
given to understand that the situation could not go on. He left
Hawker-Siddeley for a rather more flexible job with a small
firm of electrical contractors, but it was not much less difficult
to combine earning a living with the carrying-on of his
fight.

He decided to try to get a non-manual job, which, he
thought, might leave him a little freer, or at least less physically
tired. Early in 1959 a job for which he was ideally fitted was
advertised—that of Assistant Tutor at the training college run

by the Electricity Council. He applied for this post, but no reply ever came—his application was not rejected, he simply heard nothing. A few weeks later the position was re-advertised. This must be conjecture, but it is not hard to suggest what may have happened. Frank Foulkes, as President of the ETU, was a member of the National Joint Council for the Electricity Industry. The Electricity Council would not have dared to go ahead with an appointment of which the President of the major trade union for electrical workers might be expected to disapprove. All the same, it was impolite to leave Les completely in the dark about the fate of his application. The Electricity Council could at least have rejected it.

On another occasion Les answered an advertisement for a job in the Work Study Department of a large firm in the electrical industry. Again he was well qualified, as his letter of application makes plain:

I am 39 years of age.

The details of my experience and qualifications are briefly as follows:

After a three-year scholarship at the Wigan and District Mining and Technical College, which concluded when I was $15\frac{1}{2}$ years old, I began an electrical apprenticeship. I continued part-time studies at the above college in electrical engineering. The war interrupted these studies just prior to my taking the ordinary national certificate.

Between the ages of 21 and 34 I had two occupations—that of electrical craftsman and as an elected Trade Union representative. At 34 I was appointed an Education Officer of the Electrical Trades Union and later as Principal of the Union's Training College. The College was closed in 1957, ostensibly due to lack of Union funds. During the past two years I have again been working as an electrical craftsman for reasons I would explain fully should you be so good as to grant me an interview.

As an electrical worker I was engaged mainly on new installation and maintenance. I have also worked on production and assembly, gaining first-hand experience of the problems of method study and work measurement.

From the age of 21 I have been consistently elected as the

representative of the people I have worked with. I have also been elected to the following Union positions:

At the age of 21—District Committee.
At the age of 22—District Secretary.
At the age of 24—Area Committee.
At the age of 25—National Executive Council.

I held the latter position for nine years before resigning to take up the post of Education Officer.

In addition to a vast experience of negotiations at factory level, including incentives and piecework questions, I have represented the Union on a number of important national negotiating bodies, including:

NJIC Electricity supply
NJIC Electrical Contracting
NJC Civil Air Transport
Air Ministry Whitley Council, and others.

I was also a member of the General Council of the Confederation of Shipbuilding and Engineering Unions, a representative at Central Conferences under the York Memorandum procedure, and a member of the negotiations governing women's wages in the engineering industry. I am thus very well acquainted with the agreements operating in this industry.

At the Union's college I lectured on the whole range of questions covered by industrial and human relations, and was the sole lecturer on Work Study.

My theoretical knowledge of Work Study dates back to a special course for Trade Union Executives which I attended under the auspices of the Imperial Chemical Industries in 1950. Since that time I have given the subject a great deal of personal study and have taken part in major national negotiations on its introduction in the chemical and other industries.

During recent years I have come to believe that the new techniques of management offer a solution to the main problems bedevilling industrial relations, and indeed to a number of our economic difficulties. Work Study, as one of the most modern instruments of management, has I believe, according to the wisdom of its application, great power to do good for the individual, for the economy, and for industrial relations.

Having always been able to win the confidence of workpeople, and having intimate knowledge of their apprehensions in their workaday life, I feel I could be of considerable assistance to your Central Work Study Department, either in the field or lecturing at appreciation courses to your workpeople.

I would be very greatly obliged if you could find it possible to grant me an interview.

Yours sincerely,

L. Cannon

References can be obtained from Mr. J. O. N. Vickers, M.A. He was my predecessor as Principal of the ETU College and has attended a number of my lectures on Work Study. Refs can also be obtained from Mr. V. G. Feather, Assistant Secretary of the TUC, and from Mr. R. M. Currie, Head of the Central Work Study Dept., I.C.I.

What happened in this case we learned years later. It so happened that the firm, which must remain nameless, was having a certain amount of trouble with a militant shop steward, who was of course a member of the ETU. It was hinted to the management of the firm that the ETU would disown the shop steward if Les were not given the job. Les did not get it.

He made a number of other applications for jobs, some to Box Numbers, so that he did not always know to which firm he was applying. All these applications came to nothing. By this time, of course, Les was well known as a "rebel" member of the ETU, and timid managements which had to negotiate with the ETU may have considered it safer not to employ him. We smiled wryly later when some of those same managements invited Les to functions as an honoured guest. At the time, however, Les felt bitterly resentful, and I shared his feelings. These experiences of rejection left a permanent mark. They did not make him vindictive—Les was not a vindictive person, and

With Hugh Gaitskell before a lecture at the ETU College, 1962

Les welcoming George Brown, the then First Secretary of State at the Department of Economic Affairs, when he visited the Union in order to meet their Executive on January 30, 1966 (*photo Daily Mail*)

Les, R. D. Roberts and Lord Citrine at the official opening of the extension for housing the computer at Hayes Court, 1967

his own experience of rejection made him, if anything, more sympathetic to others in like case. Later, when he had become President of the Union, an employer wrote to him about an application for a job from one of his ex-enemies in the ETU: Les wrote back supporting the man's application. But the experiences of rejection did, I think, add to his impatience in dealing with those who opposed him out of prejudice or wooden-headedness. He remained conscious of the indignities that he himself had suffered from prejudice, and he could not tolerate prejudice in others. He could be insufferably impatient at times, and this quality, which some people regarded as a kind of intellectual arrogance, I think really reflected the bitterness that he had had to endure from those who were weak, timid, or corrupt.

Unable to get non-manual work, Les soldiered on with his tools, spending his evenings and weekends visiting branches, rallying supporters, worrying at the Communist grip on the Union with a sort of bulldog tenacity. It was an appalling strain, and he was kept going only by his utter determination to win. Sometimes, as in the long-drawn-out exchange of correspondence with the TUC, the struggle seemed quite hopeless and his supporters were beginning to loose heart. But Les never relaxed his grip on events, and after the Byrne-Haxell election clearly saw victory ahead. Victory, however, was still a long way ahead, and between the decision to go to law in February 1960 and the actual issue of writs in May came what seemed at the time an endless series of frustrations.

This waiting period was enlivened towards the end of February by the appearance of Frank Foulkes on television in an interview with John Freeman in *Panorama*. The interview was Les's idea; he suggested it to Freeman, who went ahead at once with an invitation to Foulkes to appear. We learned from various sources that the Communist Party was doubtful of the wisdom of Foulkes's accepting the invitation, but that Foulkes himself was keen to take part in the programme, brushing aside difficulties by insisting that he, Foulkes, could handle Freeman.

The *Panorama* interview took place on February 22. To assist Freeman in his talk with Foulkes, Les spent most of February 21

H

with Freeman in his Hampstead flat, rehearsing the interview
—Les more or less acting the part of Foulkes. It was Les's
fortieth birthday, and I was angry that he should spend it
away from home. "Can't anyone in the world do his job
properly unaided?" I asked Les rather bitterly when he
went off to Freeman's flat. When I saw the *Panorama* programme next evening I forgave him. Freeman absolutely
demolished Foulkes. It was a superb piece of work—another
devastating showing-up of the emptiness of Communist pre-
tensions. But the Communists in the ETU had been shown up
before—by Woodrow Wyatt in his pamphlet and in his own
Panorama programme as far back as 1956, and in scores of
articles and letters to newspapers since. And they were still
firmly in control. Only the law could really shake them.

There were times when it seemed that the law would never
be allowed to move. Our diary gives some indication of the
tension we lived under. Here are some extracts:

February 23. Another meeting with Ben Hooberman (the
solicitor).

February 24. We saw a play, "Hostage". Les found it
shattering in its resemblance to the situation he was in.

February 26. Ben Hooberman visits Frank Chapple to
convince him of the need for a conspiracy action.

February 27–March 3. Les again visiting branches.

March 4. Discuss with Mark Young and Frank Chapple
the *nature* of the writ to be issued.

March 7–8. Les to Gloucester, Aston, etc.

March 31. Discussion with Frank and Mark on tactics for
next E.C. meeting.

All through these weeks people were constantly having
doubts—about whether we could win an action against the
Union, about whether our working-class supporters would be
upset at the idea of invoking the courts to act against a trade
union, about whether it was proper to employ "Tory Counsel".
Discussions went on and on. Les was rock-like in his determination to act through the courts, and he spent whole days stiffen-
ing other people's resolution, steadying waverers, trying to
dispel doubts. On April 8 there was a most helpful meeting

in Lord Gardiner's[1] chambers. Lord Gardiner was confident that an action could succeed, and strongly favoured an early issuing of writs. This did much to convince the doubters in our group.

Woodrow Wyatt was present at this meeting, and I should like here to acknowledge his part in our fight. He had been a staunch ally since 1957. The democratic Labour movement in Britain owes much to him, and it has rewarded him shamefully. Because he was steadfastly anti-Communist the Left wing of the Labour Party has always tended to sneer at him. But when we were desperate for funds to continue with the posting of our circulars and with visits to branches, Woodrow Wyatt helped. Before Jock Byrne and Frank Chapple were granted legal aid for their case against the ETU, Woodrow Wyatt found the money to pay their solicitor. These facts need stating. At a time when most "respectable" Labour leaders preferred not to know us, Woodrow Wyatt remained steadfastly on our side. After our victory, when Les became President of the ETU, it was astonishing to discover how many people had "helped" us. As Les himself observed, "They managed to go about it so discreetly that we never noticed."

In mid-April we took a brief holiday in the Cotswolds. We stayed at an old-fashioned pub—it was high in the hills, and freezingly cold.

At the beginning of May there was a sudden crisis. The ETU Executive decided to charge Jock Byrne with a breach of rules, and Byrne thought that this would probably lead to his suspension. He telephoned Les from Scotland to say that he felt it would be wiser to postpone the issue of his writ. Les argued that it would be better to go ahead with the writ, which should at least stave off any question of suspension by the Union. On May 4 Byrne came to London. There was another long meeting with the solicitor, and a terrific argument about the nature of the writ, and whether it should be issued. On May 10 Les wrote four words in the diary: "Writ issued at noon."

[1] At this time, and throughout the action against the ETU, Lord Gardiner was still Mr Gerald Gardiner, QC. He is referred to here as Lord Gardiner because that is now his title.

We were under no illusion about what this meant—it meant work, and more work. We had at last invoked the law, but the law can only act on evidence. *And our enemies had most of the evidence.* Nearly all the documents, the ballot papers, and the envelopes in which they were posted, were in the hands of the ETU Executive. Our lawyers could require what the law calls "discovery" of documents—that is, they could require the Executive to produce such documents as seemed relevant to the case. But that still left things very much in the hands of the ETU administration; documents can go astray, bits of paper may be lost, and always there would be opportunities for delay. So we had to collect as much evidence as we could ourselves. That meant more visits to branch secretaries' homes to persuade them to come to court and give evidence, of the posting of ballot-papers, of the conduct of the election, and of anything else that could help to prove our contention that Haxell's victory over Byrne was fraudulent. We knew what had happened in many cases; we had still to *prove* it.

Les set off once more on his travels. When the plaintiffs in the action—Byrne and Chapple—were granted legal aid there were funds available for the collection of evidence, and Les was formally employed to help, acting in the capacity of a clerk to our solicitor. He was given a letter addressed "To Whom It May Concern", stating that he was acting as a duly authorised representative of the solicitor's office.

It was desperately hard work. June saw Les in Eastbourne, Southampton, Woolston, Crewkerne, Exeter, Bideford, Totnes and Torquay. He came back home for two days, and went off again to Swindon, Cirencester, Gloucester, Cardigan, Swansea, Newport, Ebbw Vale, Yate and Bath. His next trip, again after a rest of only a day or so, took him to Liverpool, Prescot, Widnes, Rochdale, Kendal, Penrith, Silloth and Glasgow. Then came Seaham, Newcastle, North Shields, Bishop Auckland, Leeds, Huddersfield, Barnsley, Boston . . . and so on, and on. There was an immense amount of other work as well. In his lodgings, on his travels, and whenever he was at home, Les was at work with a little portable typewriter, typing out minutes of evidence, statements, minute details of individual breaches of the rules, instances of injustice, anything that he

came across to add to the weight of the case to be presented by
our lawyers.

In July Les's own action for the restitution of his rights
within the Union came up. It was not the trial of the action
itself—it was Les's application for an interim injunction that
was heard. He conducted his own case. It was a very hot day,
and everyone in court was perspiring profusely, particularly
the judge in his huge wig and heavy robes. But the judge
remained kindly and patient, permitting Les to speak for over
an hour. In the end, though with great sympathy, he turned
Les down. As this was a complex case concerning the precise
interpretation of the Union's involved rules, Les had not expected to win it. But he was boyishly pleased with what he
felt to have been his success in acting as his own Counsel. He
hadn't succeeded in getting the injunction, but he enjoyed
being a barrister! There was always a gallant optimism about
Les, even in defeat.

We spent a brief holiday that summer in Wales. Need I say
how we spent it? Collecting evidence.

After our holiday Les was back on the road. He became
terribly tense as the year went on, and our relationship was
under considerable strain. If I could have "gone home to
mother" at this time I think I might have done so. There were
moments when I felt I just could not go on with a husband who
never gave himself a break, and who drove himself continually,
doing about five men's work. But I had to accept that I could
not change Les; I was in the fight, too, and weary as I often
was, I was glad to be fighting with him.

The High Court decided to fix the hearing of the action for
February 27, 1961. In October 1960 our lawyers got from the
ETU the envelopes we had demanded—the envelopes which
had contained the ballot-papers rejected for alleged "late
posting". They were in a bundle, not in any particular order—
there was no reason why they should be. Les puzzled over them
for two days. I had 'flu at the time, and went to bed early.
Suddenly, in the middle of the night, Les woke me up with a
triumphant shout, "*I know how they did it!*"

It was a wonderful piece of detective work. Les had sorted
the envelopes in *geographical* order, and in studying the postmarks an extraordinary thing struck him—*they had been posted*

in geographical order! He made lists of the disqualified branches, with the dates on which the branch officials said that they had posted their returns. Here is one of them:

Peterborough	December	23
Boston	,,	24
Spilsby	,,	19
Brigg	,,	20
Doncaster	,,	23
Barnsley	,,	26
Huddersfield	,,	18
Whitby	,,	21
Darlington	,,	23
Bishop Auckland	,,	24

This is a random scatter of dates, as one would expect, and all the dates were within the proper time for posting off the ballot-returns.

But here is the same list with the dates of postmarks on the envelopes which the ETU produced.

Peterborough	December	30
Boston	,,	30
Spilsby	,,	30
Brigg	,,	30
Doncaster	,,	30
Barnsley	,,	31
Huddersfield	,,	31
Whitby	,,	31
Darlington	,,	31
Bishop Auckland	,,	31

All, as alleged by the ETU, had arrived out of time, and so were disqualified. *It seemed inconceivable that such a pattern of posting could have come about by chance.* Les was convinced that it had not come about by chance; he reckoned that someone in the conspiracy, to ensure the defeat of Byrne, had set off with a bundle of fresh ballot-envelopes and posted them from town to town as he came to them. This would have produced the necessary postmarks as evidence of late posting. By collating places and postmarks on all the other envelopes Les worked out three routes—north-east, west and north-west from London—by which the systematic posting of fake ballot-envelopes could have been carried out. The envelopes were official Union envelopes, printed with the address of the ETU's Head Office, so that, apart from the postmarks, there was no way of saying whether they had been posted genuinely or not. The geographical grouping of the postmarks was damning evidence that they were not genuine—the chance of such posting in geographical order having come about naturally was so remote as to be ruled out. There was one other piece of evidence about the ballot envelopes which was also damning. One branch secretary remembered having put his branch stamp on the back of the envelope he had actually posted. *This was the one envelope from disqualified branches which had somehow got lost and was never produced in court.*

Of all Les's work in building up a hard, legal case against the Communists in the ETU, I think his reconstruction of the ballot-envelope fraud stands out as a particularly brilliant piece of sheer reasoning. He had nothing to go on but a bundle of printed envelopes, yet he made those envelopes speak—and they told an ugly story.

In November Les acquired his first decent car, a cream-coloured Ford Consul. The boys, particularly Martin, went into ecstasies over it. As far as Les was concerned the new car didn't decrease his work-load, but it did make his long journeys slightly more comfortable. He continued to work day and night. One of the trickiest jobs that had to be done was to persuade people to be willing to give evidence in court. Most of Les's witnesses were ordinary working men, with an instinctive fear of courts and lawyers. It was one thing to tell Les about what had happened at and after branch elections; to agree to go to court and to submit to the ordeal of cross-examination was something quite different. It is an immense tribute to Les that so many people did agree to come forward and give evidence—somehow they just trusted him. But he didn't always win; sometimes a potential witness could not be persuaded to give evidence voluntarily, and in such cases, if the evidence was considered important, a subpoena had to be served. Les did most of this work, too, himself.

Then there was trouble from an attempted counter-attack by the Union, with a circular telling members that it would be wrong for them to give any information to our solicitors. This turned out to be a foolish move, for it was a clear attempt to intimidate witnesses and in December Haxell and Scott (then National Officer for the ETU) found themselves summoned before the Lord Chief Justice for contempt of court. The Lord Chief Justice held that it was a contempt warranting imprisonment, but since this would only have delayed the trial the court accepted an undertaking by Haxell to send out another circular countermanding the previous one.

At Christmas Les went down with a bad cold and lumbago, but on December 31, although his back was still hurting, he set out with Oleg to serve subpoenas at Sherborne, Yeovil, Reading and Bracknell. He did the round trip in a day but it was a long day, for he did not get home until a little after 10 p.m. Next morning (January 1) he set off for Southampton, on roads that were treacherous with ice.

So it went on. On February 13, a fortnight before the date fixed for the trial, the Union applied for a postponement, on the ground that it could not possibly get its defence to the action ready by February 27. The court granted a postponement, but not until June; it fixed a new date for the trial to begin on April 17.

At the very opening of the hearing before Mr Justice Winn, the Communists tried a new tactic. They instructed the leading counsel for the Union, Mr Neil Lawson, Q.C., to say that during the inquiries preceding the trial certain "irregularities" in the conduct of the Byrne-Haxell election had come to light. They did not admit that Byrne had been elected, but they accepted that in view of the "irregularities" the result could not stand, and that there would have to be a fresh election. Obviously they hoped that this might settle the matter—there would be a new election, they might even be ready to sacrifice Haxell and let Byrne win, but this would be a small price to pay in order to prevent the whole story of Communist intrigue and fraud from coming out in court. The trick did not work. Having come so far, Les and his fellow "rebels" were not going to be put off with any patched-up compromise which, even if Haxell went (and there was no guarantee of this),

would leave the Communist Party in control of the Union.
Our leading Counsel, Gerald Gardiner, argued firmly:

> What matters very much more, in my submission, my
> Lord, is the purpose for which the action has been brought,
> namely, that after due investigation in open court, it may be
> decided whether or not, as the plaintiffs allege, elections in
> this union have for some time been rigged—by which I mean
> conducted by fraud. . . . Before any further election takes
> place the plaintiffs wish (and on my submission to your
> Lordship on public grounds it is obviously desirable) that it
> should first be ascertained whether these charges are well-
> founded or not. Therefore, my Lord, I would now propose
> to open my case.

So the trial went on.

It went on for forty-two days. The papers and documents
brought to court weighed rather more than a ton, and nearly
1,400,000 words were spoken and recorded—they would fill
some fourteen books the size of this. It was reported throughout
the world, and a substantial book[1] was devoted to a brief
summary of it. The Communists, of course, were prepared to
discount the result of the trial if it went against them by claiming that they could not expect justice from a capitalist court.
To me, having knowledge of the workings of justice under
Communism in Czechoslovakia, the trial was an impressive
demonstration of the scrupulous fairness of a British court.
Early in the trial Mr Justice Winn said that he was not going
to allow the case to be regarded as a political one, and that he
was not going to listen to any anti-Communist arguments as
such:

> Let me make it clear [he said], I am not prepared to
> equate the word "Communist" with any kind of pejorative
> significance. It means no more to me than "Conservative"
> or "Liberal". . . . I am not prepared to have the adjective

---

[1] *All Those in Favour—The ETU Trial*, by C. H. Rolph, with a preface by
John Freeman (Andre Deutsch, 1962).

"Communist" used pejoratively, nor am I prepared to allow any attempt to be made to influence my mind to suppose that because a man is a Communist he is not to be believed on oath, or trusted to conduct affairs honestly and straight-forwardly.

Those were not mere words; if ever a judge was utterly impartial, Mr Justice Winn was in this case. He was concerned with whether or not there had been fraud in the conduct of ETU elections—whether the defendants were Communist trade union officials or capitalist company promoters made not an atom of difference. If Foulkes and Haxell and their chief lieutenants had been innocent of conspiracy and fraud, they would have been found innocent.

But they were not innocent. As the facts came out in examination and cross-examination they became more and more damning. Les's detective work on the envelopes produced some compelling evidence. The Barnsley envelope, it will be remembered, was late-posted, according to the ETU, on December 31. But the Barnsley branch secretary swore that he had posted it on December 26, and he gave a convincing reason for remembering the date—*it was Boxing Day, the shops were shut, and he had bought some cigarettes from a slot-machine when he went out to post the returns*. He could not be shaken.

The most dramatic moment of the trial was evidence of extra ballot-papers being ordered from the printer and sent to St Pancras station "to be called for", whence they were collected by the Head Office of the Union. What happened to the 26,000 spare ballot-papers? Mr Gardiner called for them.

"They are not being produced," replied the Counsel for the defence.

". . . their history must be accounted for, must it not?" asked the judge patiently; and later he allowed himself a little joke: "It may be they disappeared."

"Some unfortunate sneak thief thought they were Bank of England notes. We will see what the explanation is in due course."—We did. This was a vital piece of the jigsaw, building up the pattern of fraud.

Beyond the particular issue of fraudulent elections was the question of whether the domestic affairs of the Union were controlled by the Communist Party. There was plenty of evidence of the existence of Communist Party "advisory committees" through which the leadership of the Union was told what to do.

The trial ended on June 16, and Mr Justice Winn reserved judgement. Twelve days later, on June 28, he delivered his verdict. It had been a long and immensely complicated case, and the verdict was a judgement of some 40,000 words. As the judge read swiftly and unemotionally to the reassembled court it was apparent that we had won an absolutely decisive victory. The judge found that Byrne had won the election for the General Secretaryship by a majority of at least 1,150 and probably of the order of 1,500. But the scrutineers (who were acquitted of blame) were caused "by devices which can only have been fraudulent, including some forged votes, to make their return in favour of Haxell".

There was no doubt that at least some of the envelopes from branches disqualified for alleged late-posting had been re-posted fraudulently. Precisely who had done the re-posting was not established—it was not necessary, for all that had to be proved was that fraudulent re-posting had taken place. The judge said:

> By whatever means the substitutions which I have found to have been made were achieved, several persons must have assisted in the posting. It cannot be an essential part of the plaintiffs' case to establish positively the identity of each of those persons, for it would not be inconsistent with the general probabilities that the aid of the Communist Party network was invoked. Nevertheless, it was right that the defendants who gave evidence should have had their accounts of their own movements at the relevant time probed.
> Defendant Haxell was unconvincing to the point of seeming a sorry figure in the witness box when he was asked where he had been at the material time. I noticed a nervous grin and shifts of stance. Of course, he may have been embarrassed for domestic reasons, but certainly he was ill

at ease, though he must for a long time have foreseen that
the topic would be raised.

John Frazer, the Communist who had defeated Les in the
election to the Executive Council in 1957, also came in for
sharp suspicion. As a member of the Executive he was one of
the defendants in the case. The judge said:

> Defendant Frazer is, in my judgement, no less likely than
> Mr Haxell to have posted some of the envelopes; to do so
> would not have been alien to his character as I assess it.

There was also suspicion of another ETU official who had
not given evidence because he was ill. Evidence was given,
however, that this man drew substantial quantities of petrol
and expenses for travelling somewhere over the period concerned. Of this man the judge said,

> I refrain from finding against him in his absence more than
> that he may well have had opportunity to post some of the
> envelopes.

On the larger question of Communist Party control of the
ETU, the judge found tersely that "not only was the ETU
managed and controlled by Communists and pliant sympathisers, but it was so managed in the service of the Communist
Party and the ideas of the Party".

Although they figured only incidentally in the case, the facts
brought out about the election rigged against Les in 1957 were
of particular satisfaction to us. Foulkes's statement on television, that "even if all the votes which had been invalidated
in the election had been counted Mr Cannon would not have
won", had been a continuing embarrassment to us, and his
further statement that voting figures would be published "in
full" had also cast doubt on Les's claim to have won the
election. The trial brought out that the full total of disqualified
branches had *not* been mentioned in the Press, and that in
saying that voting figures would be published "in full" Foulkes
knew that the votes of disqualified branches would not be
included. The judge said of this, "I regard this important public
statement as a lie." Geoffrey Goodman was in court to hear this

said. At last his courageous story about Les in the *News Chronicle*
four years back was vindicated.

I do not wish to harrow the feelings of those still living by
recalling more of the judge's scathing comments in the case.
We had won—it was not in Les's nature to gloat on victory.
Four years of single-minded, and often single-handed, struggle
against the whole might of the Communist Party had ended
in a triumph. But the Communists had many ways of fighting
back. Les was conscious that victory on one front does not
necessarily win a war. He knew that there were bitter battles
still to be fought.

In May Les was aware that no matter what the result of
the court action was going to be, unless there was an organised
effort to oppose every Communist and pro-Communist sitting
Executive member at the next election, there was a real danger
that the old leadership would remain and would reduce Byrne's
powers to a bare minimum.

Throughout May and June he wrote letters to friendly branch
secretaries and active members all over the country giving
names of suitable candidates to be nominated at their meetings:

Dear Joe, . . . everything now depends on the Executive
elections. With the current degree of apathy it is not impossible for the same lot to be re-elected because the members
have not been following the proceedings closely enough to
know who is at fault. . . .

Dear Derrick,
    We are feeling quite confident that we can win a majority
in the forthcoming elections. One big effort just now and we
are there. We probably won't get another opportunity such
as this to bring about a change in the direction that the
majority of the members clearly want.

Dear Ned, . . . everything depends on the Executive council
elections. It would be the greatest irony if after such an
exposure they should get re-elected . . . and start the thing
over again.

Les wrote over fifty similar letters. In addition he and others travelled to various parts of the country at weekends to press this message home.

Unfortunately some of the best potential candidates for the Executive elections were banned from standing, and it was not always easy to find candidates who had sufficient experience and weight to win the election and to do the job well, if elected. In addition, one active and able candidate died suddenly of a heart attack, another withdrew because of his wife's illness. One candidate received the bare minimum number of required branch nominations.

At the June quarterly meetings many branches nominated candidates as suggested in Les's letters and we hoped that the publicity following judgment would alert the membership to take greater interest in the September elections for the new Executive.

XV

CLEARING UP

THE TRIAL LEFT the administration of the ETU in a state of extraordinary confusion. It must be remembered that it was a civil action. The plaintiffs, Jock Byrne, as the legitimate winner of the election against Haxell, and Frank Chapple, as a member of the Union's Executive Council opposed to the ballot-rigging clique, had asked for a judicial declaration that Byrne was the properly elected General Secretary, and for certain other reliefs to secure fair conduct of elections in future. Mr Justice Winn delivered his judgment on June 28, 1961. On July 3 he sat again to consider legal arguments about the various declarations and reliefs sought. On the main issue of the Byrne–Haxell election, the judge granted a declaration in these terms:

> The purported election of the Defendant Haxell as the General Secretary of the ETU was contrary to the Rules of the Union, was and is void, and was brought about by fraudulent and unlawful devices by the Defendants Foulkes, Haxell, McLennan,[1] Frazer[2] and Humphrey.[3]

He went on to declare formally that Byrne was elected General Secretary of the Union in December 1959 and he granted an injunction restraining Haxell from doing the work of any elective office in the Union unless he had been duly elected to it. This injunction was important, for Haxell had continued to act as General Secretary even while the trial was going on, and was listed as such in the Union's May Day

---

[1] Then Assistant General Secretary.
[2] A member of the Executive since his rigged election against Les in 1957.
[3] Then Office Manager.

advertisement in the *Daily Worker*—published during the trial.

There was much legal argument about safeguards for the forthcoming elections for the Executive Council, due to be held in September. Les and his fellow-reformers wanted them to be conducted by the Electoral Reform Society, a completely independent body which conducts elections for a considerable number of trade unions. But the Rules of the ETU did not provide for this, and the judge could not re-write the Rule Book. He was, however, openly suspicious of leaving the elections in the hands of the existing Executive.

> I regard the whole lot of them [he said] with the greatest suspicion, personally, and I don't think it right that the fortunes of a most important body of working men, forming one of the healthy cells in the body of this community, should be left for a forthcoming election in the hands of these individual men.

Finally, a rule was discovered which *did* permit the Executive to appoint people to do "administrative work" in an election, and it was agreed that the election should be supervised by an independent chartered accountant.

All these were civil matters—no criminal charges were brought against the defendants, and they left the court free to carry on with their lives. Haxell was deposed as General Secretary, but Foulkes remained President of the Union, and the Communists remained in power on the Executive Council. That situation would change at the end of the year when the newly-elected Executive Council took office, but the Communists had the best part of six months to try to restore their position.

The major difference was that the anti-Communist Jock Byrne was now General Secretary in place of Haxell. The first thing he did was to appoint Les and Frank Chapple as his personal assistants. This gave him powerful allies in the coming struggle with the Communist majority on the Executive, but it was not an easy position for anyone. Frank Chapple remained a member of the Executive, but Les was not permitted to

attend Executive meetings—he had to listen from outside the
the door. Byrne also acted by suspending the Office Manager,
J. Humphrey, whose name had figured in Mr Justice
Winn's declaration as one of those who had conspired with
Foulkes and Haxell to bring about the fraudulent election
result.

It was a strange experience for Les to go back to the offices
at Hayes Court, where once he had been such an active
member of the Executive Council and where, since 1956, his
name had been abhorred. Having been under Communist
control for so many years, the staff were bewildered by what
had happened, anxious, and in some cases resentful. Les was
received in utter silence. The over-riding task in that confused
period was to strengthen Byrne's hand in doing his job as
General Secretary, surrounded by the Communist majority
still remaining on the Executive.

The Communists lost no time in striking back. On July 10
the Executive Council met and the following resolution was
proposed:

> That the Executive Council is seriously concerned at the
> action of the General Secretary, Bro. J. T. Byrne, immedi-
> ately upon assuming office, without consultation with the
> Executive Council, in suspending the Office Manager, Bro.
> J. Humphrey, who is appealing against the decision of the
> High Court, and appointing as his advisers, Bros. L.
> Cannon and F. J. Chapple. The Executive Council cannot
> admit the union's members or staff to entertain a suspicion
> that staff changes are to be determined by patronage or
> prejudice. It therefore resolves (1) that the appointment by
> the General Secretary of Bros. Chapple and Cannon as
> personal assistants is not approved and is cancelled with
> immediate effect and (2) that the suspension of Bro. J.
> Humphrey, Office Manager, is cancelled with immediate
> effect, (3) that the General Secretary be instructed to notify
> Bros. Chapple, Cannon and Humphrey of the decisions
> affecting each forthwith.[1]

Byrne argued that the staff appointments and changes were

[1] Minutes of the Executive Council of the ETU, 1961.

the prerogative of the General Secretary under the Rules of the Union, and that the rights of the General Secretary in this respect had never previously been challenged. Nevertheless, the resolution was carried by eight votes to three—the three members of the Executive standing out against it being Frank Chapple, W. B. Blairford and E. Hadley.

This resolution was, of course, sheer impertinence. Whether the Communists even expected Byrne to act on it I don't know—they can scarcely have been surprised that he took no notice. The pending legal appeals complicated matters somewhat, for it could be argued that the findings against Foulkes, Haxell and the other members of the conspiracy were still not final, and that their offences must be treated as *sub judice*. But common sense could not be ignored; evidence given in court had been so overwhelming, and the court's judgment so damning, that appeals were not likely to come to much. In the event, they did not. Mr Justice Winn's verdict was decisive, and everybody knew it. Meanwhile, the Communists were determined to make everything as difficult as possible for Byrne and the reformers. Where they could not over-rule him they tried to take things out of his hands by setting up sub-committees of themselves to deal with matters that were formerly in the province of the General Secretary. At this time Byrne was far from well, and without Les his position would have been impossible. Les, with his iron determination and his encyclopaedic knowledge of the Union's Rules, managed to circumvent many of the Communist tricks. Les's own position continued to be extremely precarious; he was merely an employee of the Union, appointed by Byrne, and with all the old hierarchy bitterly hostile to him. He was still formally barred from standing for any elected office, and while the Communist majority remained in power this ban was not likely to be lifted. He was submitted to numerous indignities. He went to give a lecture at the ETU College of which he had once been the head, but he was refused admission to the College on the ground that he had no official right to be there. A number of Area officials of the Union held a meeting and passed a resolution demanding his dismissal from the post of personal assistant to Byrne. Through it all he maintained his customary cheerfulness and optimism, but we who saw him at home knew that the strain was telling on him. Les badly needed a holiday, but he felt that he could not leave his job even for a week.

In July 1961, barely a month after the judgment, the ETU held its policy conference at Portsmouth–Southsea. Foulkes chaired the conference. Haxell sat in the visitors' gallery. The rest of the old Executive was arrayed on the platform.

Foulkes's presidential slogan was: "Don't Retreat—Mobilise". To the Press he said: "While we are recouping strength, I ask the Press to lay off a little, report some of the fine achievements our organisation has been responsible for. . . . The solidarity for which our Union was renowned, the respect in which we were held by the employers with whom we negotiate [fancy that from a Communist!], which made possible our magnificent record of achievement—can only be restored by a determined effort"; etc. etc.

Yes, Les was right: they were not going to be unduly worried about the capitalist court findings. Had Les not been on the alert concerning the forthcoming Executive Council elections, they would have started "the thing over again", as he wrote to one of his friends in May.

The vast majority of the delegates mutely accepted most of the rubbish spoken from the platform. Only 11 of the 361 voted against a composite resolution condemning the leadership of the Labour Party under Gaitskell. This too is part of Labour history; those 350 present have nothing to be proud of.

Jock Byrne had to suffer the indignity of being relegated to speak on youth training and apprenticeships, but made good use of the opportunity.

Late in the day, the General Council of the TUC stepped in once again. The ETU trial (as it came to be called) and Mr Justice Winn's verdict had attracted enormous publicity, and it seemed a public scandal that Foulkes, who had been guilty in the 1961 trial, should remain President of the Union; and that others found guilty with him should still hold office in the Union. Foulkes and his Executive were summoned to the headquarters of the TUC and subjected to severe questioning before a committee of the General Council about what they proposed to do. The examination was conducted by George Woodcock, who had been Assistant General Secretary of the TUC and who was about to succeed Sir Vincent Tewson as General Secretary. This time the General Council presented an ultimatum with teeth in it. There were three demands: 1. that Foulkes should resign and submit to a fresh election for the presidency, 2. that the ETU Executive should rescind within ten days the decisions which had set up sub-committees to undermine Jock Byrne's powers as General Secretary, and 3. that the members of the Union who had been found guilty with Foulkes and Haxell of conspiracy to rig the Byrne–Haxell election should be barred from holding any office in the Union for five years.

Still, of course, in power, the Communists used their majority on the ETU Executive to reject these demands as interference in the domestic affairs of the Union. At the annual Trades Union Congress held at Portsmouth a few weeks later a resolution calling for the immediate expulsion of the ETU from the TUC was carried by a majority of some ten to one. The ETU delegation, led by Frank Foulkes, then solemnly marched out of the conference hall. Foulkes tried to put a brave face on things, waving to the platform, and calling out to that year's President of the TUC (Ted Hill, of the Boilermakers), "Au revoir, Ted."

Looking back, it is hard to see that this dramatic expulsion of the ETU four years after Woodrow Wyatt had first tried to get the General Council to intervene in the shameful Communist running of the Union, had any particular bearing on events. Had the TUC intervened earlier it is possible that a judicial inquiry would have brought to light at least some of the facts later revealed, after such patient and painful collection of evidence, in the High Court; it is more probable that events would have followed the pattern forecast by Les in his letter to his father—the Communists would have laughed at expulsion, and carried on running the Union as before. To a strongly established union, membership of the TUC means little, apart from giving it political respectability in the Labour movement at large. The Communists did not particularly need the TUC to preserve the Union that gave them such a commanding place in the electrical industry. Affiliation was useful to them as a cloak for their real activities, and to provide a platform for political resolutions; more important, it enabled the Union to remain affiliated to the Labour Party, facilitating the infiltration into the Party of members sympathetic to the Communist cause. None of this was vital. The Labour Party could be infiltrated through Communist cells in other unions, and in other ways. In a real sense, both the TUC and the Labour Party needed the ETU more than the ETU needed either; the Union's affiliation fees, one assumes, were valuable to the revenues of both bodies, and the existence of such a large group of well-organised workers outside the fold of the TUC would have been a constant embarrassment to the Labour movement. In time, expulsion, if vigorously maintained, might have begun to erode the Union—but it would have taken a long time, and the proviso is important. Once a union is expelled from the TUC it loses the protection of what is known as the "Bridlington Agreement" to prevent the poaching of one union's members by another. In theory, then, affiliated unions would have been free to recruit members from an expelled ETU. But this would not have happened quickly, and it might not have happened at all. Unless all other major unions agreed to open their ranks to receive members of an expelled union—an agreement most unlikely to be reached, since trade unions tend to be highly jealous of one another in matters of recruiting—the "carving up" of a long-established union is improbable. For one thing an expelled union may always mend its manners in some sufficiently face-saving way to apply for readmission to the TUC; for another, there are too many personal jobs at stake. One union cannot recruit members from another on any scale without taking in some of its officials, who know the trades concerned, and the complexities of agreements with local firms. And to inject a sudden influx of new officials into an existing career-structure can upset a great many people. This is always a major difficulty when even willing amalgamations are negotiated. In time, expulsion from the TUC would lead to a drying-up of magistracies and appointments to various public bodies which normally go to "respectable" trade unionists; again, this would be a long time.

The structure of the TUC is not designed for applying sanctions. Powerful trade union leaders like to invoke the collective voice of the TUC to strengthen their own industrial or political demands, but they are seldom prepared to listen to that collective voice when it suggests a course of action they do not themselves want to take. The General Council of the TUC is not a "cabinet" of Ministers responsible to anybody in particular. It is nominally responsible to Congress, but in fact it is an oligarchy of the chief officers of the major unions, each primarily concerned with his own union's prestige and power. Sometimes a man elected to the General Council may try to act—as Les did later—as a trade union statesman concerned for the well-being of working people as a whole above all sectional interests, but this is rare, and the influence such a man can exert is hedged by sectional alliances, and the often-conflicting demands of various powerful trade union groups. The history of the TUC's protracted and ineffectual dealings with the Communists in the ETU holds many lessons indeed.

The immediate effect of the expulsion of the Union from the Portsmouth Trades Union Congress was nil. The Communists retained their majority on the ETU Executive, Frank Foulkes remained President, Jock Byrne, who was daily becoming more unwell, decided to take a well-earned holiday, and Frank Chapple also decided to have a break. Les alone stayed at Head Office, with an organised pressure group against him, and with no formal powers to do anything. He had to try to act as General Secretary, without access to documents and correspondence. The Communist Party organised a campaign of angry letters from the branch secretaries, complaining that they were unable to get replies from Head Office.

After Byrne and Chapple returned, I did manage to persuade Les to take a week off. He flew to Jersey, to stay with some friends. They told me afterwards that he did practically nothing but sleep. If he stayed indoors after breakfast, he would fall asleep in a chair. If he went out for a walk and sat on a bench, he would fall asleep as soon as he sat down. He was in bed every night before 9 p.m. and slept through till morning. He was completely and utterly exhausted.

Les got back from his week's holiday in Jersey on Monday, October 16. He went to the office next day to be told that Byrne had not come in. Byrne, whose home was in Scotland, was living in very modest lodgings—so modest that they did not have a telephone. Les drove round to Byrne's lodgings to discover that the landlady had just found him lying in a state of collapse on the floor beside his bed. He had had a heart attack, and was gravely ill. Les helped to get him into hospital, and then telephoned Mrs Byrne in Scotland, who at once came down and stayed with us for a while.

Byrne's illness made the situation in the office worse than ever. Robert McLennan, one of the Communist old guard (he had been a member of the Party since 1926), was still Assistant General Secretary, although he had been named by Mr Justice Winn as one of those who "conspired together to prevent by fraudulent and unlawful devices the election of Byrne in place of Haxell". With Byrne in hospital, the Communist majority on the Executive appointed McClennan to take over. Frank Chapple, supported by William Blairford and Ernest Hadley, opposed the Communist majority, but they were normally out-voted 8–3.

On November 12 the Executive Council met at Hayes Court and the situation arising from Byrne's illness was discussed. A resolution that McClennan should be empowered to carry out the duties of General Secretary in Byrne's absence was carried by the usual majority of 8–3. The Press got to hear of this, and there were scathing comments in some newspapers. This did not improve tempers in the office. One result was that a visit which Foulkes said he had intended to pay to Byrne in hospital did not take place. Replying to Ernest Hadley at a meeting of the Executive on December 16, Foulkes said that news of his intended visit to Byrne "to discuss union business" had been "leaked" to the Press, and newspapers had put their own construction on the purpose of the visit, none of which was true. As a result of this atmosphere he felt it necessary to cancel his visit.[1]

[1] Executive Council Minute No. 22, December 1961.

A weird example of the Communist Party standing on its head also occurred at this meeting. The re-starting of nuclear tests by the Russians was much in the news at the time, and several branches of the Union had sent in resolutions which they had passed protesting against the tests. Chapple and Hadley therefore moved "That the sentiments contained in the branch resolutions be endorsed, and a protest made to the Russian Embassy against the re-starting of nuclear tests and the explosion of the 50-megaton bomb". One would have thought that the Communists would have been eager to protest against nuclear tests—but these were Russian tests. The resolution was defeated by the standard vote of 8–3.[1]

But time was now running out for the Communists. Les and his fellow-reformers had worked hard to secure nominations and support for anti-Communist candidates for the September elections for the Executive Council, and when the results were announced in December it was apparent that the anti-Communists had swept the board. From holding eight seats on an Executive Council of eleven, the Communists were reduced to two. The new Executive took office on January 1, 1962, and it acted at once to clear up the mess. Within twenty-four hours Robert McClennan was dismissed from the post of Assistant General Secretary, and all the decisions of the old Communist Executive intended to strengthen their position were rescinded. Byrne, although still far from well, was allowed out of hospital to attend this notable meeting, and it looked as if all was now set for a clear run to the achievement of all the reforms for which Les and his friends had worked so hard and so long. Foulkes, who was appealing against Mr Justice Winn's judgment, still retained office as President of the Union, but his power was clipped—he was now in a tiny minority in an over-whelmingly anti-Communist Executive.

Things did not turn out so well for Les—for him 1962 was to be another year of frustration. People do not always reward those who have fought for them, and this was very much the case with Les. He was respected as the main architect of victory over the Communists, but he was also rather feared. Some people thought him intellectually arrogant, and a number of men with personal ambitions of their own felt privately that

[1] Executive Council Minute No. 22, December 1961.

they would be happier with Les out of the way. The old sentence of suspension which barred him from Union office was rescinded, this being part of a complicated package-deal. Several legal actions against the Union were not affected by the outcome of the main trial, and were left outstanding. Les's action for the restitution of his rights was among them. Litigation of one sort and another continued for some years, but Les was among several litigants who agreed to settle matters out of court. He simply dropped his action in return for the restoration of his rights.

Les might have his union rights back but there was no job available in the Union that he particularly wanted. He continued to act as Byrne's personal assistant, but even here relations began to be a little strained. Byrne had recovered from his stroke, but it had left him anything but fit for the heavy duties of the General Secretaryship. Les was a tower of strength to him, but, in a way, he too resented Les's help. And there were men around him who were not above suggesting that Les was really out for himself, and that if Byrne were not careful he would find that Les had taken over his job in everything but name. Les became more and more unhappy. He understood perfectly well what was happening. Machiavelli's *The Prince* appeared on his bedside table and remained there for some time! Eventually Les asked to go back to his old job at the College. Everybody agreed.

Two months after the new Executive took office the ETU applied for re-affiliation to the TUC. The application was warmly welcomed, and it appeared that a long, unhappy chapter in trade union history had closed.

At the College Les concentrated on a course of lectures setting out the lessons to be learned from the ETU trial and the events that led up to it, and these lectures were of profound value in helping to restore morale in the Union. Les also hoped that they were of real value in warning British trade unionists in general of the dangers of apathy and of letting the Communist Party gain control of their affairs.

It was astonishing how effective the repetitive propaganda of the Communist Party, advocated by a handful of regular visitors at ETU branch meetings, had been. It still had an effect after years of exposures and after a court case, where those who cared could have seen for themselves the performance of the men who claimed to be superior to other trade union leaders in Britain. Rebecca West, when reporting on the trial, described her astonished surprise at the ineptitude of Mr Haxell in the box:[1]

> ... his evidence throws a bright light on the old fiction that the Communists may be unscrupulous but do represent the intellectual élite among industrial workers, and the theory that these particular Communists were left in charge of the ETU because they were of such pre-eminent intelligence. ... Not only Mr Haxell, but also his four friends, put up an abnormally poor defence, considering that they had had a lengthy period for preparation, and that the acts they had committed were those which sane men either do not commit at all or commit only when they have thought out an answer to the criticisms. ... There was a striking incongruity in the positions occupied by these men. They have not risen to a crisis which they must have long foreseen. ...

I felt this too. I was there most of the days during the trial and though I had no great expectations I was amazed at the apparent absence of intellect in any of them.

How Les could patiently explain again and again to the stream of students that they had been duped for years I will never understand. Somehow or other he had this wonderful ability to raise his sights above the basic mundane level and look optimistically into the future.

He planned a number of innovations. Among them were included an extension of the syllabus to take in joint courses for management and trade unionists in industrial relations. These were remarkably successful when they were introduced some years later.

But work at the College could satisfy only half of Les. His driving energy wanted to be back in the fight, to make trade unions in general, and the ETU in particular, more nearly

[1] In the *Sunday Telegraph*, July 2, 1961.

the kind of institutions that he felt they should be to bring
about a better life for working men and women. He might be
detached from the day-to-day running of the Union, but he
knew everything that went on. Experience had brought home
the truth of the saying that the price of liberty is constant vigil-
ance, and he was determined to remain vigilant. The loose
grouping of reformers which had gathered round Les in preparing for the ETU trial was reconstituted into a Reform Committee, with Mark Young as its secretary. The members,
several of them ex-Communists, knew that one setback, albeit
such a major setback, was not going to finish the Communist
Party. It might have lost control of the ETU, but its political
organisation outside the Union was untouched, and its cells
within various branches of the Union remained in being.
Given the lack of interest in attending branch meetings that is
the habit of trade unionists, in time the Communists could get
back.

Reform, however, was long-term work, necessary but lacking
the urgency and excitement of the past four years. Les was also
conscious of some dangers: he had fought to destroy a private
political empire within the Union; he did not want the Reform
Committee to develop into another private organisation to
control the Union's affairs. He could trust himself and his own
small group of allies, but his political instincts were rightly
distrustful of organisations within organisations. This, indeed,
is one of the major dilemmas of democracy in its struggle
against Communism and other forms of totalitarianism. The
"cell", the "fraction", the "group within a group" are Communist weapons to destroy democracy. Can democracy use the
same weapons to fight back? The problem is as old as
humanity: can Satan cast out sin? Democracy must *learn* from
Communist tactics; it must know, precisely, what it has to
fight against; but it must be ever on its guard to ensure that
one evil is not replaced by another.

In this time of anxious frustration Les turned, as he had
turned before, to study. He decided to read for the Bar. Lord
Gardiner recommended him for admission to the Inner Temple
and he set about "eating his dinners" and attending law classes.
Cicero and works on Roman Law replaced Machiavelli on his
bedside table.

1962 was a year of tension for Les, but with his salary as Head of the ETU College—in the proper grade this time, not fobbed off as he had been before as an Assistant, Acting Head— we began to feel slightly better off. The boys were growing up, and we thought that it would be a good investment to buy a cottage somewhere in the country that we could use for holidays. For £450 we bought a cottage in a remote North Devon hamlet.

It was extremely isolated, with no indoor water supply and no electricity, but it was certainly peaceful. In term-time, of course, the boys had to be at school, but when Les could get away from the College for a few days he would go off to Devon with his law books by himself. As things turned out, he never took his final Bar examination, but he sat for the examination in Roman Law and passed it creditably. For a man who had left school at fifteen, and with all the other things that Les had to do, this was a considerable achievement.

Although Frank Foulkes, among others, had been found guilty in the ETU case in 1961, there was a feeling in the Union that perhaps he had been less guilty than the others. He was an outwardly friendly man, full of bonhomie, and he had been exceedingly popular. To what extent Foulkes was genuinely unaware of some of the things that went on under Haxell's administration I do not know, and shall not attempt to guess. He always maintained his innocence, and the new Executive, feeling that justice had been done, was willing to make things as easy as possible for him. But Foulkes would not admit that he had done anything to apologise for. He wanted to appeal against Mr Justice Winn's findings about him, but he was refused legal aid to finance his appeal. The Executive, with remarkable generosity, then agreed that the Union would pay for his appeal. He did appeal, and the appeal went against him. After this there was no more that the Executive could do. It was impossible to have as President of the Union a man whose behaviour had been so condemned in the courts. Finally, in 1963, the Executive had no other course but to expel him from the Union. This automatically ended his Presidency, and made necessary a new election for the post of General President. Les saw his chance, and determined to run for President. To his hurt surprise, he found that many of his former allies were strongly opposed to his candidature.

Les was bedevilled throughout his life by an apparent
insensitivity to other people's feelings. It was not insensitivity—
few men have ever had a deeper understanding of the motives
of human behaviour, or a more passionate sense of kinship
with others, particularly with the great mass of working
people among whom by instinct, upbringing and conviction
he felt that he belonged. From his apprentice days his work-
mates had trusted him, and to the end of his life he inspired
trust. But he was always impatient to get things done, and this
often made him seem impatient to those he worked with. This
affected all his relationships, within his family and outside it.

To him and many others it was self-evident that he should
stand for election to the General Presidency of the Union. He
had worked for the Union since he was seventeen, he had
worked on the factory floor and in the Executive Council, and
he had spent five years in fighting to overthrow a tyranny that
was betraying everything the Union stood for. Les knew that
he would be an outstanding President—it did not occur to him
that anyone who knew him could want anybody else.

But other men—quite properly—also have ambitions, and,
as I have said, some of those who knew and admired Les were
also secretly rather afraid of him. He had such a strong
personality that others feared—not without reason—that they
themselves might be diminished by it. It was possible to make
a rational case against Les's standing for the Presidency. The
Union had been rent and torn by its troubles, and this was a
time for healing. Les had successfully led a revolution—it
would be better to have as President someone less clearly
identified as the enemy of all the Old Guard. Then there was
the College: all knew well enough how valuable was his work
there. Would it not be better for him to carry on as a sort of
Elder Statesman, educating and advising?

These arguments meant nothing to Les. He had not fought
and made sacrifices for five years to be an Elder Statesman; he
wanted to be in the thick of events; he wanted a direct say
in running the Union.

The Reform Committee was directly involved in all this
because it existed to ensure that the anti-Communist (non-

Communist would now be a better term) vote in important union elections was not split, and that there should be only one non-Communist candidate in important elections.

One of the reasons advanced by some of the reformers for opposition to Les's candidacy was based on the fact that Frank Chapple had been elected to the post of Assistant General Secretary in March 1963. He, Dick Reno, and many others who were in the fight with Les supported Les for Presidency. If some were afraid of being dwarfed by Les's personality and intellect, the thought of having Cannon and Chapple in harness running the Union seemed really frightening, or so they said.

At that time it was quite clear that the ailing Jock Byrne could not cope very much longer with the demands of his position and it was only a matter of time for the natural progression of Chapple into the seat of the General Secretary. Les and Chapple, although very different personalities, both undoubtedly were personalities, each powerful in his different way. Les was impatient with people who, he felt, ought to know better, but he had within him a mechanism which governed his behaviour, and though he might have felt anger he could generally control it. Chapple could be equally impatient, but his reactions were quite the opposite. There seemed, perhaps, some excuse for feeling that Les and Chapple would run awkwardly in double harness.

Whatever the reasons, and people's real motives are never easy to understand even viewed in retrospect and with detachment, at least five former supporters of Les, some men with no more experience than a job as a shop steward or branch secretary, felt sufficiently qualified, after a brief spell on the Executive, to stand at the head of the ETU.

The arguments went on and on, and Les and his associates left for the Union's first biennial delegate conference at Scarborough at the end of May with the matter still undecided. The nominations for the Presidency were to be taken at the June Quarternight Meetings. On the eve of the conference the reformers held a meeting which went on all night. Les called this afterwards, "The Night of the Cardinals". For hour after hour they discussed whether Les should stand, and, if not, who else should stand for the Presidency. Coffee and sandwiches were brought and finished, and still the talk went on. At day-break Les brought things to an end with a practical suggestion. "Let everybody stand," he said. "Let us all stand, and see what happens."

In the end three candidates stood. In his election address Les said:

Experience is one part of the qualifications required for such high office. It does not necessarily bring with it the very high skills required in modern negotiations. Those 3,500 students who attended the Union's College during my two periods as Education Officer, know the importance I attach to the development of these skills. For my part I have consistently studied economics, Trade Union History, industrial relations and trade union law since I was eighteen years of age.

I have done this because I think it wrong to the point of deception to offer oneself for such responsible Trade Union positions without taking all the necessary steps to equip oneself to meet the professional negotiators of Employers organisations.

Les was elected by a large majority.

XVI

ACHIEVEMENT IN POWER

IN SEPTEMBER 1963 the boys and I were trying to build a pool in front of our cottage in Devon, using stones from the old quarry in the forest, when Les arrived to tell us that he had won the election for General President of the ETU. The news was not exactly unexpected—indeed, the pool was our idea of a present to celebrate his victory. Our pool, I must admit, did not wholly match the triumph; after two weeks it started leaking badly. On the day itself, however, it looked quite impressive.

Les was supremely happy with the election result, and he took us out to dinner in Barnstaple to celebrate. My own feelings were mixed. I was happy and proud that he had achieved a position from which he could influence the policy of the ETU, and, perhaps, the whole of the British trade union movement; but somehow I had hoped that he would slow down a bit, and that we should be able to enjoy all the things that we were fond of, such as theatres, opera, art. For years I had participated in his life in a field which, if not exactly alien to me, did not reflect my own interests.

"I can't wait to start work," remarked Les during our dinner, and he proceeded to tell me of all his ideas which he wanted to carry out, looking two and three years ahead. I remember thinking, "Will there never be any respite from this wretched trade union business?"

Well, I should have known better. Les did not want to become President of the ETU because of an insatiable desire for power. Whenever he was asked if he were interested in power, he would reply bluntly, "Yes. One has to be interested in power, in the proper use of the word, if one is going to do anything. I am always wary of the man who disdains power, and spends half his life trying to get hold of it." Power, for Les,

Oleg on left and Les on right, with US Labour leaders, London, 1967 (*photo Jaski*)

Lecturing at the Esher ETU College, 1968 (*photo David Ross Studios, Hampton Co*

With Shirley Williams at the Esher ETU College, 1968

meant power to do good. From doing what he believed to be good he derived a total fulfilment.

For years Les had been away from us as often as he had been at home. Now, it seemed, there would be no end to his involvement. He would go on doing several men's work, with the same devouring intensity as he had shown over the past five years. But, as I have written before, I knew that I could not change Les, and knew, too, that I did not really want to. Clearly we, his family, would have to face his continuing absences, and all the other demands of his work. But there could be no turning back.

* * *

The pattern of this book so far has been chronological. We have followed the road from Wigan Pier milestone by milestone through the Communist years, through the years of revolt against the Communists and apparently hopeless struggle, to the triumph that gave Les a commanding position in his Union, and the entry to the industrial and political counsels of the nation. The chronological pattern will no longer do. A diary of the remainder of his life, brief as it was to be, would more than fill this book. It would record this committee, that commission, this lecture, a speech at that conference, endless negotiations, endless attempts to bring some order and common sense into the chaos of Britain's trade union structure and traditional forms of bargaining. We shall, therefore, depart from the strict chronological record and attempt to assess Les's achievements under separate broad headings—his work for his own Union, for the TUC, for the Industrial Reorganisation Corporation, and so on. This can be done only briefly. A technical account of Les's work would fill not merely this book, but a whole shelf of books—his written and oral evidence to the Royal Commission on Trade Unions (the Donovan Commission) alone makes a substantial volume. We must summarise, and select. This is not a technical book, and it can convey only an impression of Les's technical brilliance of innovation in collective bargaining, work study, and related matters. Specialists and students in industrial relations, in politics, in many fields of sociology will turn with increasing

I

interest to detailed researches into Les's work for many years
to come.

The Electrical Trades Union

Les was elected General President of the ETU in September
1963 and re-elected, with an absolute majority over his two
opponents, in 1968. His term of office in each case was for five
years; he did not live to complete his second term. He had,
therefore, little more than six years to carry through the
reforms on which he had set his heart. In those six years,
however, he inspired and persuaded the ETU to carry out the
most far-reaching reforms in rules and administrative structure
achieved by any union in British trade union history.

He was both helped and hindered by the circumstances in
which he and his fellow-rebels against the former Communist
hierarchy in the Union came to power. He was helped by the
fact that the old leadership had been shown up to be corrupt,
using and abusing the rules for private political ends. The
membership was disturbed and profoundly shocked, and thus
ready for reform. He was hindered by the fact that defeat of
the Communists at the top of the Union did not automatically
remove all Communists from the branches. These remained an
embittered, but experienced and vocal, minority, eager to
resist all measures put forward by the new, non-Communist
National Executive Council. He was hindered, too, by a more
general malaise in the Union. There had been such appalling
abuse of power by the old Communist Executive that some
members of the Union remained suspicious of *all* acts by the
Executive as such. There was a feeling, understandable in the
circumstances, that one dictatorship was merely taking over
from another. Such feelings had to be understood, respected
and soothed away. That strange quality in Les that enabled
him to inspire trust was helpful here, too.

Like many—indeed, most—of the older trade unions in
Britain the administrative structure of the ETU had never been
thought out; it had simply grown, a patchwork of expedients
tacked on to the original rules of 1889. The basis of early
trade unionism had to be geographical. Membership was small
and scattered in small pockets up and down the country; there
were no cars, travel was difficult and expensive, and a branch

could be formed only by members living within walking—or at least within bicycling—distance of the pub (it was usually a pub) that was their meeting place. Moreover, in those days almost all employment was local, and no manual worker could afford to live more than a walk, or short bicycle ride, away from his work. There were fewer skills; a craftsman was doing much the same job for whatever firm he worked, and there was a natural community of interest between men working in the same locality.

With the growth of industry and the technological and social developments of nearly a century, all this changed. Electrical skills multiplied and multiplied again—the needs and problems of the man working in a factory making television sets are by no means the same as those for workers in a power station. Yet the geographical basis of the Union remained basically unchanged. As the Union grew District Committees were imposed on branch committees, and then Area Committees were superimposed on the old District Committees, but real community of interest—the natural community of interest of men and women working in the same industry, or one large company—was ignored. Thus when a particular industrial problem came before an Area Committee it was quite likely that only one or two of its members would have any personal experience of the industry concerned.

Les had recognised for years that this structure was out of date and totally unfitted to the needs of the Union in relation to modern industry, and his Reform Group set about suggesting changes as soon as the new Executive that replaced the Communists took office. After the trial in 1961 it was clear that major changes were needed in the conduct of Union elections. A Rules Revision Conference was called in 1962, before he became President and while he still had to influence the Executive from outside, and a start was made in instituting reforms. The 1962 Conference agreed to take all balloting out of the hands of the Union itself and put it in the hands of the impartial Electoral Reform Society. A repetition of the ballot-rigging that had kept the Communists in office was thereby rendered impossible. The trial, and the events leading up to it, had also shown that the system of appeals within the Union, whereby the Executive was both judge and jury, offered scant hopes of justice to any member who was at odds with the Executive itself. This system was replaced by the institution of a Final Appeals Committee, composed wholly of rank-and-file members of the Union, whose decision on any appeal that came before it was immediately binding.

Until 1962 the Union held an annual delegate conference at which matters of general policy were discussed, and periodic Rules Revision Conferences. These were irregular and infrequent—between 1889 and 1962 there were only twenty-three occasions at which changes of rule could be discussed. This, too, was changed in 1962. The annual delegate conference was replaced by a biennial conference, and it was enacted that the agenda of every other biennial conference should include provision for discussing changes of rule. Thus there would be regular and known opportunities for reconsidering the Union's rules. No organisation can be effective if its rules are subject to constant change, but equally no organisation can be effective if its rules are so rigid that changes cannot be instituted reasonably promptly to meet changing needs. Opportunity for revision every four years was a notable improvement on the previous system.

The change from annual to biennial general conferences was only part of more fundamental changes in the government of the Union and, in particular, in the opportunities given to rank-and-file members to influence policy. In 1962 an entirely new form of conference was introduced. This was the National Industrial Conference, an assembly of delegates not from geographical areas, but from particular industries. The first of these industrial conferences to be held was for the electrical lift industry, and others early in the field included electricity supply, engineering and shipbuilding, iron and steel, and electrical contracting. Provision was made for adding other industries to the list, and over the next few years the range of special interests represented at these industrial conferences covered radio and television servicing, the film industry, Independent Television, the BBC, the exhibition trades, and paper and boardmaking. In addition, there were industrial conferences for members of the Union working for big individual companies. These included Courtaulds, the Ford Motor Company, Associated Electrical Industries, Massey Ferguson, and Standard Telephones.

It was arranged that these separate industrial conferences should be held in the years between biennial conferences. This provided a continuing opportunity for delegates from the branches year by year to influence policy, both on matters of special concern to the industries in which they worked, and on the general affairs of the Union.

All this was no more than a start. The most far-reaching reforms, creating effectively a New Model Union, were introduced (after Les had become President) in 1965. He prepared the way very carefully. In 1963 he wrote and circulated a long document for discussion, setting out the form of structure that he considered most suitable for the Union. Briefly, he argued that the old, sprawling, horizontal structure should be replaced by a line organisation, with direct links between the biennial delegate conference, the Union's supreme authority, and the man on the job through a series of industrial groups, each having a sub-committee of the Executive Council for itself. Changes began with the branch. Wherever possible (obviously this could not apply in all areas) the old, purely geographical branch was to be replaced by an industrial branch, grouping the members working in particular local industries, or big firms, in branches sufficiently large to permit the employment of a full-time elected branch official, who would be able to specialise in matters of particular concern to each branch. Policy would be co-ordinated, again industry by industry, through meetings of Area shop stewards, Area industrial conferences and National industrial conferences, all this work being the direct concern of the appropriate industrial sub-committee of the National Executive. This required two more major changes: making membership of the Executive Council a full-time, salaried job, and extending the term of elected office from two years to five. It also meant the complete abolition of the old, geographical Area Committees.

Any tinkering with the organs of democracy, however badly they may work, is bound to provoke opposition. On paper, what could be more democratic than unpaid Executive Councillors elected for only two years at a time? In practice, what could be less efficient? A man elected for only two years has to spend half his time electioneering if he wants to stay in office; he has no time to master his job before the next election is upon him.

And while in theory an unpaid Executive has all the merits of disinterested service to the community, in practice a man has to live; if he spends any material amount of time on union business (and if he is to be any good as an Executive Councillor he must spend a great deal of time) he can only recoup himself by drawing as much as he can in delegation fees, travelling expenses and the like—an evil system which has plagued trade unions for too long. Les's reforms demanded a full-time National Executive, but it was not easy to get people to understand this.

There was no place for the old Area Committees in Les's proposed line-organisation, but these threatened committees had their friends, who genuinely believed in them. At the same time they had long been cherished by the Communists as convenient stepping-stones to local power in the Union, which could be used to thwart the policies of the non-Communist National Executive. When the Communists realised that the Area Committees were likely to be abolished they went into action, and the Party issued a document entitled *Amendments to Rule* which was circulated round the branches. It listed a number of amendments to the rules in preparation for the 1965 Rules Revision Conference. Some 243 proposed amendments were sent in by the branches, and when these were examined it was found that ninety were either worded precisely as in the Communist Party document, or so thinly disguised that they had clearly been taken from it.

This Communist counter-attack called for decisive action to meet it. The Executive Council considered the situation and concluded that "there has been outside interference by the Communist Party in the internal affairs of the Electrical Trades Union, calculated to determine a substantial part of the agenda of the Rules Revision Conference". It was then decided to conduct a ballot on whether members of the Communist Party should be eligible for office in the Union. This question was decisively answered in October 1964 by a vote of 42,187 to 13,932 in favour of banning Communists from holding office. Existing office-holders were then given three months in which to comply—that is, those officers of the Union who were members of the Communist Party had to choose between resigning office or resigning from the Party. Two full-time officials in the London area decided to resign their posts, but by January 1965 they had changed their minds, and the election to replace them was called off.

There was no persecution—rather, the whole matter was handled in keeping with the British tradition of fair play and of gentlemen's agreements. Originally, it was felt that it would be necessary for members of the Communist Party who wished to stay in office to make individual declarations that they no longer belonged to the Party. Then it was decided that they should be required simply to advise the Executive Council whether they were disqualified from continuing to hold office as a result of the new rule. This generous attitude on the part of the Executive undoubtedly saved much heartburning. The former Communist Party members who stayed in their posts appeared to be quite happy with their lot. Some of them probably felt a genuine relief to be free of the burden of being Party members.

While all this was being settled, Les's paper on the reorganisation of the Union, which had been recommended for discussion by the Executive in 1963, was being studied and discussed. It was printed in the Union's journal, and hundreds of branch, district and area meetings were held at which the proposals could be criticised, and doubts discussed and explained. Les felt that never before, in any trade union, had the members had so much opportunity for democratic discussion of proposals affecting their future.

In his presidential address, opening the vital 1965 conference, Les said:

We now have probably a once and for all chance to reform the internal structure of the union. If we fail in this task, we fail in all the great possibilities before us. . . . Delegates know that the new leadership took office in the least fortunate circumstances, and have succeeded in a short space of time in restoring the name of our union in the eyes of everyone. Indeed, more so—our union is held in greater respect than ever before. What is not so widely known is that in addition to the publicly-exposed scandals we also inherited organisational stagnation and maladministration which has stunted the growth and development of the union. . . . We live at a time when every thinking person in the country is anxious to see Britain modernised as quickly as possible. Governments will be elected or rejected depending on the fulfilment of their pledge to do just this. Every man in this conference shares this view, surely. But for Britain to be modernised it means not only our economy, but our ideas and our institutions, including the trade union movement. One of the most important organisations in the country is the union which organises workpeople in the electrical, electronic and telecommunication industries. So many people are all for modernisation except when it affects themselves. But I am confident that in this critical moment of the union's history this conference will show that when it speaks of the new modern Britain it recognises the need for a new modern electrical workers' union.

His confidence was justified. After a long debate on the abolition of the Area Committees and a speech from him which he described as "one of the best I have ever made", the reforms were approved and adopted. Pointing out that there were now tens of thousands of jobs in the electronics industry but that no trade union in Britain had the name "electronic" in its title, he also succeeded in getting the name of the Union changed to "The Electrical, Electronic and Telecommunication Union".

A sad accompaniment to the events of this important year of 1965 was the continued ill-health of Jock Byrne. He had never been really well since he took office after the trial, and at the beginning of 1965 his doctors advised him that he was in need of immediate rest. He was offered six months' leave of absence, which he accepted. In the autumn he was still not well, and his sick-leave was extended. Towards the end of January 1966 he wrote to the Executive Council saying, "The fact of the matter is that the improvement in health which I had hoped for, and which would have enabled me to resume my duties, has not been obtained. I therefore, regretfully, advise the E.C. that I desire to relinquish office on the grounds of ill-health." Sadly, his resignation from the General Secretaryship had to be accepted. Four years later—in February 1970—he died. Success came to him too late.

In September 1966 Frank Chapple became General Secretary of the Union.

Given the framework of his New Model Union, Les set about making it work. Such a radical transformation of a human institution that had been living and forming habits and traditions for over three-quarters of a century was an immense task, but he and the colleagues who worked with him succeeded wonderfully well. By the time of his death the EETU and the Plumbing Trades Union, with which it amalgamated in 1967, was the most efficient trade union organisation in Britain. And efficiency was not accompanied by any loss of democratic control—rather, the New Model unionism gave a greater say to individual members than they had ever had in the past. Of course, all this was not the work of Les alone. He had able colleagues, but no one would question that the inspiration and drive came from Les.

With the reforms to the Union's structure, a recruiting campaign was instituted which substantially increased membership. The administrative side of the Union was steadily tidied up and improved. On discovering that it took several people several days to establish just how many members the Union had on any given date, a computer was installed to handle membership records and other statistical work. It soon paid for itself, because the Union was able to lease computer-time to other bodies. Les and the new Executive also carried out a major reconstruction of the Union's finances. With the help of an able accountant a new investment policy was introduced, substantially increasing the value of the Union's funds.

None of these activities lessened Les's interest in education, and to the end of his life he maintained close links with the College at Esher. The change of rules in 1965 allowing for the employment of more full-time branch officials meant even more emphasis on training, and the work of the College was adapted to meet this need. Courses in work study were introduced in

1963, and three years later, regular joint courses for trade unionists and representatives of management. Whenever a new agreement was signed Les always tried to arrange for the company concerned to send representatives to a joint course at Esher to study precisely how best to work it out, and to discover in advance any snags that might be met in practice. These courses represented a wholly new conception of trade unionism, and were of inestimable value to shop stewards, management and all concerned in making agreements work. Les usually gave up part of his Sundays to the College to address new courses as they assembled, and he would spend a weekday lecturing, if he thought a course particularly important.

Comparison of average weekly earnings from decade to decade is at best a rough guide to living standards, because so many other factors have to be taken into account. But a comparison of earnings in the Electricity Supply Industry in the last four years of Communist control of the ETU (1958–61) with earnings in the comparative period (1968–71) after Les's reforms is interesting. Taking an index figure of 100 for the average weekly earnings of adult males in 1958, the index figure in 1961 had risen to 121·4, an increase of 21·4 per cent Between 1968 and 1971 the index rose from 164·2 to 243·4, an increase of 48·2 per cent.[1] Inflation must, of course, be taken into account in comparing these figures; even so, the relative improvement in the lot of electrical workers under non-Communist leadership is marked.

Engineering and Shipbuilding

The ETU (now the EETU) has members in virtually every industry in Britain and is constantly concerned in negotiations involving a number of other unions. Multi-union negotiations are a particular problem in the engineering and shipbuilding industries, where the unions concerned are grouped in the Confederation of Shipbuilding and Engineering Unions (CSEU). Les considered—and many would agree with him—that this vast conglomeration dealing with the wages and

[1] Figures from Electricity Council Industrial Relations Department and *Status, Productivity and Pay* by Sir R. Edwards and R. D. V. Roberts.

conditions of roughly one-fifth of the nation's working population, in situations as diverse as small workshops employing a handful of men and the great motor factories and shipyards, works extremely badly. The Confederation is supposed to promote common action, but communications between officials and members vary from union to union, there is never enough money for adequate research and secretarial work, and the complexity of agreements, with all the difficulties of interpreting them in diverse situations, frequently leads to trouble. These difficulties are compounded by a similar federation on the employers' side, ostensibly uniting all engineering employers from one-man businesses to gigantic companies. Les gave a great deal of thought to improving things, and submitted detailed proposals to the Royal Commission on Trade Unions. He tried hard, too, to persuade the other unions involved to consider reforms. A few of his ideas have been carried out but many, alas, have not, and the engineering industries remain in a kind of trade union jungle. His ideas, however, are on record in the Proceedings of the Royal Commission, and in his own voluminous memoranda and articles, and they may yet inspire others to promote reform.

Les was instantly sympathetic to Mr (Lord) George Brown's attempts in 1966 to rescue Fairfield's Shipyard on the Clyde by forming a consortium of Government, private industry and the unions to inject fresh capital. The ETU agreed to provide £50,000 towards the venture. A special course on how work study and critical path analysis could be applied to the shipyard was arranged at the ETU College, and attended by representatives of management and of all the thirteen trade unions involved in shipbuilding.

Wage Bargaining

Les was a hard bargainer, but he wanted a bargain, not a killing. He wrote,

There are conflicts within industry. Where these are damaging to the interests of both parties they should be eliminated, if at all possible. It is neither possible nor desirable, however, to eliminate all conflict. Conflict properly contained can be creative. The aim of a good system of industrial relations is not to blur the lines of conflict, but rather to contain it within an institutional framework, so that it may be fought out without spilling over into other areas. Almost by definition, employers and employees cannot have an identity of views on every subject. Clearly there are many things on which they ought to be, and indeed are, united. On other matters they must differ. It is our contention that the tensions created by these differences are both healthy and creative. A balance must be kept between employers and employees. If this balance is lost it will, in the first instance, clearly be against the interest of whichever party is placed at a disadvantage. In the long run, however, it could easily be destructive of both parties.[1]

He believed that the organisation of human work is generally inefficient; that it is nearly always possible to find a better way of doing things; and that the better organisation of work is not only more profitable in the sense of producing higher earnings and increasing productivity, but more satisfying to those who have to do the work. This was the basic philosophy behind his approach to all wage negotiations. The result was that virtually all his wage settlements were true bargains, in that his members got more pay and that management—and the community— got higher productivity for that pay. He was never afraid of innovation. In 1966 a remarkable agreement was made for the Electrical Contracting Industry, doing away with the traditional but somewhat nebulous status of "electrician's mate" and providing for a recognised system of grading for all workers in the industry. Men with five years' experience were up-graded to "Approved Electricians", mates with four years in the industry became "Electricians" and those with less than four years could become "Trainee Electricians" with up-grading to "Electrician" after two years' training. Rates of pay were agreed for each grade, and any employer violating the agreement was liable to a fine of £1,000, to be imposed by the Joint Industry Board (with equal representation of employers

[1] Written evidence to the Royal Commission on Trade Unions.

and the Union). It was also agreed that an employee persistently violating the agreement could become liable to a fine of £100. This somewhat startling clause provided opponents of the non-Communist leadership of the Union with much ammunition for misrepresentation and abuse. In the Union's Journal for November 1967 Les replaced the usual editorial with an open letter on the subject. In this he wrote:

> Much has been made of the £100 fine. . . . It could only happen in the event of an individual over a long period of time repeatedly organising resistance to the agreements, organising unofficial strikes, refusing to follow the procedure of the industry and thus defeating the whole object of the agreement to bring radical improvements in pay and conditions based upon increasing efficiency in the industry. The members, I feel sure, will not be prepared to give up the enormous benefits in this agreement in order to protect the odd person out of 60,000 who is bent on destroying the procedures and the benefits. Moreover, it must be understood that the major addition to this disciplinary procedure which our members have constantly urged us to achieve—namely, that employers should be disciplined in the event of their violation of the agreement—will be lost, for if the discipline provided for a handful of people in the industry were to be removed, then, at the same time, the heavy discipline against employers violating the agreement must also be removed.

Courage and imagination paid off. That agreement turned out to be of immense benefit to everybody in electrical contracting.

Les became Chairman of the trade union side of the National Joint Council for the Electricity Supply Industry in 1967. Mr R. D. V. Roberts, chief negotiator of the Central Electricity Generating Board, writes of him:

> Although we were engaged in an activity where protocol required that we speak from a different standpoint, our basic philosophies were very similar, and had, at their centre, the

dignity of the working man and a burning desire that he should not be exploited by opportunists in either the political or the economic sense. The similarity of our philosophies did not become at once apparent to each other, but evolved in the course of some interesting, and, from my point of view valuable, intellectual swordplay that took place on issues which were related to the Electricity Supply Industry. This was the beginning of a deep and lasting personal friendship, based on a meeting of minds but which, in my case, soon became submerged in a sense of admiration, which was related to the highest reaches of human courage. For me, he was like some comet; once one had developed an intellectual relationship with him one could never really be the same again.

A study of Les as a negotiator, by Mr Roberts, from which this extract has been taken, will be found in Appendix I at the end of this book.

The Industrial Reorganisation Corporation

In 1966 Les was invited by Mr George Brown, then Minister of Economic Affairs, to become a part-time member of the board of the IRC. This was an assignment close to his heart, and he approached it with a kind of passionate realism which was extremely valuable to the Corporation. Professor W. G. McClelland, who served with him on the board, writes:

Les made a great impression on me, as on others, through his integrity and commitment and also through the intellectual power and mature judgement embodied in what he had to say. Time and time again in Board discussions his contribution provided the rounded appraisal or key consideration which showed us all the way we had to go, and the respect in which his depth of knowledge and his judgement were held by his colleagues who were "Captains of industry" was quite evident. Without looking back over the files, I am not sure that I can quote particular examples of this but of course the range of industries of which he had first-hand knowledge through the employment in them of ETU members was vast and included some with particularly knotty problems, such as Nuclear Power. His insight into the situation and problems of top management, his ability to appraise their calibre in particular cases, and his sense of what was appropriate or inappropriate organisationally, were all impressive.

His special contribution to IRC included, of course, a special concern for questions of redundancy and consultation with the Unions. Whilst he was realistic about cases of over-manning and non-viability Les never allowed the Board to forget the special considerations that applied in the case of regions with high unemployment. You ask about his role vis-à-vis his trade union colleagues. I was not myself present when the TUC General Secretary and others came to lunch at Pall Mall, but I know that there was a general disposition, both on the part of the IRC Board and Managing Director and on the part of the TUC, to ensure effective consultation and collaboration. I think indeed some "ground rules" were drafted which recognised the impossibility of advance information about confidential negotiations. I don't think Les was or would have wished to be in any way the sole link or initiator on this front, but his advice and good offices were highly valued on the IRC side. Where he did render enormous service to IRC was in defending its desira-bility and orientation and record publicly at one (at least) of the TUC Annual Conferences. I might say that I was present at his last appearance at the NEDC when we were discussing the measures introduced by the new Conservative Govern-ment in the late summer of 1970. His attack on the decision to axe the IRC was enormously powerful. The Chancellor and John Davies visibly wilted under it and really had nothing to say in reply. Les told me afterwards that he had made no notes for this contribution, but that did not stop its being a masterly performance.

Particularly in the first year or so of IRC's existence, Les and I were thrown together somewhat with each other and Frank Schon, as a result of the latter's initiative.... We three were those most clearly committed to a radical line. Les's contributions to these discussions were penetrating but balanced and realistic. At that time, though IRC was to some extent still feeling its way, there was emerging in the Board a clear difference of opinion between those who preferred a cautious approach and those who favoured a more active, interventionist, and necessarily controversial one. After some months of this Les made a very significant contribution at one Board meeting, the nub of which was, so far as I remember it: "We have to decide whether to be hawks or doves and I for my part am a hawk." One by one other weighty members of the Board, each in his own way, supported him and I think that was a real turning point for IRC and perhaps Les's single most significant contribution.

Les had great courage and honesty. At the same time he had an acute sense of the long-term adverse repercussions of non-egalitarian steps which might seem to be justified in the short term. I have in mind matters like the salary and taxation arrangements that might be necessary to get first class executives into the right places. . . . The IRC administration generally lined up with the high ability/high pay equation of merchant banking circles rather than manufacturing industry. Les was in a minority in respect of some IRC executive salary increases but he made his witness. In respect of the remuneration of Board members he made a similar egalitarian witness but qualified it by reference to the amount of work required of Board members compared with that from part-time members of electricity boards. On one further Socialist issue he carried his point that IRC should not give financial assistance to a private company without an undertaking that it would go public within a definite term of years.

The TUC

Les was elected to the General Council of the TUC in September 1965. It was a dramatic election. The Council is composed of representatives of industrial groups or sections—mining, railways, textiles, etc. Candidates are nominated by the unions within each section, but voting is by the Trades Union Congress as a whole, so that (in theory) the Council is fairly representative both of certain industries and of the trade union movement as a whole. With industrial change over the years, the structure of the Council is liable to become unbalanced, with declining industries over-represented and developing ones under-represented. Since the Second World War the main growth of trade unionism has been among non-manual workers and in the technological industries, most of which barely existed when the TUC was established. In 1965, to cater for the affiliation of the National and Local Government Officers' Association, and the rapidly expanding electrical trades, the General Council proposed two new "constituencies", one giving an additional place to unions representing Public Employees, and the other creating a new industrial group for electricity.

The ETU was already the sixth largest trade union in Britain, and its claim to be represented on the General Council was obvious. But the domestic politics of the TUC are not simple. There are delicate alliances to be maintained, and the most powerful unions are reluctant to see their power in any way diminished. Les was naturally a candidate for the new electricity section, but the great Transport and General Workers Union preferred to put its voting strength behind a nominee from another union, the Engineers, Firemen and Electrical Workers, which is an affiliate of its own. Two other giant unions, the Amalgamated Engineering Union (now joined with the Foundry Workers) and the National Union of Mineworkers, decided to vote with the TGWU. These decisions are taken at pre-Congress delegation meetings and students of political arithmetic can usually forecast pretty accurately how elections for the General Council are going to turn out. There was a third candidate, from the relatively small Electrical Power Engineers' Association, but he was not, as it were, a front runner. The chief contestants were Les and the candidate favoured by the TGWU and its allies. It seemed inconceivable that a man with the votes of the TGWU, the AEU and the NUM behind him could be defeated, and it was generally pre-dicted that Les was out.

When the card votes were counted, however, Les was in. His majority (about 600,000 in a card vote of several millions) was fairly narrow, but it was decisive. Alone of the giants, the National Union of General and Municipal Workers voted for him, and the rest of his vote came from numerous smaller unions, who saw in him a counter to the entrenched forces on the General Council. It was a remarkable triumph.

Les had only five years left to live—not a long time to play himself into the complex power-groupings on the General Council. Many of his colleagues were, perhaps, a little afraid, and a little suspicious, of him. He remained a somewhat isolated figure, but his influence grew and, had he lived, it would have become more profound. He was one of the very few trade union leaders who understood the creative aspects of Labour's economic policy in the sixties and he gave unstinted support to Labour's National Plan—the great constructive effort of the Labour Government of 1964–66, which became a casualty in 1967 with the demise of the Department of Economic Affairs set up to carry it out. After devaluation in 1967 and the winding up of the DEA, two instruments of the once all-embracing National Plan remained—the Industrial Reorganisation Corporation and the Prices and Incomes Board (under Mr Aubrey Jones) established to administer Labour's incomes policy. Les was directly concerned with both, as a member of the board of the IRC and as a trade union leader who believed whole-heartedly in a *creative* incomes policy. To most trade unionists, however, "incomes policy" was simply wage-freezing under another name, and it was hard to explain that although in the short run the practical results might seem much the same, there is a world of difference between self-restraint and restraint imposed from outside. Les did his best. In his view an incomes policy must be voluntary, but it must also mean genuine readiness by the more powerful groups of workers to stand aside in favour of the less powerful. In his written evidence on behalf of the ETU to the Royal Commission on Trade Unions in 1966 he put it thus:

We are in favour of an incomes policy because we accept the general proposition that if the gross national product is expanding at a certain rate, increases in income must be contained within the boundaries of that rate of expansion.

There has in the past been no written policy on what unions should or should not do. To find out the unwritten policy you must look at past behaviour patterns. In relative terms, those workers within well-organised, sensitive industries have done well, while the worst organised, in less sensitive industries, have done very badly. Quite apart, therefore, from injustices between different sections of society, this policy has led to considerable injustices within the wage and salary classes. As well as being a means for keeping incomes increases within the bounds of gains in output overall, an incomes policy must, therefore, have two main aims. One, it must further the cause of social justice. Two, it must encourage increases in productivity.

It will further social justice by raising the level of incomes of the lower-paid. If the exercise is to be in any way worthwhile this will involve restraint on the part of the better-paid. If a norm is to be laid down, the fact that some people are getting above it must mean that others are going to receive increases below the norm, or none at all. More than this, however, an incomes policy must also take account of those outwith the wage and salary earning framework. It will also concern itself with the levels and standards of pensioners and others dependent on welfare benefits.

This was hard to put across to a movement passionately concerned to preserve its old-established differentials. That Les and his National Executive persuaded the ETU to support an incomes policy is a measure of the quality of their leadership. The TUC, with no coherent leadership, was another matter. "The law," as Anatole France put it, "with magnificent impartiality, forbids both rich and poor alike to sleep under bridges and to beg for bread." That "magnificent impartiality" applied equally to free collective bargaining. Les tried to bring this home to the Trades Union Congress in 1966, concluding a notable speech:

I say this finally, that quite apart from this nation needing, as it desperately does, an incomes policy, this trade union movement needs an incomes policy so that those who have been in the weak positions can receive help from those of us who have the strength to give it.

It was at that Congress that he had a clash with Frank Cousins, then leader of the Transport and General Workers Union. The TGWU, the largest union in Britain, is itself a kind of TUC, grouping workers in hundreds of different trades into one "general" union. Some of its members, in tightly-knit groups like the dockers, have done well out of free-for-all wage bargaining; others, in more dispersed trades, much less well. Les said that he could understand how some unions liked "anarchic collective bargaining" but he could not understand the attitude of the TGWU "whose members, in a majority, have suffered for a century because of uncontrolled collective bargaining and the absence of an incomes policy inside the trade union movement".

Cousins replied with a bitter accusation that Les was in favour of productivity agreements which gave his own members more money. That, of course, was the point. Les believed that no incomes policy could succeed unless it offered incentives for genuinely increasing productivity, and he would apply work-study and every tool of scientific management to that end. But to say that men who help to increase industrial productivity should benefit from it is not to say that *all* the benefits from increased productivity in a given industry should go solely to those working in it. There are many jobs and services—the hospital service is a good example—where productivity cannot be directly measured, and is not, in any case, the right criterion for assessing human skill. In Les's view the gains from increased productivity should be shared, part going to the workers directly responsible, part to the industry itself, and part to the community in the form of higher incomes for those less able to fight for themselves. It was a creed demanding hard reasoning and considerable self-sacrifice, neither quality conspicuous in the modern trade union movement. The Cousins approach to trade union politics was foreign to Les. He was not much given to thinking in terms of personalities, but he once described Frank Cousins as "like a boy who says in the middle of a game when losing, 'I want my marbles back, I'm going home'".

Les did not consider that the General Council of the TUC was the right body to "vet" wage claims, nor would he have anything to do with suggestions that some tripartite body representing the TUC, the Confederation of British Industry and the Government should do so. In his view an independent Prices and Incomes Board was the right organisation to investigate and pronounce on wage claims, and he wanted its approach to be positive, recommending higher increases in some cases than those sought as well as whittling down claims in others.

Had he lived, he would probably have turned his mind towards attempting to reform the structure of the TUC, but he had so much else to do that he had no time for working out more than an outline of his ideas in this direction. The reluctance of the General Council to intervene in his struggles against the Communist Party in the ETU left him with a mixture of exasperation and contempt. He regarded the General Council as, on the whole, an ineffective body, lacking some powers that it needed and often reluctant to use such powers as it had. Moreover, even in its representative capacity, he did not consider the General Council to be adequately representative of the trade union movement. It was ridiculous that the supreme authority of British trade unionism should have proved quite incapable of effective intervention when the affairs of a constituent union were as grossly mismanaged as the ETU under Communist control. It was equally ridiculous that promises of support for Government action as in the TUC's adherence to the Declaration of Intent in 1964 on a policy for productivity, prices and incomes should turn out to be largely meaningless. There *can* be no effective trade union policy on anything if individual unions insist on absolute independence in all circumstances. Freedom of this sort is simply anarchy. Les would have sought changes along the lines of the reforms in his own Union, replacing an inchoate structure, united only at the top, by some kind of line-organisation, linking the individual Union more directly with the TUC through a series of industry groups and conferences. That he did not live to promulgate his ideas is a tragedy.

Geoffrey Goodman, one of the ablest of industrial journalists, who knew Les over twenty years, contributes a perceptive note. He writes:

He had a certain brusqueness, almost a crudity of manner, which at times didn't help him, and this manner later on tended to develop into a kind of arrogance, which, I suspect, put serious obstacles in his way. It was almost as if a certain natural arrogance became formalised when he was firmly established as President of the union. When he eventually moved on to the TUC General Council this arrogance certainly proved a handicap in his relationship with other members of the TUC leadership.

My own assessment is that it was an arrogance based on defensive mechanisms. Such mechanisms are present in all people who have been through the Communist Party machine and have rejected it for intellectual reasons. Equally, I think, it has roots in men of great ability who have risen from humble working-class backgrounds. They are both defensively aware of this background, and, at the same time, arrogantly assertive about its virtues and values.

Such a background builds up a certain brittleness of character; perhaps even a harshness in personal attitudes. None of this is surprising, and I think it is to Cannon's great credit that he was beginning to overcome these personality failings. Indeed, in the last two years of his life my own view is that he was maturing so rapidly that these old personality defects were being increasingly submerged.

He was an outstanding President of his union, and an equally outstanding member of the TUC General Council. His natural qualities of leadership made this inevitable. Nonetheless, he suffered fools as well as critics badly. Again I would attribute this to his defensiveness. To my mind this came out particularly on certain political issues where he felt, perhaps subconsciously, that it was necessary to take an anti-Left view. I think there were times when it would have been better and more healthy for him to have adjusted more slowly to the Right-wing position he held; or, indeed, to have corrected it publicly from time to time with more radical, Left-of-Centre views. I never regarded him as someone who had, in terms of the cliché, "switched to the Right". I don't believe this to be true. It is not necessary to be Right wing in the generally understood sense in order to be critical of Communists.

If I criticise Les Cannon at all during his period as President it would be because he allowed others to believe that he had become as obsessed with Right wing politics as he once was with Communist politics. Of course it is easy for an outsider to make these criticisms. The pressures on him were enormous—pressures of power and influence and flattery—and it would have been superhuman for him to have resisted all the blandishments. I am convinced that, had he lived, he would have succeeded in rising above all this, probably settling in a more Left-of-Centre position. He understood profoundly the value of the democratic right to say "No".

Victor Feather, General Secretary of the TUC, writes:

I never saw any sign that he was disconcerted by opposition, or that he was alarmed at the prospect of becoming involved in controversy. Indeed, I believe he relished argument—not for its own sake, but because he knew that this was the way that truth would break out from the bonds of prejudice and dogma, and the way that the right course of action would be found. His keen analytical brain was never at rest. This approach of his made him a stimulating member of the TUC General Council and a formidable contributor to the debating and discussion processes of the trade union movement.

Les Cannon was not only a man of great intellect and physical courage, he was resourceful as an organiser and skilful as an administrator. As a negotiator, too, he was shrewd and far-sighted, and when he had concluded an agreement for the benefit of his members, he was as tough in ensuring its observance as he had been in the negotiations. He was an active man. He had always driven himself hard and was untiring in his work. He was unrelenting in his efforts in pursuit of the causes he thought right. And in a period when he, and other colleagues in his union, were fighting for changes in its structure and democracy, I recall how he obtained employment on night shifts only, so that he could devote the whole of the day-time to pursuit of those aims. He had loyalty. Humour and wit were there in his make-up, and with his friends he could enjoy laughter.

XVII

THE LAST YEARS

THE PREVIOUS CHAPTER was mainly impersonal. In this Olga Cannon returns to her personal narrative.

*   *   *

Our life, materially, changed little with Les's election as General President of the Union. Financially, we were only slightly better off. The boys both went to boarding schools, initially because it was recommended that Oleg would be better off at a boarding school because his father was away so often, and Martin insisted on following his elder brother. School fees took a fair slice of our income, and we were also contributing to the support of my parents. Otherwise, our lives flowed on more or less unaffected by Les's new status in society.

We tried not to get too involved in the sort of social life that a prominent trade union leader can have. We remembered the bitter years when Les was virtually an outcast from society, and we felt mildly amused at the invitations that poured in. It would be wrong to give an impression that we did not enjoy meeting all the interesting new people who now came our way. We did. But we always remained conscious of how easily one can become severed from all these social elevations. This is something that has helped me a great deal since Les died, for a widow, even the widow of a famous man, is no longer at the top of the invitation lists.

Les was austere about spending the Union's money on himself. In spite of all the travelling he had to do he continued to drive his car himself until I got worried about his tiredness and insisted that he should have a driver. He had a single dining credit card, which he used sparingly, generally contriving to get himself invited to dinners and lunches so that no cost should fall on the Union's funds. He disliked lavish functions and receptions, and none were given by the ETU under his presidency.

We stayed on in our house at Chessington because it was conveniently near to the College at Esher, though we did modernise it. We did not buy our present, larger house at Dorking until a few months before Les's illness in 1970.

Geoffrey Goodman's note about Les in the previous chapter is perceptive, but he is wrong in suggesting that Les ever identified with the political Right. Rather, the terms Left and Right themselves require definition. Some reflections of Les's own, in an article he wrote in the winter of 1966, are relevant here:

Are the old terms "Left wing" and "Right wing" any longer meaningful in Labour politics? This question sprang to mind after a television programme in which I took part recently. On the same programme Michael Foot asserted that the Right wing always wishes to disown the label, or to prevent the label being attached, and that there is generally a clear argument between the Right and Left. I am very sceptical about this. Ten or twelve years ago, perhaps, it could be done—the term "Bevanite", for example, usually denoted opposition to German rearmament, and a distinctive stand on a whole range of issues. Today, on the question of incomes policy, Michael Foot, Frank Cousins, Clive Jenkins, the Communist Party, Enoch Powell and Paul Chambers of ICI are all firmly united. Indeed, when Frank Cousins made his speech resigning from the House of Commons, we had the strange sight of Enoch Powell sitting nodding in agreement with almost every word he said. The Communist Party, and other members of the so-called Left, oppose an incomes policy because they say they are pursuing the class struggle, and this is one element in their fight. The question must be asked, however, how the class struggle can be pursued against capitalism when many of the most forthright and convinced advocates of the capitalist system are ranged firmly on their side.

The impossibility of drawing a strict distinction between Left and Right is not confined to an incomes policy. The Prime Minister's[1] announcement in the House of Commons

[1] Mr Harold Wilson was then Prime Minister.

last month that Britain would make a new attempt to enter the Common Market illustrates the point once again. The Communists and the so-called Left wing in general are opposed to it along with the Right wing of the Conservative Party. . . .

The same alliance of so-called Left and Right can be seen in the opposition to the Industrial Reorganisation Corporation. The Communist Party opposes it because it appears to them to be an attempt to bolster capitalism. The Conservative party opposes it because it appears to them to be an attempt to destroy capitalism. They cannot both be right.

In foreign affairs the views within the Labour Party of Frank Cousins on the Left and Christopher Mayhew[1] on the Right are remarkably similar to those held by Enoch Powell on the Right wing of the Conservative Party. Once again we have a range of views from the extreme Left to the extreme Right, taking in supporters in the centre from all parties as well.

From all this it must be perfectly clear that there cannot be a distinctive Left and Right attitude on every subject, and that those who, in their rather smug way, regard themselves as the defenders of the only true faith, should think again before they say that they are the holders of a distinctive point of view.

Les's true political place was as a radical reformer. He was a radical in the sense of the strong radical tradition of British politics, working for reform, but conscious always that the good in British institutions must not be thrown away with the bad. He could not have reached this thinking without his Communist experience. That showed him the evils of bureaucratic dictatorship, from Left or Right.

Les distrusted emotion in speechmaking and packed his addresses, speeches and lectures with hard facts and ideas. He never went in for hackneyed emotional perorations, but ended a speech on, as it were, a "flat" note, leaving his hearers to feel the emotional content for themselves.

He built up a new relationship with the Press. This had problems, because newspapers became rather tired of ETU

[1] Minister of Defence (Navy) in the Labour Government.

news once the trial of 1961 was over. The Communists in retreat fought back with a spate of counter-accusations and the public, which the newspapers simply reflected, became a bit bored with the whole thing. But Les remained in demand for articles and interviews, and he maintained a good relationship with the journalists he knew. He was scrupulous to ensure that any Press statement should be factual and accurate, and he never tried to put a convenient gloss on inconvenient facts. He was trusted by the Press because he was trustworthy.

Television was a challenge. At first he found TV appearances rather an ordeal, but the medium suited him and he became almost a TV personality. He appeared regularly in discussion programmes, and he took these occasions very seriously, making copious notes beforehand. When he got to the studio he would never use his notes, but they had helped to clear his mind.

He often asked me or one of the boys to come to the studio with him. If, for some reason, I couldn't be with him, he would telephone immediately after the programme to ask, "How did it go?" There was nothing personal or vain about this; he wanted to know if he had managed to express his Union's point of view clearly and convincingly.

On a few occasions Les took part in the radio programme "Any Questions?" and as the years went by we got to know quite a number of producers and TV and radio personalities, and always enjoyed meeting them. Among our friends was Sidney Harrison, the music expert, and another interesting person who often takes part in "Any Questions?", Anthony Hopkins, who once amused us by playing the piano faultlessly with his back to the keys. I shall also never forget meeting Freddy Grisewood, who, although badly crippled with arthritis and walking with two sticks, refused all help, and allowed Martin to carry his bag to his car only to please the boy.

In January 1964 we applied for visas to visit Czechoslovakia. It was six years since I had last seen my parents, and we set off in May with the car loaded with every imaginable item that I knew to be unobtainable in Czechoslovakia. Martin, who travelled with us, had barely enough space to sit on the back seat. We travelled in a new car, and on a motorway in

Bavaria one of the blades of the fan broke off. We were towed to the nearest village which had a garage, and spent five days in a pretty place called Rosenheim, waiting to get a spare from England. When he met employers in the car industry Les always liked to quote this incident, as illustrating the inefficient distribution of spare parts abroad.

Our enforced stay in Bavaria, however, was enjoyable enough, for the weather was beautiful and the mountains stunning. The gorgeous weather, alas, was not so beneficial to some of the perishable foodstuffs we were carrying, and we had reluctantly to dispose of some of the goodies we had brought—particularly the cheese.

The fan replaced, we drove on into Austria and then crossed the border into Czechoslovakia. The contrast between impoverished Austria and "progressive" socialist Czechoslovakia was marked—it was like progressing from an oasis into a desert. Czechoslovakia in 1964 still suffered from the material shortages which we in England had long forgotten. I remember how shocked Martin was at seeing his grandfather standing in a queue outside a butcher's shop at 6.45 in the morning; he insisted on queueing in his place on the two days in the week when meat was available.

My parents were finding life hard. They had aged sadly, and their home was comfortless and neglected. I wanted to stay to help decorate their house, but Les felt that we must go back after a fortnight, because he had to attend a conference of electrical contractors at Harrogate. We drove back through Prague, and called to see Sir Cecil Parrott, who was then British ambassador there. He had a great love for Czechoslovakia and cared enough to have learned the language well. I found him extraordinarily sensitive and well-attuned to what was going on. In 1964 the system was slowly being liberalised, but it was scarcely visible to me then, and I argued vehemently with Sir Cecil in the face of his optimism. I was wrong, of course, as the events of the spring of 1968 were to prove.

Prague, like so many cities, was not (and still is not) a suitable place for the accommodation of the motor car, and we had to leave the car in the street for the two nights we stayed there. One of our friends suggested that we should park in front of the offices of the Communist Party, because there was a night watchman on duty, and the car would be safe. In the morning we found that the car had been broken into. It had been done through the quarterlight, with the most delicate expertise, and without causing any damage. Everything inside, except the car's documents, had been taken. The police were apologetic, but assured us cheerfully that this was something that was happening all the time, particularly to foreign cars!

I went back to Czechoslovakia in November 1964 to take my mother to hospital and after that returned for regular short visits as often as I could, travelling with suitcases loaded with the everyday things that people in Czechoslovakia simply could not get. I could not send things by post because that meant paying a heavy duty, which my parents could not afford. I was torn between affection for my parents and my own family. Had I had a brother or sister, or had my parents lived in a different society, my concern would not have been so great. As it was, I lived in a constant state of tension about them.

But in Czechoslovakia itself things were gradually getting better, and I was happy to see the relaxation of the regime which eventually disposed of Novotný and brought Dubček to the fore.

My mother died in the summer of 1967. Her death was a tremendous personal loss to me, even though we lived so far apart. We had carried on an intensive correspondence, and when she died I realised how much this contact had meant to me. A few weeks after my mother's death my father suffered a mild heart attack. I couldn't dream of leaving him in Czechoslovakia, so I brought him, travelling in a wheelchair, to stay with us in England. His health recovered rapidly, and the only drawback was that I could not find anyone speaking Czech who could help me with him when I needed to be away. Eventually he decided to return to Czechoslovakia.

In the autumn of 1967, while attending a conference in Paris, we drove to Auvers to visit the graves of the Van Gogh brothers. We bought an armful of anemones from the owner of a small cottage facing Dr Gachet's[1] house, and we walked past the famous church which Vincent had painted, and up to the graveyard on the hill. The two brothers are buried side by side, their graves overgrown with ivy. We called at the little inn

[1] A close friend of Vincent Van Gogh.

where Vincent had lived, and went up to the tiny dark room where he had died. Les had always felt sympathy for, and a certain affinity with, Vincent Van Gogh, and on the wall of his office hung a copy of Vincent's self-portrait (with the grey hat) which Les had bought in Holland.

The neglected graves, the dismal room where this great artist died, the profound tragedy of the two brothers' lives, touched us deeply, and we returned to Paris in a rather sad mood. At the hotel a telegram was waiting for us: Jim Cannon Senior had died suddenly of a heart attack. We had seen him only a few weeks before, taking my own father with us. We had been worried then by Jim Cannon's appearance; his health seemed to have deteriorated, and he had lost his lively interest in life. We had feared that he might not have much longer to live. It was good that he had lived to see Leslie's achievements.

My own father went back to Czechoslovakia in the spring of 1968. I was able to go there several times that summer because I had taken a job as an export adviser to firms doing business with Czechoslovakia. The prospects for British exports then seemed very hopeful, for the Czechs in the Dubček era were anxious to extend their trade with the West. I toured the country extensively in July and early August 1968 conducting market research.

I find it difficult to describe the difference between the Czechoslovakia of 1967 and that of 1968. The Communist Party, after years of unpopularity with the vast majority of the nation, was looked up to with new hope that it would find a form of Socialism which would be just and humanitarian, embracing the best democratic traditions of the Czechoslovak people. For me, the most touching thing I saw was groups of old-age pensioners—a section of society which had been treated abominably under Novotný—going into national banks to give trinkets of gold or money as gifts to build this new, truly Socialist State. This sort of action was going on all over the country. If ever there was a threat and alternative to capitalist society it was in this new concept of "Socialism with a human face".

I left Czechoslovakia ten days before the Russians, flanked by the armies of the other East European governments (East Germany, Poland, Bulgaria and Hungary), descended on my homeland. The date of the invasion was Wednesday, August 21, 1968.

On this day the General Council of the Trade Union Congress started its meeting at 10 a.m. We had heard the news of the Russian occupation of Czechoslovakia before Les went to the meeting. From the minutes of this meeting, held at Congress House in London, it can be seen that the meeting proceeded in a normal fashion, discussing various proposals concerning Incomes Policy and Nationalised Industries. One of the items on the agenda happened to concern Czechoslovakia—a more or less routine matter regarding a trade union visit. When the Council reached this item on its agenda, Les said that the situation in Czechoslovakia had now changed dramatically with the invasion of troops of the Soviet Union and other countries. He suggested that the General Council should pass a motion condemning this action and withdrawing the invitation to the Soviet equivalent of the TUC, to be represented at the forthcoming Centenary Congress of the TUC in Blackpool in September. He also suggested that unions should reconsider exchange visits with movements in the countries involved in the invasion.

The General Secretary of the TUC (then George Woodcock) suggested that "very little official information was available and that advice should be sought from the Prime Minister". This was agreed. At a later stage of the meeting Mr Woodcock said that his office had been in touch with the Prime Minister, who said that "very little was known about the situation in Czechoslovakia, but the newspaper reports confirmed what the Government knew at the moment. He understood that the Czechs had been told not to resist the invasion. The matter would no doubt be referred to the United Nations. He (the Prime Minister) would see a deputation from the General Council if it was thought necessary when more information was available later in the day."

Les's motion condemning the invasion was then read. The General Secretary suggested that the discussion should be an open one and not confined to the motion or amendments to it.

I quote now directly from the minutes of that meeting:

Mr Cannon said he had *moved a motion* and he would like

The last photograph, April 1970 (*photo Lawson Gibbs & Co.*)

At the TUC, 1969 (*photo The Guardian*)

it to be discussed until he was convinced that it should be in any way changed.

Mr Cousins said he both condemned and regretted the action of the Soviet Union. He did so with some sadness because he felt that in the long run the losers would be the Russians themselves because it would be working people who would get killed in any fighting that might develop. There were progressive forces in Russia which had been looking forward to a closer relationship with trade unionists of other countries, and they too would be saddened by the events. He would support a motion of the Council regretting and condemning the action of the Soviet Union attacking a Sovereign state, but he would not wish to support an instruction to unions to break off all relations with the Iron Curtain countries. He was supported by Lord Collison. Lord Collison said that his union had had approximately fourteen exchanges with the unions in the countries behind the Iron Curtain. These would not continue, but he thought it was unnecessary to advise unions as to their course of action.

Mr Jones of the Transport and General Workers Union said that although it appeared that the action of the Soviet Union was indefensible, he did not wish to vote for or against Mr Cannon's motion until more facts were available.

Les would not have any of this. He said that Prague radio was still operating, it was possible to listen to Czechoslovakia, and there was no doubt about the situation. The arguments went on and on. Les strongly urged that any statement from the TUC must condemn the action of the Soviet Union, that the invitation to the Soviet TUC must be withdrawn, and that he saw no reason why affiliated trade unions should not be asked, as suggested in his motion, to reconsider their activities concerning delegations to and from the Iron Curtain countries.

The minutes again:

He [Les] was supported by other speakers and after a long discussion it was agreed that the office should draw up a statement publicly condemning the invasion of Czechoslovakia by the Soviet Union and the satellite countries, and expressing sympathy with the Czechoslovak people; declaring

K

that because of their action no useful purpose would be served by continuing contacts with the trade union movements of these countries, and that the invitation to the Soviet TUC to attend the 1968 congress should be withdrawn; and finally suggesting that affiliated unions should reconsider their attitude about visits of delegations to and from any countries which had invaded Czechoslovakia.

When Les came home from that meeting he said that he had been as near to tears as ever in his life.

And so it came about that on the one o'clock News on that August 21, 1968, the day when Czechoslovakia was once again invaded, Britain did find a voice to condemn the act of aggression. Parliament was not sitting. The voice of condemnation was not the Government's. It came from the TUC—but it was the authentic voice of Britain.

At the Trades Union Congress in September Czechoslovakia was discussed again. Les listened to a sort of pro-Communist apologia. Then he strode to the rostrum, and as he flung his notes on the speaker's stand, they scattered and floated down below him. Without pausing for a second he delivered a passionate speech—for once without interruptions from the so-called militants in the hall.

In August 1967 Les was elected a Visiting Fellow of Nuffield College, Oxford, and in December of the same year the University of Oxford conferred on him an Honorary MA Degree. I think these two awards gave him a great deal of personal pleasure. He had left school at fifteen and had had no chance of going to a university. Half of him had always hankered for an academic life—now his academic distinction had been recognised.

We had our share of travel. In June 1966 we were flown to Tangier, on an inaugural flight for a new route in conjunction with the Ministry of Tourism of Morocco. It was one of those "perks" which trade union officials are offered, and which enable them to see something of the world at the expense of various organisations. I used to wonder on these occasions what the nineteenth-century pioneers of the trade union movement would make of these junketings, so completely removed from the original concept of trade unionism. I must hasten to add that trade unionists from Russia and other Communist States are subjected to the same VIP treatment as their colleagues in the capitalist world.

In November 1968 we went to Nigeria. Les and Jack Lee, a Past President of the Institute of Personnel Management, were invited to lecture at an advanced course on industrial relations arranged by the Nigerian Employers' Consultative Association. Les gave two lectures, one on "The Role of Trade Unionism in Modern Society" and the other entitled "A Trade Unionist's View on Collective Bargaining". He also took part in discussion and acted as an assessor in practical exercises in negotiation. In addition to attending the course on industrial relations, Les addressed the inaugural meeting of the Nigerian Union of Commercial, Technical and Allied Employees. We were not able to see much of the country, for the war in Biafra was still going on, and there were protests and demonstrations not far from Lagos—the issue, we were told, was higher taxes. At the time of our stay a large Russian delegation was visiting Lagos, discussing trade and Soviet economic help.

Les was blunt with the British business representatives he met—about their lack of involvement in education, and in the training of new, native personnel. The segregation of society continues, and the British businessman lives in blissful isolation from the future problems of the country. He meets his African equal, who is a prosperous businessman or highly-placed administrator, but the gap between the urban élite and the peasant mass is greater in Africa than in Europe or America. We liked the smiling, joyous Nigerians, but we left the country after a short spell concerned and wondering what the future held for them.

We called at Uganda, where Oleg was doing a spell with VSO, not very happy with the circumstances, and too young at eighteen to make a real contribution. Looking at those young, eager people one could not help thinking that it was an insult to the Africans to send such immature youth to educate and to advise them. It was the young British who benefited from the experience, not the other way round. I believe that the Voluntary Service Overseas organisation has now raised the age-level to a graduate standard, as has the American Peace Corps.

I often think of Africa and wonder about its future. Economic help alone is not enough, and much already given has been wasted. Too often such assistance helps to keep in power corrupt regimes. There should be *some* control over economic help, but not with political strings attached. The priorities should be the village school, the agricultural colleges, rural clinics, carts, hoes and spades. Instead we were shown impressive universities, a super-modern hospital, American-type hotels and luxurious Government offices. As John Hatch has written, "The social and economic revolution needed to break the stranglehold of African poverty can only come from idealism, self-sacrifice, and dedication."[1] Of Africans and ourselves alike.

Later that year Les visited the United States and Canada. He wrote to me from Canada, "Like the USA, this country is a mixture of overt wealth and unaesthetic monstrosities. Toronto and Ottawa, just like Detroit, have overhead lines sprawling spider-like all along the main shopping streets. For me, I must say I'm as 'conservative' as ever about the merits of the UK. It must be my age. . . ."

In New York Les took part in a nation-wide radio programme—one of those fast-moving, all-embracing, high-pressure programmes, fruitily mixed with verbose advertising. "They don't pay you, you pay them for the honour of using their hospitality," Les said afterwards.

After lengthy discussion on the internal affairs of Britain from the school-leaving age to colour prejudice, the interviewer moved to Britain's relationship with the United States and the question of Red China. The interviewer was critical of Britain's acceptance of open trade with China. Les defended the British position firmly, and insisted that the United States would never be able to resolve the war in Vietnam without talking to China. At the time it required considerable courage to say things like that in the United States. President Nixon's visit to China in 1972 was an interesting justification of Les's convictions.

Our last trip abroad together was a lightning visit to Australia in April 1970. Les, who had been tired in the weeks before we set off, enjoyed every minute of this exhausting "See Australia

[1] John Hatch, "A Note on English-speaking Africa".

in Six Full Days" affair. I would drag myself reluctantly out of bed after a late-night expedition somewhere or other, to find Les shaved, dressed, packed and ready to see more of Australia. At the uncivilised hour of 8.30 in the morning he would jolly me along to get to the waiting bus on time (or at least with the minimum of delay). He swam for hours in the sea at the Golden Beach, off the Great Barrier Reef north of Brisbane, ate hearty meals, and seemed fitter than ever.

On our way home we called at Fiji, where Les wanted to attend the annual conference of the Fijian Public Employees Union. The union had 4,500 members—Fijians, Indians and Europeans—and the one-day conference was held in an aircraft hangar. It was an impressive gathering of some 600 members, many of whom had travelled long distances from all the scattered islands of Fiji to get there. Les addressed the conference, and conveyed greetings on behalf of British trade unions. He got a tremendous welcome, largely, no doubt, because he was the first British trade union leader who had ever officially attended such an event.

Two weeks after our return we were at the College at a small gathering, and I looked across the room at Les. His face was ashen. Next morning I telephoned the hospital for an appointment. Prolonged tests were carried out, but no one believed that there could be anything seriously wrong. Eventually an operation was arranged at the end of May. Cancer was diagnosed, too advanced for any hope of recovery. By early autumn Les knew that he was dying. He faced death with nobility and with the same courage he had displayed throughout his life. It came to him on December 9, 1970, 21 years and one day after that cold grey evening of my arrival at Victoria Station.

XVIII

REFLECTIONS

Two or three times in his life Les contemplated writing a book. In 1958 he began to set down his thoughts on leaving the Communist Party, but events crowded so fast upon him that he did not get beyond the opening chapter. Brief as this is, it contains some of his most reflective writing:

For two years I have pondered over the question as to whether I should add to the fairly considerable ex-Communist autobiography. A number of considerations have urged delay, some to be cautious, others not to write at all.

The counsels of delay are wise. It is ill-conceived to rush into print immediately after having rejected a system of ideas built up over a period of many years. Many of the ideas are still held—they are good, provided they are allowed to stand up for themselves. It is the dogmatic system of contemporary Communist theory and practice, into which many noble ideas were packed, alongside historically outworn and rejected concepts, which has disintegrated. It requires time to set down the reorientation of ideas, to show by reason and not emotion, the shallowness of those ideas which have been rejected. It requires patience, too, to explain why once unacceptable propositions are now regarded as indispensable to a theory of social advance. . . .

There can be few topics more worthy of exploration than the problem of how it came to pass "that a band of British citizens could sacrifice themselves so freely over a period of forty years to the service of a dictatorship in another country"—Henry Pelling, in the closing lines of his book *The British Communist Party*.

Whilst not denying the truth of the assertion that the British Communist Party has rendered service to the Soviet Government over the past forty years, I am, just the same, quite certain that an exploration along the lines suggested above is like looking for rhino in scented water. . . . No two people join the Party for precisely the same reasons. They can, however, be brought under fairly broad headings: those who are impressed by the ideology of Marxism, those who are at the wrong end of the anomalous features of society, and those who are generally anti-social and regard the Communist Party as the authentic anti-society party.

The majority, including myself, belong to the second category. What always annoys me are those wiseacres who never suffered a day's hardship in their lives, who don't know how brutal society can be to wide sections of the population, sneering at those who take up the fight; who condemn the sincere sacrificial efforts of the victims of social injustice as queer people with a chip on their shoulders. These not only don't know why people join the CP—they just don't know the country they live in.

To take care is advice of which I have certainly not been left wanting, and not just by faint hearts. Many well-intentioned friends have expressed concern for fear that what I have to say might be used by enemies of democracy and of the interests of ordinary working people. To hearken to this plea, however, would be to continue, in a sort of way, the means-justifying-the-ends conduct. If it is true (as the friends mentioned above believe) that Communist theory and practice lead to corruption, bureaucracy, and a stifling of democracy, to say nothing of their mythical claim to be a panacea for all social ailments, then surely, in the long run, it cannot serve any reactionary purpose to write of one's experiences, if showing this to be true. . . .

I vaguely remember reading a review of Howard Fast's book in the *Observer*, and I was left with the impression that the reviewer was contemptuous of Fast, not for what Fast has come to believe, but that he ever believed differently. I seem to remember also that he, like the Communist Party, is a bit sick of these so-called recantations. . . . The trouble with those who don't understand, and don't want to understand, the different reasons why people of different walks of life have found their way into the CP is that, however much they protest, they don't really understand those social anomalies which are the recruiting agents of the CP; nor do they really care to remedy them.

Les's book breaks off here. His analysis of those factors in society that he called "the recruiting agents of the CP" would have been a considerable addition to political and social literature. To complete it, however, he needed at least three months of undisturbed peace; and he never had those months.

Ten years later he returned to the theme when he was interviewed on television by Christopher Brasher. "What," Brasher asked him, "is your vision of the Golden State?"

Les: I don't think there is any Golden State, and that is one of the ideas I rejected when I ceased to be a Communist. I believed then that there was a system of society which resolved all problems of conflict, of poverty, of culture, of opportunity, and so on. I don't believe that is the case any more. I do believe that society evolves and is never the same one decade from another. If one compares our so-called capitalist society in the later 1960s with the sixties of the nineteenth century, one sees the effects of this transformation. And in the next century it will not be the same. . . .

Brasher: But as a Communist you did have this vision of the future. What is your vision now?

Les: Well, in some ways it's the same kind of vision. You must remember my vision was one that I held in the 1930s, when I was surrounded by . . . poverty; most of the families surrounding my own home were unemployed, the children, like myself, didn't have any opportunities. I had a vision then of a society of nice houses, each with gardens, and everybody at work, and working less hours, and having an opportunity for culture and education, children with equal opportunities, and so on. I have the same kind of vision. I certainly don't believe that it will be achieved in that way. . . .

Brasher: It's a materialist vision, in a way—nice houses . . .

Les: Materialist, if you like, as against religious, but not materialist in the sense of being opposed to a cultural life.

I've always believed that life doesn't have much meaning if it merely means better food and a better house and a better job; if it doesn't mean getting a wider experience of the world in which we live, and developing appreciation of music and literature.

Later in the programme Brasher asked, "How did you lose your faith in Communism?"

Les: A number of reasons. One was an increasing recognition that the British Communist Party was really alien to the political development of workers' organisations in this country. Looking over the last century one can see the Labour Party as an evolution of the Chartist Movement of the radical Liberals. In the second half of the century this evolved into the Labour Representative Committee. This is the part that clearly the British people chose, and all the crises that have occurred in the Labour Party have not interrupted this relationship between working people generally and the Trade Unions and the Labour Party. The Communist Party was an importation of a party developed by Lenin from the Czarist days of Russia when all organisations were illegal. It never was able to take root, because it's really not part of our traditional growth; it's not part of the way people conceive political organisations, political struggle within our democratic society. This took over me in the early fifties. I did tend to think, notwithstanding these frustrations within the British Communist Party, that the world movement of Communism might begin to show even workers in advanced countries that Communism was a good system of Government, and likely to bring the millennium, the vision. . . . However, I had very serious political experiences in Czechoslovakia, and I also suffered from the traumatic impact of Khrushchev's speech in 1956. . . . It became clear to me, and it has become increasingly clear ever since, that a Communist Party, so highly disciplined, with power at the centre, when it comes to power transposes these principles into every facet of social, economic and political life. . . . The economy is run not by experts in management and engineers, but by Communists who carry a card, and the whole society is one dominated by an élite, which might be skilled in the art of getting power within the Communist Party, but is certainly not skilled in running the country. . . .

Brasher: So really you saw the millennium arrive in Czechoslovakia, and then saw what it was like in reality?

Les: Well, I saw virtually the precursor to George Orwell's society of 1984. I was astonished, too, because I met Novotný and I had a discussion with him through a highly-skilled interpreter—I was astonished at the level of his intelligence. Apart from anything else I found him an extremely unintelligent man. I wondered how [such a] man could even get to such a position of power, until one sees the way power does move by intrigue and cabal inside the Communist Party. . . .

The personality has all-but evaporated in this transcription of an interview, though enough remains to suggest what Les could have made of his theme had he been given time. But life did not give him time.

The quality of Les's thought is clearly outlined in what is left of his writings, and the impact of it is still one of the really formative influences in British trade unionism since the Second World War. That influence is not easy to define, for it was expressed mainly through his own personality, and with the living man no longer there to compel agreement in committee by the sheer logical force of his argument, or to hammer away at sloppy thinking from the rostrum of the Trade Union Congress, it may seem that the power of his thought has waned. But it has not waned. It has been clouded by the dismal lack of self-confidence that has afflicted the Labour movement since electoral defeat in 1970, but the inspiration of his thought will return. Above all, perhaps, the inspiration of his *example* will remain, to inspire younger men with the courage that he showed in securing the triumph of reason and human decency over what seemed for so long to be insuperable odds.

Where personality counts for so much, it may be fitting to record the views of some of those who worked with him in life. Lord Gardiner, who was leading Counsel for the plaintiffs in the ETU trial and who later became Lord Chancellor, wrote in a letter to Olga Cannon:

I was immensely impressed with the grasp which your husband showed of all the intricate details of an unusually complicated case. The work he personally did on it was prodigious, and it is not too much to say that I gravely doubt whether the case could have been won without him. It was because I had such a high opinion of his abilities and social sense that, when Lord Chancellor, I put his name forward to the Queen as a member of the Royal Commission on Assizes and Quarter Sessions. I told him at the time that I would rely totally on him to safeguard the interests of the parties, jurors and witnesses, whose interests, I am afraid, have not always received from the lawyers the consideration they deserve. As you know, the report of the Royal Commission, which recommended the largest reform of our legal system for at least 100 years, was warmly acclaimed by all the political parties, and by the judges and the legal profession, and has now been carried out. A Royal Commission is work which involves a great deal of thought, and many meetings, and I shall always be grateful to him for taking it on in addition to everything he had to do.

Jack Lee, Past President of the Institute of Personnel Management, writes:

When I was President of the IPM, on many occasions I used to act either as Chairman to Les, or else introduce him, to the meetings or conferences of the Institute.

I vividly remember the National Conference of the IPM at Harrogate when I was taking over the Presidency in 1967. John Davies, now the Minister for Trade and Industry, was then Director General of the CBI. John was the last speaker at the plenary session of Conference, and he immediately followed Les Cannon. That particular morning Les was at his most brilliant; perhaps it was one of the best speeches he ever gave, certainly the most outstanding I had ever heard him deliver. It was as if he were saying to John Davies, "Now

beat that" (for Les always loved to win). John Davies followed
and he acquitted himself well. Nevertheless he came to me
afterwards, quite sincerely, and said, "Jack, if ever you ask
me to speak at IPM meetings again I will do so, but never
ask me to speak after Les Cannon."

Another incident comes to mind when we were together
on a lecture tour in Nigeria. One evening in Lagos we had
been asked to meet privately a number of leading employers,
most of whom were British. About a couple of dozen management men assembled at a house in Ikoyi, the fashionable
suburb of Lagos, eager to listen to this TUC General Council
man, who had brought with him to Nigeria a reputation for
straight shooting and honesty. After supper, when we were
sitting in the lounge and preparing ourselves for a lengthy
discussion on labour relations, one man said, "Mr Cannon,
why is the British economy in such a sorry state? Isn't it
because of the outrageous demands of the trade unions and
the lack of exports?"

Without a smile Les turned to his questioner and replied,
"The same thought about the poor state of British exports
was also crossing my mind tonight, in fact within the last
few minutes. I watched all you gentlemen arrive and was
amazed by the number of Cadillacs, Volkswagens, Renaults,
Simcas and Mercedes Benz cars in which you all came."

Another personnel manager of long experience in the
electrical industry, Terry Lyons, was particularly impressed by
Les's "remarkably constructive" approach to industrial relations. Terry Lyons observes:

He had a tough, agile mind, winkling out the tiniest weakness in one's case, but trying always to integrate management's objections with his own, and concentrating on any
elements of common interest. He did not supplicate on behalf
of his members; he wanted no charity—he wanted a business
deal. Of course his members would give more; he wanted
them to, and he wanted them to get more in return.

Lyons and Les were invited to give a demonstration of wage-bargaining to students at a training centre. Describing this, Lyons adds:

> We found the exercise engrossing. Between us, our student teams occasionally getting a word in edgeways, we reorganised the fictitious company, and did a deal. We enjoyed it, and we agreed to perform again another time. Eventually, it became a travelling duet, and our case studies got harder. We never knew what they would be, and the Institute of Personnel Management, who started preparing them for us, gave us some tough assignments.
>
> The most fascinating aspect of these teaching exercises was the fact that we both forgot that the situation was fictitious. Course organisers would tear their hair over the gravely-threatened timetable as Les and I, by now oblivious of the students, insisted on bringing the negotiations to a conclusion.

Les's last public appearance was at a meeting of the National Economic Development Council on November 4, 1970, a few weeks before his death. This was a meeting at which the Conservative Government's plans to dismantle the IRC was to be discussed, and Les, who believed passionately in the value of the IRC, was determined to speak. Lord Robens, who was present, contributes this moving note:

> The last time I saw Les Cannon was on an occasion that no one who was present will ever forget. It was at a meeting of the National Economic Development Council on 4th November 1970. The Chancellor of the Exchequer, Tony Barber, was in the Chair and there were two other Cabinet Ministers: John Davies (Department of Trade and Industry) and Robert Carr (Department of Employment).
>
> The meeting started without Les, but the Chairman indicated that Les Cannon had indicated his intention of attending for the item in connection with the dissolution of the IRC, of which he had been a member since its inception, and to all accounts a vigorous and outstanding member. About eleven o'clock Les came in and took his seat. There were nods of greeting and smiles as he sat down which he

acknowledged in his usual boyishly cheerful way. I don't know how many others knew—from his demeanour it was impossible for anyone even to guess—but *I* knew that he was dying. (I had reason to know because I had been able to help in a very small way with a problem of his medical treatment. I knew that the dreadful disease from which he was suffering was a terminal one. And so did Leslie, but no one would have thought so as he took his seat.)

The Chairman invited him to speak and all those who were present, his trade union colleagues from the TUC, the business men from the CBI, the academics and the specially selected staff who were present on that occasion together with the Ministers listened, with a silence and intensity that you could feel, to the finest exposition of the great advantage to the national economy of the IRC. No one could have deployed with better skill the cogent arguments for its retention in the light of the Government's declared intention to wind it up. He buttressed his arguments with concrete examples of business successes. A stranger listening to it all might well have imagined that he was listening to a professional economist, a management, or a business tycoon— he would never have guessed that this was the full-time President of the Electrical Trade Union.

It was a fairly lengthy exhortation and when finally his voice ceased there was a silence in which you could have heard a pin drop, and then a chorus of approval around the table, in which Ministers joined. The approval, however, was for the man whose tremendous courage took him to that meeting that morning.

The die had been cast, the Government had already taken its decision. The IRC was doomed and the advocacy of Les Cannon was a last despairing effort on the part of a brilliant and courageous man to save an organisation which he was convinced rendered great service to the industrial life of the nation. It was his last great effort in advocacy. Within five weeks Les Cannon was no longer with us.

As events have subsequently turned out, and the "lame ducks" that John Davies said it was not part of Government Policy to aid have turned out to be firms like Rolls Royce and Upper Clyde Shipbuilders, and he found it impossible not to provide very substantial aid, I have often thought how benefited the Government would have been if they had accepted the firm, strong and powerful plea of Les Cannon to keep the IRC in being.

Mr Charles Lovell, General Secretary of the Plumbing Trades Union before its amalgamation with the ETU and late National Secretary of the combined Union, saw Les in a different context. He writes:

Les was not the easiest of people to understand, except by those who were on the same intellectual plane as himself, and I suspect that even these people found it hard to keep abreast of his thinking. To me, he appeared as a man born before his time.

On occasions Les would call into my office on his way out after normal office hours and would chat about many things. He knew I had originated from Tyneside and liked to talk about his stay in the area whilst working as an electrician during the war years.

Les derived pleasure from the simple things in life; I suppose he found them relaxing. For instance, during Conferences the Union usually provides light refreshments for the delegates and their wives on one evening, and invariably they provide their own entertainment. This follows the traditional pattern: one or two solo efforts from the more talented and brave delegates, concluding with the usual community singing in which the whole company joins in. Les loved this, and took part with great gusto. He had a good memory of the songs from the 1930s onwards.

I shall always remember his last visit to the Executive Council. It was a sad occasion, if not a slightly macabre one. It demonstrated the courage of the man: he knew he was dying. I suppose we all knew, really, but were hoping we were wrong. He spoke of the future structure of the Union, advising us, in effect, what we should do following his death. He spoke calmly and deliberately, if a little more slowly than he usually did prior to his illness. My admiration for the man as President and chief negotiator for the Union was already very high and it was enhanced by the great courage and fortitude he displayed towards the end of his life. The memory I shall keep is of his hesitating at the door of the Board Room, turning, and waving his final farewell to the EC members.

Messrs N. G. Bailey and Company, electrical contractors, of Ilkley, Yorkshire, is one of the firms which has regularly sent shop stewards to training courses at the ETU College. Mr N. S. Bailey, the managing director, himself attended several of the courses. Describing the first course, he writes:

It was a week which went a considerable way to extending and broadening my education, and a week which made a very considerable impact on the Company. We had representatives from Site Agent and Branch Manager categories, as well as our Personnel Director, and none of us knew exactly what to expect. We broke a lot of ice that week, we all received a severe "dunking" in very cold water, and fortunately recovered to make what I believe to be very constructive progress.

Mr Bailey found it a most valuable experience to meet shop stewards personally at the College, and he believes that it is equally valuable for shop stewards to meet representatives of management on the same terms. Here are the views of some shop stewards:

(A shop steward from Yarrow's Shipyard) I wondered what the blazes I was letting myself in for, but as the week progressed I saw a new field of thought opening up. People who don't take the opportunity to be educated today will be poor in mind as well as pocket.

(From Glasgow) I would like to bring my Manager to Esher. He would open his eyes, he would get the shock of his life.

(From Electricity Supply) Management used to push me around on productivity questions. Now I find I am pushing them around. I find myself in a good negotiating position.

(Another shop steward in Shipbuilding) I learned that if

only ten per cent of my skill and half my time at work is used effectively, that is all I am paid for, no matter how good my officials are in negotiation. This is the result of poor management, and it helps to keep my wages down. I used to think that productivity was their problem. Now I know it's mine.[1]

Les truly broke new ground with these joint industrial courses at the ETU College. They gave management and workers an entirely new insight into each other's problems. This valuable work goes on.

Les Cannon was only fifty when he died. He was forty-three when he was first elected General President of the ETU, and he lived to enjoy barely seven years of power. His achievement in those years was immense, his range of activity—from complex negotiations on wages and productivity to membership of the Royal Commission on Assizes and Quarter Sessions—enormous. He had little time for reflection in tranquillity and the ordered exposition of his thought. He wrote a good deal and spoke more, but his speeches were for particular occasions—Presidential addresses to his Union, in debates at the Trades Union Congress, in the cut and thrust of wage negotiations—and his writings are scattered in the files of trade union journals, a few newspapers and other periodicals. Many of his more important writings were letters or memoranda.

His lectures at the ETU College and at seminars concerned with labour relations and business administration were memorable, but his work here (like the work of all great educationists) lives in its influence on the thinking of those who attended his lectures. That influence is real and lasting, but impossible to quantify.

He was interviewed fairly frequently for television and sound radio, and transcripts or recordings of some of these programmes remain. But a television interview in cold typescript is a poor thing, the verve and vitality of the living speakers lost. A recording of a sound programme has more of the quality of the original, but an interview is an unsatisfactory form of conveying thought, and the controller of the thought that is

[1] These observations by shop stewards are quoted from *Contact*, published by the EETU–Plumbing Trades Union.

conveyed is the interviewer as much as the interviewed. A television or radio interview may be moving, dramatic, effective in
making this or that point; it is not, it cannot be, a coherent
statement of philosophy. Les was not given time to complete
his own books, but the legacy of his thought is still tremendous.

It remains to speculate a little on might-have-beens. Had
that strange road from Wigan Pier taken a different turning,
Les Cannon might have been a Labour Prime Minister. Or he
might have been an able lawyer, or a university professor.
He would have been outstanding in many walks of life. As it
was, he put all his gifts to the service of trade unionism, in
which, he believed, lay the best hope of advancement for
Britain.

APPENDIX I

Les Cannon as a negotiator in electricity supply

by R. D. Roberts

MY FIRST CLOSE contact with Les Cannon as a negotiator was in the Autumn of 1963 when he became one of the twelve members of the trade union side of the NJIC. He remained a member until he resigned through illness in September 1971. Between January 1967 and that date he and I alternated annually as Chairman and Vice-Chairman.

The whole period was one of intense negotiating activity so that I saw a lot of Les. When he joined us we were in difficulties. Earlier in 1963 we had begun negotiations on staff status for manual workers and as the months had gone by the gap between boards and unions had widened, not really over principles but through a series of misunderstandings and external pressures which had a damaging cumulative effect. One of the first things Les did was to take his own union out of the negotiations on the grounds that there had been un-necessary delay and that tentative proposals made by the boards' side did not adequately recognise his members' skills. I am sure he thought that this action was in his members' interests, but I criticised it at the time as hasty and ill-judged and it also aroused opposition from his own side whose solidarity he had breached. In March 1964 negotiations broke down and the Union side imposed a work to rule and ban on overtime. A court of inquiry under Sir Colin Pearson was set up and Les gave oral evidence.

His performance was characteristic: he was self-assured, quick, rational, relevant and courteous. One of the main impressions he created on this occasion and on many future ones was that his mind, which was exceptionally quick, easily lost patience with the relative slowness of speech, so that, rapidly though he spoke, his thoughts would always seem to be racing ahead of his tongue and occasionally he would have to hesitate while his words caught up with him. This is among my most vivid recollections of him.

In recalling this particular occasion (and re-reading the evidence) I remember especially the complex comparisons he made between rates, earnings, costs and so on in electricity supply and electrical contracting: he made little or no use of notes, yet when we checked his apparently off-the-cuff statistics we found, as we often did later, that they were accurate, although like many facts presented in negotiations, selective! He enjoyed himself on that occasion and no doubt impressed the court.

His evidence gave us our first insight into his thinking at that time. His main aim as a negotiator, like other union leaders, was of course to get the best deal he could for his members and, in spite of his previous political attachments (perhaps indeed as a reaction against them), his approach to this objective was at this stage almost entirely pragmatic. He made it clear to the court that he was neither wedded to staff status as an ideal nor hostile to this or any form of productivity deal in principle, but prepared to look at them as sources of benefit to his members. "As I say, I am not terribly concerned about the form this takes—status or anything else. . . . It is all a matter of price. This is the crux of the matter." He was asked about the over-time ban and replied that this was simply "one of the legal methods of exerting pressure" aimed at lifting earnings in electricity supply "up to comparable levels with other like industries". He dismissed too readily, I thought, the arbitration procedure in the NJIC constitutional agreement, although in this he was of course following the decision of his side.

Helped by the Pearson Court we got over our immediate difficulties and in three stages in 1964 and 1965 negotiated a staff status agreement. In February 1966 a further agreement provided union backing for the use of work study, although not in a form which provided for the payment of bonuses to individuals for the achievement of measured performance, the emphasis initially being much more on method improvement. Les was much more deeply involved in this negotiation than in the status negotiations and the agreement owed much to his knowledge of work study and his urge to see it applied widely in electricity supply.

In November 1966 Les gave oral evidence on behalf of his union to the Donovan Commission. Re-reading now his evidence both to Pearson and to Donovan one can see how experience and events had in the meantime influenced his thinking. The Labour Government had introduced its policy on productivity, prices and incomes and Les, as he told the Commission, was a supporter of that policy. He acknowledged that the national interest required a period of restraint in prices and incomes. But like us he saw that a period of restraint could be used to create legitimate opportunities for advance by making the utmost out of productivity improvement. He certainly agreed with our own view that, in electricity supply, as elsewhere, there was great scope for this, and that if it could be achieved the Government would be satisfied and both the consumer and his members would gain. And it was a happy circumstance that the qualities which effective productivity bargaining demanded of the Union negotiator were exactly the ones he possessed in abundance: a capacity for clear economic analysis, a practical knowledge of productivity techniques, and an ability to lead the unions and their members successfully into new ground.

In January 1967, during the "period of severe restraint", the industry's one-year agreement on pay was running out and Les, on behalf of his side, put forward a claim for a substantial increase in pay which he specifically requested should be examined in the context of the Government's incomes policy. Les clearly saw the prospect of a big new productivity deal, but in fact some of the arguments he used could not be confined within the framework of the current incomes policy. The claim also seriously under-rated the problem of measuring changes in labour productivity in a form which would be acceptable under the Government's incomes policy by the NBPI. For our part we were keen to make a productivity deal if the right watertight conditions could be found.

In that and the next two years we made pay and productivity deals which transformed relations and productivity levels in electricity supply. They were years of long and difficult negotiations and in the course of them I learned a lot more about Les's qualities as a negotiator. These qualities I should like to try to bring out.

Les was leader of a union side made up of representatives of five unions. But so far as we on our side could see, there was at this time simply no questioning of his leadership. He was their spokesman in joint session and whatever differences they may have had at their own meetings were not apparent to us. His senior colleagues were men of experience and stature in their own right and the acceptance of Les was both a tribute to him and a measure of their judgement in recognising his qualities.

In multi-union bargaining situations, individual unions, in their separate conferences, often seek to outbid each other in the size of pay claims that they advocate and this, as we know, has often been an embarrassment to the negotiating team later. Les was able to discourage this and it stood him and his colleagues in good stead both in and after negotiations. He was also keen to increase the authority of the trade union side throughout the industry by such means as fuller and more frequent direct communication from his side to the district and works committee representatives (rather than solely from individual unions to their own members) and by annual conferences between the union side and such representatives.

In September 1967 we negotiated a productivity deal which gave the full backing of the unions to management's use of various productivity techniques and the more flexible deployment of the labour force. This was only achieved after tough negotiations, the intervention of the Government and a reference to the NBPI, and it would not be accurate to assert that Les and his colleagues were keen on these conditions. Throughout the lengthy negotiations Les had been determined to get written into the agreement a commitment to the industry's use of work study-based incentive payment schemes and he was successful in securing this commitment in principle. And before the ink was dry on the 1967 agreement we opened discussions on an agreement governing productivity payment schemes. In March 1968 the agreement was made: it provided for the piece-meal introduction of schemes, all under the firm control of the NJIC. I think that the agreement would have come eventually without Les, but I know that he had great influence on both its timing and its form. By the end of 1971 over half the industry's employees were on work study-based schemes and by the end of 1972 the great majority will be.

The successful negotiator requires ability to judge the logical effects of agreements made on the future negotiating situation and at this time Les displayed this ability quite markedly. For instance, we stressed throughout the 1967 and 1968 negotiations that, with the work load expected to increase only slowly and productivity very rapidly, numbers employed would have to fall. It could have taken a long time for the Union side to accept the full implications of this. But Les recognised the force of the boards' members' arguments and while both sides rejected compulsory redundancy in a productivity context Les led his side to accept proposals for bringing down manning levels, culminating in a voluntary severance scheme.

A further example concerns non-unionism, a subject on which Les was very strong. We did not have a closed shop agreement, but there was a very high Union membership and we on our side did all we could to encourage this. But there were some non-unionists and Les believed that in the end really effective productivity agreements, with the commitments they imposed on industrial staff, required a closed shop to sustain them. He disliked the thought that Union members who did not like the commitments were free to leave the Union without penalty and that they and the non-unionists could in effect get away with minimum co-operation while their union colleagues carried them. The result was that in 1969 we agreed, backed by the Donovan recommendations, to introduce a modified trade union shop agreement.

I may have given the impression that Les, in the later sixties, had eschewed industrial action—working to rule, overtime bans and strikes—as instruments in negotiation. But that would be wrong. What Les believed was that these were weapons in the trade union armoury to be used with the utmost tactical skill, and, especially in electricity supply, in a highly sensitive and controlled way.

At the first stage of a negotiation Les always mustered his facts and deployed his arguments with the utmost care. When our side had replied he searched for common ground and the area where negotiation was required. He pushed his strongest arguments hard and probed what he thought were the weaknesses in our case. But there was a limit to his patience and at what he calculated to be the right moment he did not hesitate to threaten an overtime ban, working to rule or both.

Les had acquired by this time a sure instinct about the dangers of arousing elements among the rank and file which might get out of control, and was strong and effective (particularly at the end of 1969 when a difficulty of this type arose) in his condemnation of small militant movements which could emerge at critical moments, damage the unions' cause and then lapse into obscurity.

Most important negotiations reach a critical point when the two sides look at each other over what appears to be an un-bridgeable gap. It is at that stage that informal discussions between the leaders are not simply useful but essential. Off the record, two leaders can discuss the whole situation and at that moment the belief that each has in the capacity and integrity of the other is critical. For one wants to know where, if anywhere, the point of settlement will be and that when the final offer is made it will result in an agreement acceptable to both sides. Les, as I say, was a tough man in negotiations who knew how to build up maximum pressure so as to push the area of possible agreement nearer to his side's initial position. But he knew how far we would go and the point at which a settlement was a better thing for the membership than the alternative.

How in the end do I assess Les as a negotiator? To his job he brought to bear outstanding qualities of leadership, integrity and toughness. He helped to achieve, by his skill in negotiations, a great improvement in the social status, the working conditions, and the standard of living which the industrial staff in electricity supply now enjoy. In the fullest sense he can be said to have made a good bargain for his side. These simple words cover the whole range of negotiating skill, and I watched Les progress from a more limited conception of what constituted a good bargain to the growing awareness of the relationship of a particular negotiating issue to the long-term interests of his members, broadly conceived to take account of the health and efficiency of the industry and the background of economic trends and Government policies. Because of his skill and integrity he was able to take this broader view of his role without losing the confidence and support of his side, and increasingly towards the end of his life he was playing a part in the national policy-making discussions which formed the framework of negotiations in electricity supply and elsewhere. I am sure that Les's skill and vision were still developing rapidly when his career was brought to such a sad and untimely end.

APPENDIX II

APPENDIX II

An article by Les Cannon on Strike Law, reprinted from the Sunday Times, *October 11, 1970*

LEGISLATION IN INDUSTRIAL relations has always been controversial, but never more than during the past decade. The controversy reached a point in 1965 where the classic remedy of a Royal Commission under Lord Donovan was invoked. The Commission reported to a mixed reception, since when a Labour Government has made an abortive attempt to establish a legislative framework for an industrial relations system. Now a Conservative Government, this time with a mandate from the electorate, is to make a further attempt with measures even more radical than the Donovan Commission's recommendations.

In spite of the supreme confidence of those for and against, I do not believe anyone can be nearly so certain about the outcome. It will be judged by how it helps to deal with situations seemingly intractable at present.

It will be judged also by the extent to which new contracts are fair and rewarding and the procedures for dealing with grievances lead to speedy and just settlements. If these things do not happen the legislation will have failed, even if the days lost in unofficial strikes diminish as I believe they will anyway.

One thing certain is that it is no substitute for intelligent, competent management nor for responsible trade union leadership. This must lead its members from the front within a proper trade union power structure rather than a new vogue of so-called democratic trade unionism, which consists of nothing more than leading workers from behind.

There are three general arguments which have been widely used in this debate. *One—That it will seriously undermine the power and authority of the unions built up over a century.* This I regard as nonsense. Even if all the proposals of the consultative document were implemented in legislation, the trade union movement would have sufficient power exercised legally to have a devastating effect on important sections of the economy.

Two—The legislation is an unwarranted interference in the field of collective bargaining. This really is an irony because during the 1960s legislation had to make up for serious shortcomings in the collective bargaining system. Take the Contracts of Employment Act, the Industrial Training Boards, the Redundancy Payments Act, and equal pay for equal work. Every trade union negotiator knows that the only way to get a universal right of independent appeal against unfair dismissal is through legislation.

Three—That it is an interference in the internal affairs of trade unions. Again the 1960s have many cases of injustice against trade unionists who have gone to law and where the union rules have had to be construed by the High Court either because of their ambiguity or inadequacy. There is nothing I personally welcome more than the right to be given for trade unionists to challenge a fraudulent leadership such as existed in the Electrical Trades Union in the 1950s, which could not be resolved within the trade union movement at that time and which could not be resolved by the TUC even today.

Five weeks now remain, within which the TUC must impress the Government with its views on Mr Robert Carr's consultative document. I believe this time must be extended.

What tactics will the TUC employ or can it employ during this period of consultation? Eighteen months ago it won what can now be seen to be a pyrrhic victory against the Labour Government's proposals set out in the White Paper "In Place of Strife".

On that occasion the TUC was uncompromising throughout the negotiations on the main features of the White Paper. From the beginning they made it clear that they would never accept penalties against workpeople or trade unions and would therefore not accept the industrial courts, nor would they accept a legally enforceable cooling-off period or compulsory strike ballots.

The withdrawal of these main features of the White Paper was, and according to the TUC and Labour Party conference decisions still is, the TUC's negotiating position.

The situation now, however, is very much different. Mr Carr, who does not fear a backbench revolt, has said that he would welcome constructive consultation about the details and went on: "But the main principles are firm and there is no going back."

Those who have studied the document know that it includes and even extends those principles to which the TUC is implacably opposed.

In these circumstances can there be a constructive dialogue? It is hardly likely. What seems to me to be inevitable is that the five weeks will go by during which the TUC will re-state its position of 18 months ago and at the end of which the Government will not be moved one inch. This leads inexorably to a confrontation between the TUC and the Government and it also raises a constitutional issue of the highest importance.

Having been invited to consult and try to modify details of this programme, will the TUC be right in the event of not having all its demands met to decide that it will use its great power against the fulfilment of a mandate which the party now in government sought and received from the electorate? I think not.

Millions of trade unionists whose working lives will be much affected by this legislation have the right to expect that their leaders will go through the entire document with the Government, submitting reasoned amendments to its proposals. If the TUC stands on principle in total opposition to the document I fear the case of these millions of workers on many unsatisfactory features of the document will go by default.

L

INDEX

INDEX